Corrstown: a Coastal Community

Corrstown

A Coastal Community

Excavations of a Bronze Age Village in Northern Ireland

Edited by

Victoria Ginn and Stuart Rathbone

Archaeological Consultancy Services Ltd

With contributions by

Örni Akeret, Eoin Grogan, Martin Halpin, Ella Hassett, Maria Lear, Stephen Linanne, Stephen Mandal, Cormac McSparron, Maria O'Hare, and Helen Roche

Oxbow Books
Oxford and Oakville

Published by
Oxbow Books, Oxford, UK

© Oxbow Books and the authors, 2012
ISBN 978-1-84217-464-7

This book is available direct from:

Oxbow Books, Oxford, UK
(Phone: 01865-241249; Fax: 01865-794449)

and

The David Brown Book Company
PO Box 511, Oakville, CT 06779, USA
(Phone: 860-945-9329; Fax: 860-945-9468)

or from our website

www.oxbowbooks.com

Front cover: Reconstruction of the Corrstown settlement, artwork
by Lizzie Holiday based on an original drawing by Ella Hassett
Back cover: Aerial photograph of the site: © Archaeological Consultancy Services Ltd;
Reconstructions of Type 1 & 2 structures: artwork by Lizzie Holiday based
on original drawings by Ella Hassett

Printed in Great Britain by
Information Press, Eynsham, Oxfordshire

This volume is dedicated to all the inhabitants of Corrstown and Hopefield, past, present and future, and to Adam Miguelle, who was made there.

Contents

List of Illustrations

Appendix I

Appendix II

Appendix IIII

List of Tables

Acknowledgements

The authors would like to thank Dr Chris Lynn from the Northern Ireland Environment Agency for his clarity and extensive advice on the Final Excavation Report and on this volume. The advice and useful comments from Robert O'Hara and Stephen Linanne, both formerly of Archaeological Consultancy Services Ltd, from Dr John Ó Néill (University College Dublin) and Dr Phil MacDonald (Centre for Archaeological Fieldwork, Queen's University Belfast) on earlier drafts were also most appreciated. Dr Phil MacDonald also kindly provided unpublished information and radiocarbon dates on the site of Knockdhu, Co. Antrim. Dr Nicki Whitehouse, Dr Helen Roe and Dr Gillian Plunkett (Queen's University Belfast) provided advice and direction on the palaeoenvironmental background of the area. Thanks also to Dr Eoin Grogan for being continually supportive and encouraging.

Archaeological Consultancy Services Ltd would also like to express their sincere thanks to key project personnel, including Brian Williams, Paul Logue and John O'Keefe from the Northern Ireland Environment Agency, as well as The Kennedy Group Plc for their involvement and support.

The publication would not be possible without the dedication of the site-based project managers, directors Malachy Conway (The National Trust) and Audrey Gahan (Gahan and Long) and the excavation team. Rachel Sloane and Maria Lear, both formerly of Archaeological Consultancy Services Ltd, worked ceaselessly in the post-excavation department to ensure the completion of the specialist reports. Martin Halpin, formerly of Archaeological Consultancy Services Ltd, produced the illustrations and Ella Hassett the reconstruction illustrations.

Thanks extend to Professor Paula Reimer and The Chrono Centre, Queen's University Belfast, who kindly provided a further eight radiocarbon dates as part of the PhD research of Victoria Ginn and also gave permission for their publication here. Extreme gratitude is expressed to Lorna O'Donnell who provided the species identifications for these particular samples.

The continuing support of Donald Murphy and Deidre Murphy of Archaeological Consultancy Services Ltd in funding the completion of the drafting and the cost of this publication is gratefully recognised.

Any mistakes and errors in the text remain the authors' own.

Chapter 1

Introduction

A total of 76 Bronze Age structures, including 74 roundhouses, were discovered at Corrstown, Co. Londonderry (site centre NGR 28609 43914), representing a site which is hitherto unique in the archaeological record of the British Isles (Illustrations 1.1–1.5). A number of additional contemporary features included a large cobbled road surface and numerous cobbled pathways as well as dispersed postholes and pits. Early medieval activity was represented by a ringfort, a rock-cut souterrain and a large square structure. A Neolithic presence on the site was represented by a small pottery assemblage.

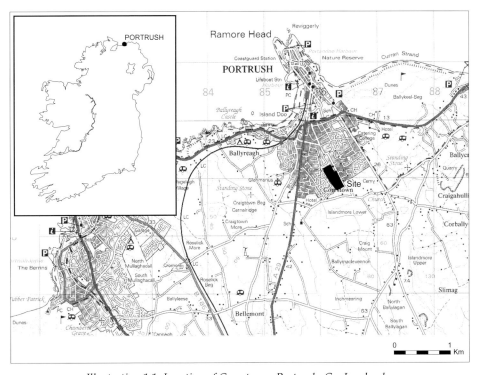

Illustration 1.1: Location of Corrstown, Portrush, Co. Londonderry

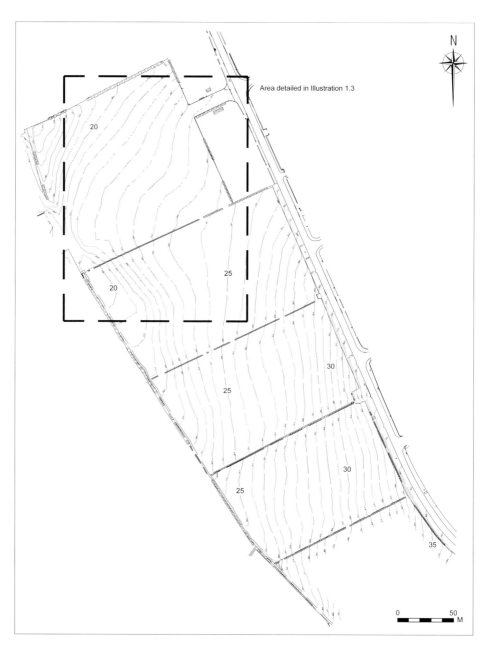

Area detailed in Illustration 1.3

Illustration 1.2: Contour survey of the site

1.1 Background to the archaeological excavation

In 2001 and early 2002 small test excavations were carried out under the direction of Malachy Conway for Archaeological Consultancy Services Ltd (ACS) in the townland of Corrstown at the southern limits of the small town of Portrush, Co. Antrim, on the north coast of Northern Ireland. Portrush is typical of many towns along the north Antrim coast which were major tourist destinations in the late 19th and early 20th centuries but which have suffered from the mid-20th century onwards, partly due to the development of the overseas tourist market and partly as an effect of The Troubles in Northern Ireland which dissuaded holiday-makers from visiting the area. Following the cessation of violence in the mid 1990s Portrush, the adjacent coastal town Portstewart, and the larger inland town, Coleraine, began a significant period of redevelopment, based on re-invigorated tourism and the influx of students to the University of Ulster Coleraine Campus. Large housing and commercial developments were built in all three towns and archaeological investigations took place in advance of these developments, identifying and recording numerous new archaeological sites. The test excavations at Corrstown (Licence Number AE/01/82) were undertaken in advance of the construction of *c.* 200 new houses in four adjacent fields, representing a large sub-rectangular block of land measuring approximately 600m in length (north–south) and between 150m and 190m in width (east–west), giving a total area of 7.4 hectares. The area of excavation was delimited by pre-existing housing along its western and northern boundaries and the northern part of its eastern boundary along Hopefield Road. That the site had great archaeological potential was already known, as a large circular enclosure had been recorded in aerial photographs of the site and the enclosure was listed on the Sites and Monument Record (SMR LDY 003:26). In addition, excavations had been carried out in 1999 in the adjacent townland of Magheramenagh, immediately to the west of the Corrstown site. These excavations were carried out by Alan Reilly for Northern Archaeological Consultancy Ltd in advance of an earlier housing development and had uncovered several prehistoric houses, a sizeable early medieval souterrain and a large number of pits, postholes and other features (Reilly 2000, 130).

The archaeological testing of the Corrstown site was undertaken in two phases, the first of which comprised a fluxgate gradiometer survey conducted in order to locate the previously recorded enclosure. Phase 1 also incorporated the collection of artefacts from the ploughed surface of the fields, the excavation of four archaeological test trenches, and the archaeological monitoring of four engineering test pits. The fluxgate gradiometer survey successfully identified the enclosure, as well as several other features, including at least one possible souterrain. The second phase of archaeological testing included the excavation of 22 archaeological test trenches, further collection of artefacts from the ploughed surface, and the archaeological monitoring of topsoil removal in the two southernmost fields. The results of both testing phases indicated the presence of significant numbers of archaeological features in only two of the four fields, although large quantities of lithic material were recovered from the topsoil across the whole site. This indicated that the site had been heavily ploughed and suggested that the archaeological features may have become truncated as a result, a process confirmed during excavation. At this stage, a sizeable prehistoric occupation site was discernable, as well as evidence for an early medieval settlement. A full excavation of the archaeological features was scheduled for the later part of 2002 to be funded by the developer of the housing scheme, The Kennedy Group Plc.

Illustration 1.3: Post-excavation site plan

1.2 Surprising results

In October 2002 a small team of archaeologists consisting of the site director Malachy Conway, site supervisor Stuart Rathbone, and four site assistants arrived in Portrush to begin excavation of the small prehistoric settlement and the early medieval ringfort (Licence Number AE/02/100). Topsoil stripping began in the approximate centre of where the prehistoric settlement was deemed to be located and several large circular buildings were revealed. As excavation began on the first structures, Structures 1–4, topsoil stripping continued, slowly expanding the excavation area on all sides. Each day new building foundations were revealed and the estimated total number of buildings present was constantly being revised upwards. After several weeks of topsoil stripping it was clear that the settlement consisted of many more buildings than could have ever been expected and that the site was of far greater complexity and scale than had been previously envisaged for the Irish Bronze Age. It was clear that the assembled archaeological team was much smaller than was needed and while progress had been made with the first six buildings uncovered a considerably larger team would be required if the site was to be completed within the next decade! Late in December 2002 the number of identified houses had risen to above 30 and several emergency meetings were held between the developer The Kennedy Group Plc, the management of ACS, and various members of the archaeological staff at the Northern Ireland Environment Agency. In December 2003 the excavation team was increased by the addition of two new site supervisors, Chris Conway and Maria Lear, along with the addition of 15 new site assistants.

With increased team members excavations proceeded at a greater pace and progress on site could be measured on a daily basis, despite the incredibly hostile winter with its seemingly constant heavy rain and daily hailstorms. The level of the truncation and the effect it had on the extant archaeological evidence varied across the site. Early modern field boundaries and pipe drains also traversed the site and had an adverse effect on the archaeological remains, often obscuring and truncating the structures. Topsoil stripping continued throughout the early spring and it was then that the extent of the settlement was eventually revealed. In June 2003 Malachy Conway left the excavation in order to take up a position with the National Trust for Northern Ireland, and the rest of the excavation was directed by Audrey Gahan of Gahan and Long Ltd. Excavations at the site were finally completed in late August 2003 and all involved were aware that, at least in some small way, the Irish Bronze Age would never look the same again.

1.2.1 *Bronze Age occupation*

The excavated structures, described in Chapter 2, were oval or circular in shape and as such were classified as roundhouses (Illustrations 1.3–1.4). Large quantities of domestic pottery were recovered from most of the structures which suggested that they had functioned as houses. Seventy four of these roundhouses were revealed along with several more irregular groups of features, the exact nature and function of which have still not been established. Although a small number of the buildings were of a well-known Bronze Age type defined by a circular slot-trench with vertical sides and an internal postring (described in this volume as Type 2), the majority were of a type that had not been previously recognised (described in this volume as Type 1) (Illustration 1.6). These consisted of wide ditches of a peculiarly segmented form and a multitude of

Illustration 1.4: Simplified post-excavation site plan

pits and postholes that formed no easily interpretable pattern. Several of the buildings consisted of concentric rings of these segmented ditches and one stood within a deep horseshoe-shaped enclosure. Some of the buildings were clearly grouped into pairs or short rows. Many of the buildings had long, sunken porches flanked by pits and postholes, with fine cobbling covering the base. Long, sunken pathways connected some of the entrances together and the bases of these pathways were also covered in the same fine cobbling. A large, roughly cobbled road surface (over 70m in length by 10m in width) ran through the eastern side of the settlement. A second un-surfaced road was suspected to be present along the western side of the site; it was defined by an absence of features in this area.

The manner in which the houses were connected by pathways and grouped into pairs and rows, as well as the very rare occurrence of individual buildings overlapping each other, suggested that much of the settlement was occupied contemporaneously. Twenty-four radiocarbon dates were obtained from 22 of the roundhouses and the dates were found to be tightly clustered in the Middle Bronze Age, supporting the excavation team's impression that the majority of the buildings would have been in use at the same time, and that what had been excavated was the first indisputable evidence in Ireland and Britain of a large Bronze Age village. A reconstruction of the village is shown in Illustration 1.7 (no evidence for field systems was forthcoming from

Illustration 1.5: Aerial photograph of the site

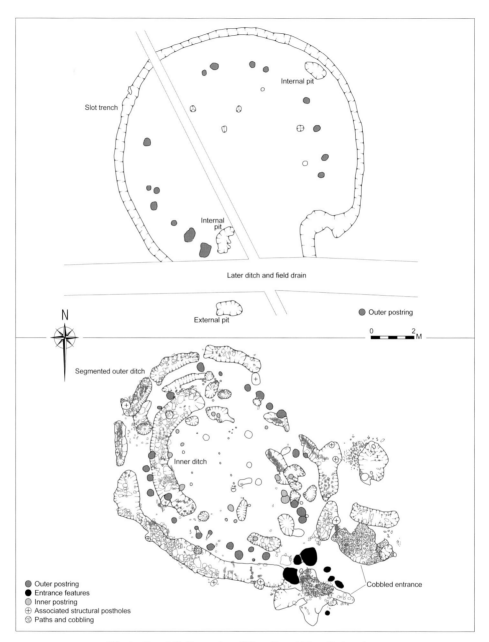

Illustration 1.6: Examples of Type 1 and Type 2 structures

the excavations but these have been included by the reconstruction artist. A view to the sea from the site was discovered using Google Earth).

The artefact assemblage from the site was dominated by pottery and lithics. Over 9,000 sherds of mainly undecorated pottery were collected and identified by Helen

Roche and Eoin Grogan. The pottery represents a highly significant assemblage of a newly recognised plain domestic ware, dating from the Middle Bronze Age, and deriving from the cordoned urn tradition. Bipolar reduced flint artefacts were recovered in such large quantities that it was not possible to assign a separate artefact number to each piece but it is estimated that over 16,500 pieces were collected. A sample comprising 65% of the total assemblage has been analysed by Maria O'Hare, and it represents one of the largest assemblages of Middle Bronze Age flint that has currently been examined in Ireland. Four stone moulds, two complete polished stone axes, five polished stone axe fragments, and a large polished stone macehead were recovered from the site, along with four stone moulds for casting bronze objects. Despite the presence of the moulds no metal artefacts were recovered and no slag was identified. These more elaborate stone artefacts were examined by Eoin Grogan and Stephen Mandal.

Unfortunately, animal bone – either burnt or otherwise – was almost completely lacking from the excavations. Therefore, little information regarding the diet or farming practices of the inhabitants was discerned, although a small quantity of carbonised seeds from the Bronze Age occupation was recovered. No waterlogged deposits were discovered that would allow for the preservation of organic material, although a small number of burnt stakes and timbers were discovered. No human bone was recovered from the site and it is not known if it was originally excluded from the site or has simply not survived. The reason for the poor representation of plant macrofossils, bone and metal artefacts from the site may be partly linked to post-depositional processes

Illustration 1.7: Reconstruction of the Corrstown settlement (Ella Hassettt)

and to the general acidic soil environment in the area, both of which appear to have been significantly affected by the arable farming undertaken across the site over the recent decades and even centuries.

1.2.2 Early medieval occupation

In addition to the Bronze Age settlement the early medieval ringfort was fully excavated, along with a small partially rock-cut souterrain which was located in the interior. An unusual set of shallow ditches that formed a large rectangular arrangement possibly represented the foundations for a building and also dated to this period. It was associated with a large number of carbonised seeds which may indicate that it had a crop-processing or storage function. An early medieval kiln was also identified and excavated.

1.3 Post-excavation processing

The completion of the Corrstown excavations was a major achievement, but as with any excavation of this scale the fieldwork was only one part of a large and complicated process that would lead to the eventual publication of the results. In the years following the excavations, the stratigraphic report was slowly compiled, the massive artefact assemblage was processed and analysed, the environmental samples were studied, and the large archive of drawings was digitised and prepared for eventual publication. In 2004 the Council of British Archaeology recognised the importance of the site and the quality of the work that was undertaken. The excavations received a commendation for high standards in commercial archaeology at the annual British Archaeology Awards, held that year at Queen's University Belfast. An initial account of the site was published the following year in *Current Archaeology* as part of the coverage of the awards (Conway *et al.* 2004) which complemented the summary accounts in *Excavations Bulletin* (Conway 2003, 2004). A further, succinct account was published in *Archaeology Ireland* in 2006 (Conway 2005). A brief discussion of the site was also included in Cleary's article discussing Irish Bronze Age settlements (Cleary 2006, 20). Details of each of the Bronze Age buildings and a limited account of the site have been included in John Ó Néill's recent *Inventory of Bronze Age Structures* prepared on behalf of the Heritage Council (Ó Néill forthcoming). In 2010 a summary account of the excavation report was also included in the Northern Ireland Environment Agency's inventory of recent archaeological discoveries in Northern Ireland (Conway 2010).

A major milestone for the project was the submission of the full stratigraphic report for the site to the Northern Ireland Environment Agency, in 2008 (Conway *et al.* 2008); however, there was no illusion that that report could simply be reproduced for publication, primarily due to its size. It should be noted that the original post-excavation budget was entirely spent, and much more besides, on simply obtaining specialist reports detailing the artefacts and ecofacts and that publication of the results had not formed part of the original contract. Efforts were made to secure funding for the publication and The Heritage Council Ireland granted funding for the production of an education pack based on the site. This was compiled and freely distributed to schools and education bodies in Northern Ireland and in the border counties in the Republic of Ireland; it was also available on the ACS website (as ACS Ltd no longer operate, electronic copies are available by contacting Victoria Ginn). Much of this current volume has therefore been completed in the spare time of the authors and other contributors who believed that the site should be published and not left to languish as 'grey literature'. An unfortunate consequence of the lack of funding is the limited number and variety of accompanying illustrations to this volume, but such illustrative work is simply not feasible under these publication restrictions.

With such a wealth of data it is perhaps not surprising that the current volume has gone through an often labourous editorial process. New evidence from the specialist reports has consistently required alterations to be made throughout the body of the text, while advice from numerous colleagues working in the field of the Irish Bronze Age has repeatedly altered the way in which the site has been interpreted and presented. New excavations in Ireland and Britain added important evidence that required parts of the text to be substantially rewritten, while new articles and papers affected the way in which different elements of the site were envisaged. In 2007 it became clear that new information could not continue to be included into the text and so the implications of several important new projects published after this date have not been included.

It should be recognised that what is presented in this volume has never been intended as a definitive statement about the site. Instead, it is hoped that this volume represents a beginning of the study of Corrstown. By producing this account it is hoped that all those involved in studying the Bronze Age in Ireland and Britain will be able to examine the evidence and contribute new interpretations and explanations. An example of this can already be seen in this volume; the delay in the publication has allowed the application of Bayesian statistics to the radiocarbon dates to provide a much sharper definition of the site's chronology than would have been possible if this report had been published several years earlier. Secondly, as part of Victoria Ginn's PhD research an additional eight radiocarbon dates was kindly funded and processed by The Chrono Centre, Queen's University Belfast (species identifications generously undertaken by Lorna O'Donnell) as the initial set of dates were derived from unidentified charcoal and potentially suffering from the 'old wood' effect. The samples are all from the same contexts as the initial dates and they represent the only surviving environmental material from the site (see below). Indeed, a ninth sample was identified as containing oak (*Quercus*) and it is therefore probable that some of the initial dates do suffer from the 'old wood' effect. The new dates have been incorporated alongside the others throughout this volume. All dates have been analysed by Cormac McSparron (Appendix I). It is hoped that after publication other researchers can use the information contained here to undertake new studies of the site. In particular, it is suspected that statistical analysis beyond the expertise of the original team may provide new insights, while the site clearly provides plentiful scope for further spatial analysis and discussion of population density.

It should also be noted that the project in its entirety did not run without several regrettable problems. Firstly, the photographic archive from the early part of the excavation was sadly depleted when a camera bag was stolen from the site which contained several rolls of film. Secondly, it has to be confessed that a large number of environmental samples became unavailable after ACS Ltd underwent office re-organising. Thirdly, the manner in which the soil samples were processed was limited to simple tank floatation with only plant remains visible to the naked eye being collected, and no samples were subjected to microscopic analysis which somewhat limited the amount of information that could be generated from this material. Fourthly, the illustrations and photographic record of the pottery assemblage are still forthcoming (although see Grogan and Roche 2009 for a full and illustrated account of plain Middle Bronze Age domestic ware). Fifthly, it has not been possible to properly incorporate the evidence from the 1999 excavations that took place in the field immediately west of the Corrstown site. Unfortunately, only very brief accounts of this excavation are available and it is not possible to determine at present how the houses identified in Magheramenagh townland may relate to the Corrstown settlement. The current authors hope that they have managed to complete the project in a way which is acceptable to the original site directors (whose involvement in the publication has been regrettably limited) and have attempted to present the site, as much as was possible, in a way that follows their original interpretation.

1.4 Structure of this volume

This volume focuses on the Bronze Age material from the Corrstown settlement, due to the sheer scale and importance of this evidence. Chapter 2 comprises a gazetteer of the individual structures recorded on the site, each accompanied by a detailed plan. This provides a synopsis of the primary data (the full stratigraphic record is available for public consultation in the Northern Ireland Environment Agency, Belfast). The specialists' analysis of the artefacts and ecofacts is given in Chapter 3 and Chapter 4 discusses the nature of the structures and attempts to reconstruct the buildings based on the archaeological evidence. Chapter 5 incorporates analysis of the site as a whole, including some detail on the surrounding landscape and contemporary environment. It also attempts to estimate the size of the population that occupied the site, gives a consideration of the social status of the occupants, and an examination of the processes by which the site was abandoned. Chapter 6 places the results of the excavations at Corrstown within a local, regional and British context and incorporates some of the evidence for contemporary activity in the region of Portrush and Portstewart which has hitherto not been readily accessible. Chapter 6 also includes a discussion on how the settlement should be classified.

   As noted above, a variety of early medieval archaeological features were also excavated at Corrstown; as this volume concentrates on the Bronze Age evidence details of the early medieval features are located in Appendix II. Appendix IIII provides a summary account of Steve Linanne's excavations of a Bronze Age settlement and possible ritual complex at Cappagh Beg in Portstewart. This site was excavated simultaneously with the Corrstown excavations and was also undertaken by ACS Ltd on behalf of The Kennedy Group Plc. Taken together these two sites represent a remarkable increase in our knowledge of Bronze Age activity in this region.

Chapter 2

Excavation Results

2.1 Summary

This chapter presents a summary of the prehistoric structures excavated at Corrstown during 2002–3 which has been derived from the Final Excavation Report written and compiled by Malachy Conway, Audrey Gahan, Stuart Rathbone, Maria Lear, and Victoria Ginn.

In total 76 structures (74 roundhouses and two 'W'-shaped structures) and a contemporary road surface, F100, were identified, either on site or during the post-excavation analysis (Illustrations 1.3–1.4). Several early, pre-publication accounts of the site at Corrstown unfortunately only cite 'forty' (Bradley 2007, 196) or '52' (MacDonald *et al*. 2005, 57) roundhouses and to some readers the estimate of 74 such structures may seem inflated. In fact, it would perhaps be even more appropriate to view these 74 structures as 74 house platforms as the multiple modifications and replacements would have increased the total number of structures built on the site even further, possibly to over 100. The archaeological footprint of these structures was often complex and varied. Pits, postholes, ditches, and stone sockets cut each other and often features were so truncated that they were difficult to categorise and to assign to particular phases. It is therefore important to note that in many cases the features that were excavated on each house platform represent the culmination of several successive buildings, the final phase of which had typically destroyed many of the preceding features. Although some structures on one platform may have been rebuilt, there was little sign that the position of the platforms migrated as there was no evidence that they overlapped any neighbouring house platforms. Therefore, in most cases what is described is the final construction phase and a number of rather random features which can be assigned to earlier phases but which cannot be brought together to form complete plans. In other instances, in particular with the rings of postholes, it is clear that so many features were present that they must belong to several successive phases, but there was no way to attribute many of the postholes to particular phases. In addition, it should be noted that some buildings appear to form contemporary pairs or members of small groups. While this is briefly discussed in each structure's description, it is more fully discussed in the following chapters. It is therefore likely that each house platform was occupied simultaneously at the zenith of the settlement's occupation as it is unlikely that a new house would be built on the perimeter if there was a more centralised vacant site; the issue of contemporaneousness is explored further in Chapter 4.

There were numerous isolated and clustered features (pits, postholes, stakeholes, etc.) which were linked to but did not form part of the 76 structures and only some of these are discussed below. For the purposes of presentation, this chapter details the structures in ascending numerical order and not by chronological or geographical sequence. Structure numbers are prefixed with a capital S.

2.2 Structure types and terminology

The majority of these structures were roundhouses and had similar constructional features (outer ditch, outer postring, inner ditch, inner postring, etc). Consistency of terminology has been maintained as far as possible for the sake of clarity and understanding but it should be noted that there were design elements of different structures and some phases of structures which were either unique or were difficult, sometimes almost impossible, to decipher. Despite these interpretative problems, two broad discernable structure types (Type 1 and Type 2) emerged. Type 1 structures were defined by wide segmented ditches and at least one concentric postring, and Type 2 structures were defined by narrow, vertically sided slot-trenches and a single, internal postring.

2.2.1 Type 1 structures

The principal structural components of the Type 1 roundhouses are as follows (Illustration 1.6):

Outer ditch – this was often segmented and formed the perimeter of the structure and was therefore an external feature (the area enclosed by the outer ditch was taken as the structure's external dimensions). In some examples the outer ditch was associated with drainage.

Outer postring – the first ring of postholes located inside the outer ditch was designated the outer postring. This ring of posts supported the weight of the roof. There was evidence to indicate that these posts were modified, strengthened and replaced on numerous occasions.

Inner ditch – some structures had evidence for a second, inner segmented ditch which was concentric with the outer ditch and which was positioned in the interior of the building. Where this occurred often a bank existed between the two ditches, on which a low, non-load-bearing wall was possibly placed. In some structures this inner ditch may actually have belonged to a different phase of activity / occupation, representing successive structures built on the same spot. However, clear demonstrable evidence that any of these buildings concentrically expanded over different phases, although theoretically possible, was not forthcoming. In other structures, e.g. the final phase of S4, the inner ditch was integral to the design concept of the structure. Where greatly segmented, the inner ditch segments may represent internal storage.

Inner postring – some structures had evidence for a second, inner postring which would have further supported the roof or which would seem to represent evidence for a different phase of activity or successive structures built on the same spot, although again the stratigraphic evidence for this was somewhat lacking.

There are two main architectural points of interest with the Type 1 structures: the segmentation of the ditches and the occasional presence of two concentric ditches. The segmentation of the outer ditches poses interpretative problems, but is a phenomenon found occasionally within the archaeological record and is currently evidenced as far west as Sligo (McCabe 2005) and as far south as Meath (Kelly 2008). In some examples these ditches may have had a triple purpose, acting initially as source pits from which constructional material was obtained, before then functioning as drains during the occupation of the structure, with cobbling laid to facilitate drainage, and thirdly, serving as convenient receptacles for household waste (large quantities of pottery and lithic material were found in many of the outer ditch segments). The incompleteness of the inner ditch circuit, where identified, was such that it seems much more likely to have been an inherent design attribute rather than the result of partial truncation of an earlier phase; however, its exact function remains somewhat elusive. It is possible that the inner ditch segments in the buildings with contemporary concentric ditches were used for storage or even as sleeping compartments.

The entrances to Type 1 structures were all similar: they were mainly east facing and they were often elaborate; many were two phased with a sunken, cobbled entrance being replaced by a longer, paved pathway, which in some examples extended into the interior. Paired postholes aligned along the entrance suggest that many of these pathways would have been covered with a porch.

2.2.2 Type 2 structures

The Type 2 structures (S18, S33, S49, S63, and S64) had rather different archaeological footprints (Illustration 1.6) and consisted of a simple, single slot-trench and an internal postring.

Slot-trench – narrow with vertical sides and held a vertical timber wall which would have borne some of the weight of the roof.
Postring – functioned with the slot-trench in holding up the roof.

These structures were rare compared to those of Type 1: only five were positively identified, and they generally occurred around the southeastern periphery of the site. S63 was a hybrid form with its outer ditch sharing similarities to the segmented outer ditches of Type 1 structures but also to the narrow slot-trenches of the Type 2 structures. Overall, artefacts, including pottery, from these Type 2 structures were few, although S33 and S38 did contain pottery sherds.

Radiocarbon dates were obtained from both types of structures and these ranged from 1665–1497 BC (UB-6247; associated with S19) to 1261–935 BC (Beta-190132; associated with S1) with an apparent concentration between 1300 and 1200 BC. There was no discernable variance between the radiocarbon dates of either structure type and it is likely that they were occupied contemporaneously. Perhaps they differed in function, as evidenced by a considerable lack of associated artefacts from the Type 2 structures (Chapters 3–4). It is also possible that, although broadly contemporary, the Type 2 structures were among the last to be constructed at Corrstown, before abandonment of the site, and that this subtle difference in chronology is not apparent in the radiocarbon dates.

2.2.3 Other structures

In addition to the 74 roundhouses, in the southern half of the settlement there were two unusual W-shaped structures: S24 and S26. S24, at the west of the site, consisted of two conjoined semi-circular ditches facing towards the south. S26 was located at the east and was very similar, consisting of two conjoined semicircular ditches facing towards the north. The function and date of these two structures is unknown and they may represent unfinished buildings; their descriptions are included below.

Structure No.	Size	Dimensions (m)	No. O.D.S.	No. O.PR.P.	No. I.D.S.	No. I.PR.P.	Entrance	No. Pottery Sherds	Amount Strat Flint (kg)	No. Possible Phases
1	Large	10.6 × 8.6	3	34	-	11	SSE	294	30.354	3
2	Large	11.5 × 9.5	8	27	1	15	SE	90	8.242	3
3	Medium	8.6 × 7.8	6	-	1	-	ESE	195	2.05	1
4	Large	11.4 × 9.5	7	12	3	16	S	711	41.179	2
5	Large	11 × 10.8	8	15	3	3	E	268	37.572	2
6	Medium	9 × 8.5	3	26	1	-	S	291	13.682	2
7	Medium	10 × 7.9	2	14	-	-	SSE	79	10.229	2
8	Large	11 × 8	5	21	-	-	SE	193	21.189	1
9	Medium	10 × 8	8	11	-	-	SE	53	2.286	1
10	Medium	9.2 × 9.2	6	-	-	-	SE	3	5.562	2
11	Small	8.8 × 6.4	4	6	-	-	SE	8	1.938	1
12	Medium	8.4 × 8	5	10	-	-	SE	198	10.89	1

Structure No.	Size	Dimensions (m)	No. O.D.S.	No. O.PR.P.	No. I.D.S.	No. I.PR.P.	Entrance	No. Pottery Sherds	Amount Strat Flint (kg)	No. Possible Phases
13	Large	11.2 × 11	10	22	5	29	SE	697	30.23	2
14	Medium	9 × 8	5	16	-	-	SE	26	10.036	2
15	Medium	9.4 × 7.8	5	29	1	8	SE	173	6.968	3
16	Medium	9 × 8	3	3	-	-	SE	95	13.81	2
17	Medium	10.4 × 9.6	6	18	-	-	SSE	83	2.565	2
18	Slot-trench	11.6 × 11.4	1	15	-	-	SSE	-	-	1
19	Large	10 × 10	7	22	6	13	SSE	166	5.794	2
20	Medium	8.29 × 8.29	3	1	2	-	SE	6	0.256	2
21	Medium	7.43 × 7.43	2	8	-	-	SE	55	2.859	1
22	Medium	7.7 × 7.14	3	10	-	4	SE	24	0.128	2
23	Large	11.14 × 11	4	9	-	6	SE	38	1.239	1
24	W-shape	-	-	-	-	-	-	5	0.230	
25	Large	10.9 × 10	3	11	-	6	SE	-	-	1
26	W-shape	-	-	-	-	-	-	102	0.254	
27	Incomplete	-	2	-	-	-	SE	31	0.250	1
28	Small	6.2 × 6.2	3	2	-	-	SE	140	3.957	1
29	Medium	8 × 8 terminal–terminal	4	2	3	-	S	28	8.755	1
30	Small	6.8 × 6	6	3	-	-	SE	8	1.097	2
31	Small	7.71 × 7.71	4	14	-	8	SE	21	4.894	1
32	Medium	-	4	2	-	-	-	-	-	1
33	Slot-trench	12.57 × 11.7	1	4	-	-	SE	83	15.222	1
34	-	-	1	6	-	-	-	1	1.605	-

Structure No.	Size	Dimensions (m)	No. O.D.S.	No. O.PR.P.	No. I.D.S.	No. I.PR.P.	Entrance	No. Pottery Sherds	Amount Strat Flint (kg)	No. Possible Phases
35	-	-	5	5	-	-	E	26	2.342	1
36	-	-	-	8	-	-	S	1	-	-
37	Large	10.29 × 10	4	5	1	-	E	196	33.266	1
38	Large	11.14 × 10.86	7	12	-	-	SE	226	50.799	1
39	Large	10.29 × 9.71	2	2	-	-	-	-	-	-
40	Medium	10.6 × 8	4	28	-	-	S	29	2.394	2
41	Medium	9.14 × 8	2	7	-	-	E	42	2.377	1
42	Medium	9.14 × 8.86	6	2	3	-	E	66	10.795	1
43	Large	12 × 10	4	21	1	3	SE	25	3.531	2
44	Large	12 terminal – terminal	4	4	-	-	SSE	2	-	1
45	Medium	9.1 × 8.4	5	9	3	3	E	26	4.61	1
46	Small	7.4 × 7	7	5	-	-	SE	15	4.039	1
47	Small	8 × 7	4	11	-	-	E	18	5.772	1
48	Medium	8.3 × 8.3	1	31	-	-	E	35	10.621	3
49	Slot-trench	9.2 × 9	1	10	-	-	-	-	1.439	1
50	N/A	12 × 12	1	-	-	-	-	1	-	1
51	Medium	9.5 × 9	3	-	-	-	SSE	37	2.034	2
52	Medium	9.8 × 8	5	9	-	-	SSE	57	8.878	1
53	Medium	9 × 8	5	18	1	-	SSE	94	2.891	3
54	Small	8.2 × 8	4	13	-	-	SE	264	4.627	2
55	Medium	10 × 8.6	7	18	-	-	SE	86	6.54	2
56	Medium	9.8 × 8.4	4	13	-	-	S	119	11.799	1

Structure No.	Size	Dimensions (M)	No. O.D.S.	No. O.PR.P.	No. I.D.S.	No. I.PR.P.	Entrance	No. Pottery Sherds	Amount Strat Flint (kg)	No. Possible Phases
57	Small	7 × 6.4	5	7	-	-	SE	33	2.985	1
58	Large	10.8 × 9.3	7	20	4	-	SSE	265	21.431	2
59	Medium	9.2 × 9.2	8	12	-	-	SSE	161	10.192	2
60	Large	11 × 8	1	8	1	-	SSE	15	-	1
61	Small	8.4 × 8.2	5	1	-	-	SSE	-	7.517	1
62	Small	7.4 × 6.5	2	1	-	-	SE	4	0.314	1
63	Medium	11 × 9.4	6	9	-	-	S	-	0.266	1
64	Medium	10.4 × 9.1	1	5	-	-	SSE	5	-	1
65	Small	8.3 × 6.6	4	6	-	-	S	29	0.863	1
66	Medium	8.8 × 8	4	3	-	-	SSE	-	2.761	1
67	Small	6.8 × 6.8	3	3	-	-	S	-	0.255	1
68	Medium	10 × 8	5	16	-	-	SSE	-	0.383	2
69	Large	11.2 × 11	6	5	1	-	SE	114	2.009	2
70	Medium	10 × 8.4	2	11	-	-	SSE	146	5.08	2
71	Medium	9.2 × 9.2	5	3	1	-	S	27	0.500	1
72	Small	7.6 × 6.86	4	9	-	-	SE	51	3.356	2
73	Medium	9.26 × 7.43	3	10	-	-	SSE	20	1.282	1
74	Small	6.6 × 6	4	5	-	-	-	2	-	-
75	Small	7.71 × 7	3	4	-	-	-	12	1.12	1
76	Large	12 × 12	1	4	-	-	SE	-	0.208	1
-	Road	-	-	-	-	-	-	176	0.048	-

Table 2.1: Summary of excavation results (O.D.S. = outer ditch segments; O.PR.P. = outer postring postholes; I.D.S. = inner ditch segments; I.PR.P. = inner postring postholes)

2.3 The structures

A more in-depth analysis of the above-mentioned features and the constructiona techniques they represented is provided in Chapter 4. A summary of the results is presented in Table 2.1.

All radiocarbon dates in the text are quoted in calibrated form at two sigma (for full detail see Table 4.3). Context numbers are given in brackets. Unless otherwise mentioned, the identified pottery was Middle Bronze Age in date. Further Middle Bronze Age pottery was derived from contexts associated with the ringfort, including the remains of four barrel-shaped vessels and an additional four vessels. Details regarding each structure's artefacts are located in Chapter 3.

Structure:	**1**
Illustration:	2.1
Shape:	Sub-circular
Measurements:	10.6m × 8.6m
Location:	S1 was adjacent to and respected both S2 and S8. Road surface F100 lay immediately east of S1; the cobbled entrance path of the SSE-facing entrance extended south, then east, onto this road.
Outer ditch segments:	n=3
	In several places single and double rows of boulders ran along the centre of these segments and the covering ditch fills contained further large stones.
Outer postring:	n=34
	The fill of one contained a small quantity of unidentifiable burnt bone These postholes occurred in small clusters e.g. [197], [184], [201], and [199 or [639], [640;1], [604;2], and [604;4] and are likely to represent more than one phase of construction/repair.
	Inner ditch: No definite inner ditch segments were identified. Many of the internal pits could represent the remains of such segments but with so many postholes cutting the pits it was difficult to identify with any certainty which pits may actually represent inner ditch segments.
Inner postring:	n=11
	The fills of these postholes contained frequent stones, including packing stones. Some of these postholes occurred in clusters, e.g. [178], [180] and [182] as well as [190], [192] and [188], which suggests multiple (most likely three) phases of modification. These clusters are positioned adjacent to notable groups of outer postring postholes as described above and these areas may indicate the position of rafters.
Entrance:	SSE
	There were two phases to the entrance: the first comprised a shallow sunken pathway which extended south [196] then curved eastwards on to road F100. A layer of close-set cobbles was present at the base. During the second phase, paving stones were laid on top of the cobbling to create a large, flat area [262] (*c.* 2m length × 1.8m width). A number of postholes at the entrance gap probably represent successive doorjambs rather than a porch. Four postholes [608;18] and [608;20–22] and a pit [9122] located in a cluster on the western side of the entrance are presumed to mark the locations of the former western doorjambs. On the eastern side of the

Illustration 2.1: Structure 1

Additional features:

Artefacts:

Radiocarbon dates:

Notes:

entrance gap two postholes [608;11] and [608;23] were presumed to mark the position of the eastern doorjambs. It seems that the presence of adjacent S2 to the south prevented the creation of an elongated entrance.

Two segments of external ditch (which contained stone settings) located to the north of the outer ditch segments may represent a later modification or extension to the structure beyond the line of the original outer ditch, although one segment did not maintain a constant distance from the main outer ditch segment, which could suggest that the external ditch post-dated the principal occupation phase of the structure.

A large, polished macehead (147mm × 115mm × 62.5mm) was discovered in the interior of S1, being utilised as a packing stone in posthole [608;105]. The macehead has been assigned an Early to Middle Bronze Age date. A palstave mould fragment (90mm × 48mm × 18.5mm) was recovered *c.* 1m north of the structure, is of Middle Bronze Age date and is therefore likely to be contemporary with S1's main occupation. The majority of the pottery from S1 was derived from the outer ditch segments. The pottery represented 12 barrel-shaped vessels, two straight-sided vessels and two rimmed vessels, as well as nine bodysherds of fine fabric, two base fragments of medium fabric, 74 bodysherds of medium fabric, and 129 fragments of medium fabric, and three bodysherds and fragments of coarse fabric.

A charcoal sample from the fill of this outer ditch returned an Early Bronze Age radiocarbon date of 2016–1772 BC (UB-6230); however, it is at considerable variance to the other dates from the site and may be from old timber recycled or the centre of a long-lived wood species.

The number of outer postring postholes suggests that the structure was rebuilt, or at least structurally modified, on more than one occasion, with no single, cohesive ground plan discernable from the internal features alone. Clustering was particularly noticeable at the southwest of the structure and postholes from both the outer and also the inner postring were grouped together. The premise that the house was modified or rebuilt is further supported by the existence of the above-mentioned external ditch found in two segments located around the north and east perimeter. The resurfacing of the entrance path from a fine cobble to a more substantial stone paving also indicates that modifications took place.

Structure:	**2**
Illustration:	2.2
Shape:	Oval
Measurements:	11.5m × 9.5m
Location:	South of S1, to the east of S12, to the north of S16.
Outer ditch segments:	n=8

The fill in each of these segments contained medium-sized and large stones positioned along the bases. Patches of fine cobbling were noted in areas and several sherds of prehistoric pottery were recovered from the fills.

Outer postring: n=27

Only one obvious cluster was noted: [4418], [4412] and [4414], located near the entrance, and this suggests that there were approximately three construction / modification phases, at least in this area.

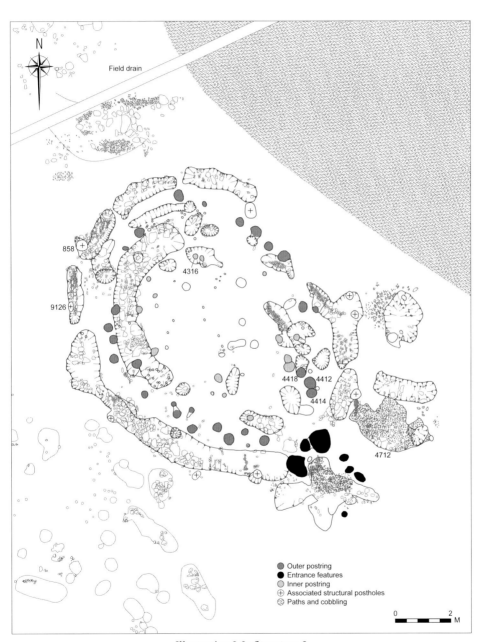

Field drain

858

4316

9126

4418 4412

4414

4712

- ● Outer postring
- ● Entrance features
- ● Inner postring
- ⊕ Associated structural postholes
- ⊚ Paths and cobbling

0   2

M

Illustration 2.2: Structure 2

Inner ditch:	n=1
	It was similar in form and size to the outer ditch segments and also contained a stone setting or wall foundation and therefore may have been related to a different phase of occupation or modification. This layer of large, flat stones was similar to those in a feature observed within S13 and S5, although in these cases the stones were well-laid and resembled paving or a surface, suggesting that these were storage or work areas.
Inner postring:	n=15
	The majority contained considerable quantities of charcoal in their fills.
Entrance:	SE
	Twelve features comprised the entranceway, including a possible door jamb and a large pit with a partially cobbled base. Cobbled patches were noted in several other features, most noticeably the shallow irregular feature [4712] which may have been an entrance from an earlier phase.
Additional features:	Nine substantial postholes lay within and adjacent to the outer ditch segments, particularly at the south, and some of these were cut by the ditch. Although inconsistent in arrangement, and with two postholes, [9126] and [858], clearly sealed by stone settings within the outer ditch, it is possible that these represent an initial phase of an exterior wall which was defined or supported by wooden posts.
	There was also a high concentration of internal features within S2, mostly small shallow pits that were circular, elongated or irregular in shape, and which were of undetermined function.
Artefacts:	The pottery from S2 represented three straight-sided vessels and five barrel-shaped vessels as well as a ninth vessel (V25) and 43 sherds/fragments of varying fabric.
Radiocarbon dates:	N/A
Notes:	N/A

Structure:	3
Illustration:	2.3
Shape:	Sub-circular
Measurements:	8.6m × 7.8m
Location:	S3 was partly overlaid on the western side by the entranceway of S42.
Outer ditch segments:	n=6
	Three of the segments contained pebbles, a moderate amount of larger stones and occasional charcoal flecks and flint flakes throughout. A large amount of prehistoric pottery (173 sherds) was recovered, the majority of which came from the northwest section of the outer ditch, and which may have been discarded from the temporally later S43.
Outer postring:	n=0
Inner ditch:	n=1
	Cobbling and larger stones were laid on the base.
Inner postring:	n=0
Entrance:	ESE
	This consisted of a large irregularly shaped cut [263] (4.98m × 0.89–2.5m × 0.2–0.25m) forming a pathway. Like many of the other entrances on the site, it appeared to be two phased. The first phase consisted of simple cobbling but this was later superseded by a layer of large flat stone which

N

B
B1

285

A1

263

A

⊙ Paths and cobbling

0   2
■—■—■—■ M

PROFILE OF ENTRANCE FEATURE   PROFILE OF INNER DITCH SEGMENT

A   A1   B   B1
22.236m OD +   +   21.970m OD +   +

0   1
■—■—■ M

Illustration 2.3: Structure 3

survived particularly well towards the southeast end. Occasional charcoal flecks and flint flakes were recovered, along with 13 prehistoric pottery sherds. No porch or postholes for doorjambs were evident.

Additional features: The internal area of the structure was 7.7m north–south by 7m east–west and contained various features (postholes and pits) contemporary with the occupational use and an additional feature [285] of probable modern date and insertion. No hearth was identified.

Artefacts: The pottery from S3 represented seven barrel-shaped vessels along with a further vessel and 123 sherds and fragments of varying fabrics.

Radiocarbon dates: N/A

Notes: The precise relationship between S3 and S42 is unknown as, during excavation, this area was waterlogged. It is possible that S3 pre-dated S42, but it is also possible that the two structures were contemporary and associated, at least for part of their occupation.

Structure: **4**

Illustration: 2.4

Shape: Sub-circular

Measurements: 11.4m × 9.5m

Location: Northeast of road F100 and northwest of S50.

Outer ditch segments: n=7

The outer ditch was considerably deeper than the inner ditch and subsequently the bank ran down to the top of the edge of the outer ditch. The outer edge of this ditch had been revetted with large, flat stones which survived particularly well around the northwest. A series of small stakeholes was found around the base of the outside slope of these ditch segments and these may have been used to secure the revetment in some manner. An earth-cut drainage channel [377] extended northwest, down slope, from the ditch and terminated in a shallow sump below the road.

Outer postring: n=12

These postholes were interspersed with stakeholes. Postholes were located immediately inside the inner edge of the stone wall set on the middle bank. The stakeholes indicated the probable presence of wattle panels. Packing stones were few and only one [350] contained any pottery (three sherds).

Inner ditch: n=3

The base of the shallow, segmented inner ditch contained a fine cobbled surface and it was considered during excavations to represent an internal division of space.

Neither the outer nor the inner ditch extended around the eastern side of the structure; a particularly curious arrangement. An external stone wall was located on the middle bank between the two ditches (which later slumped into the outer ditch fill). The middle bank had a consistent form all around the western and northern circumference of the structure. It was a narrow, flat area, level with the top of the outer slope of the inner ditch.

Inner postring: n=16

The fill of posthole [529] contained two charred grains of barley (*Hordeum distichon* L./*H. vulgare* L) as well as charred wood fragments and six

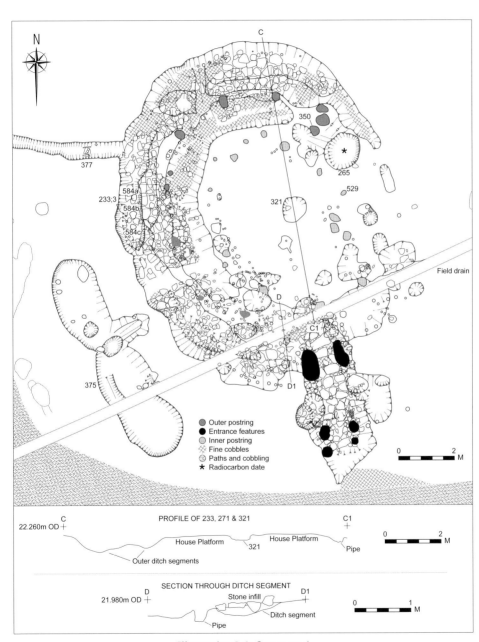

Illustration 2.4: Structure 4

Entrance:

poorly preserved charred cereal grains (one identifiable as barley). This inner ring was also interspersed with numerous stakeholes, suggesting an internal screen or partition wall for the central space.

S

The entrance was 5m long by 2m wide and was represented by opposing pairs of postholes, indicative of a porch, associated with a sunken, finely cobbled entrance path. As with S3, the fine cobbles had subsequently been covered over by a layer of large flat stones, some of which overlay the paired postholes, suggesting that the porch had been dismantled before this occurred. A shallow slope with a sub-triangular shape, just beyond the entrance in the interior, is probably the result of erosion caused by people entering and leaving the structure. The entrance led on to a fine cobbled trackway, which connected to the entrance of S52, situated to the east, and to the major road surface to the southeast.

Additional features:

No hearth was located within the structure, although a substantial pit [321] filled with sterile material was located close to the building's centre.

Investigation of the join between the drain [377] and outer ditch segment [233;3] showed that the outer ditch was deepened by at least 0.1m in some areas, making it much deeper than the drainage channel and thus rendering it redundant. The interface of the drainage channel and the ditch was then blocked using a triangular-shaped, flat stone set on end, and it is thought that this stone was placed at the same time as the revetting stones were positioned against the outer edge of the outer ditch. A large ceramic vessel (recovered as a concentration of 51 pottery sherds) had been placed into this drain 1.2m from the eastern end, presumably at the same time as it was blocked, and this possibly represents an act of structured deposition of which there is so little evidence across the site (see Chapter 5). Three truncated postholes [584;a], [584;b] and [584;c] which survived to a depth of just 0.1m were discovered sealed beneath the stones of the collapsed revetment and outer wall at the east of the structure. These had obviously been truncated when the outer ditch was deepened but it is not clear if they belonged to an earlier phase of the building or pre-dated it entirely. If dug from the original ground surface these postholes would have been very deep, perhaps as much as 0.7m or 0.8m. A similar deep posthole was found underlying the ditch at the northeast of S52.

Between 1.2m and 1.4m to the west of the southwestern side of S4's ditch [233;1–6] was a large, elongated pit [375] (7.6m × 1.7–2m × 0.4–0.69m) and because of its proximity it is suspected that its use was contemporary with at least one phase of S4. It contained large stones and a moderate amount of charcoal throughout with much larger quantities of charcoal occurring at the southern, deeper end. It also contained 38 pottery sherds and several postholes were cut into its base. An unusual feature, its purpose remains enigmatic and it is not known whether this feature was associated with the final phase or an earlier one. Only a large pit, half the size of [375], located to the east of the equally large and complex S13 provides an approximate on-site parallel.

Artefacts:

Over 700 prehistoric pottery sherds were recovered from contexts associated with this structure, including 360 sherds discovered in an internal pit [265] which had a well-like profile (1.36m diameter × 1m depth with vertical sides and a flat, cobbled base). Pottery from S4 included a sherd from an Early Neolithic carinated bowl, 26 barrel-shaped vessels including several large examples, and a further 10 vessels including flat-rimmed, round-rimmed and straight sided examples, as well as 680 sherds/fragments of varying fabric.

Radiocarbon dates: A radiocarbon date of 1431–1270 BC (UB-6231) was derived from pit [265], although it is highly unlikely that this pit was contemporary with the structure's occupation, and it presumably post-dates its abandonment. Charcoal (hazel (*Corylus avellana*)) from the same context was radiocarbon dated (by Chrono as part of Ginn's research) to 1424–1302 BC (UBA-16615).

Notes: The archaeological footprint of S4 is complicated and there is definite evidence for multiple phases of modification to the structure. During excavation two episodes of considerable rebuild where the inner ditch was an integral part of each phase were acknowledged; during post-excavation analysis Chris Lynn suggested an alternative proposal (Chris Lynn, pers. comm.). Lynn suggested that the inner ditch may have represented the perimeter of a smaller, earlier structure, which was supported by the inner postring. Indeed, he points out that the inner postring appears orientated on a different entrance axis from that of the outer postring, thus providing further evidence for a separate structure. This structure could then have been replaced by a larger structure, the perimeters of which were defined by the outer ditch. In this scenario the available space was increased with the construction of the later, larger structure. It should be noted that during the excavation the cobbles and stone features in the inner ditch and on the middle bank were seen to blend into each other and likewise features on the middle bank blended into features within the outer ditch. It is therefore unlikely that the inner ditch as recorded is not directly associated with the middle bank and the outer ditch. However, these features may have removed a small ditch that formed the perimeter of a small oval structure associated with the inner postring. The shallow feature immediately east of the northern end of the entrance [9018] could therefore relate to the entrance of an earlier structure rather than the perimeter of the double ditch structure.

Structure: **5**
Illustration: 2.5
Shape: Sub-circular
Measurements: 11m × 10.8m
Location: Towards the northwest of the settlement, to the east of S6 and the west of S45.
Outer ditch segments: n=8
Patches of inlaid cobbling and deposits of stones were identified throughout the outer ditch segments. Deposits of charcoal and pink ash were found in the southern segments. The outer ditch was cut by or cut through the southern-most ditch segment of the inner ditch, suggesting that originally S5 consisted of a small building defined by the inner ditch segments which were replaced by a larger building at some stage.
Outer postring: n=15
Many of the postholes contained packing stones.

Illustration 2.5: Structure 5

Inner ditch:	n=3
	The base of the inner ditch segments contained patches of inlaid cobbling. A further two patches [693] (1.12m length × 0.7m width) and [693a] (0.75m length × 0.5m width) were noted towards the southeast of the interior. A single deposit [692] consisting of charcoal-rich, sandy clay with ash and patches of red oxidisation was discovered above [693]. Numerous pits, possible postholes, stakeholes and deposits, including deposit [253] from which 89 prehistoric pottery sherds were collected, cut the inner ditch.
Inner postring:	n=?3
	A series of stakeholes ran between [702] and [688].
Entrance:	E/SE
	The entrance consisted of a simple 1.35m-wide gap in the ditch segments, flanked by two large postholes. S5 may not have had an extended entrance because of the presence S45, if it was pre-existing. An unusual shallow oval pit with a cobble-lined base and a layer of large flat stones at the south was located immediately north of this structure. This pit had clear parallels to some of the entrance features seen on other structures, but no associated structure was identified.
Additional features:	N/A
Artefacts:	Pottery from S5 included 22 barrel-shaped vessels and two vessels and 214 sherds/fragments of varying fabric.
Radiocarbon dates:	N/A
Notes:	A small building, S46, was built immediately south of S5 and is suspected to have been added sometime after S5 was constructed but then used simultaneously.
Structure:	**6**
Illustration:	2.6
Shape:	Sub-circular
Measurements:	9m × 8.5m
Location:	NNW of S5.
Outer ditch segments:	n=3
	The ditch contained a blackish-brown, loosely compacted, clayey loam with frequent charcoal inclusions. Towards the bottom of the fill there were large quantities of medium-sized and large stones thought to represent a collapsed wall foundation. Underneath these stones was a cobbled layer. The ditch contained 116 sherds of pottery.
Outer postring:	n=26
	These postholes were grouped in clusters of two, e.g. [3448] and [3280], and three, e.g. [3050], [3052] and [3046]. Many contained packing stones and charcoal and eight contained prehistoric pottery sherds in various quantities of one to 13. Two of these sherds represented the remains of an Early Neolithic 'cup'.
Inner ditch:	n=1
	There were two concentrations of small and medium-sized stones resting on the base of this feature. Nine sherds of pottery were recovered.
Inner postring:	n=0
Entrance:	S
	The entrance to this structure [3316] (3.8m length × 1.6m width) was located at the south and extended into the interior for an additional 2m.

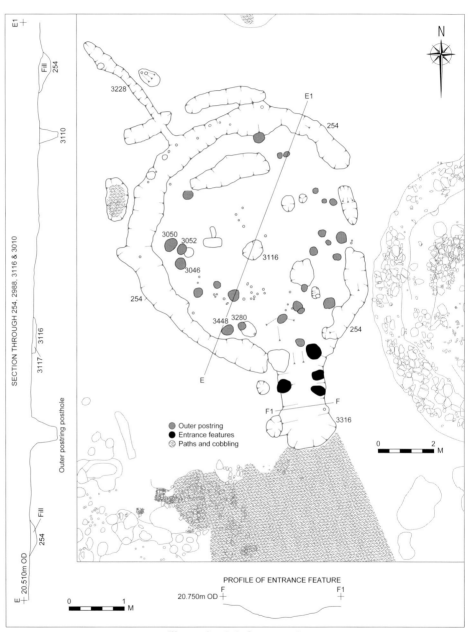

Illustration 2.6: Structure 6

The base was covered in a layer of cobbling, part of which was continuous with the cobbled trackway (which connected to S48) to the south of the structure. Postholes which were associated with the entrance provided evidence for a porch.

Additional features: In the approximate centre of the structure was a sub-oval hearth [3116] (0.7m × 0.6m × 0.13m). The fill consisted of a brownish-black, loosely compacted, clayey silt, with frequent charcoal and occasional small and medium-sized stones. The base of the feature was burnt to a bright orange colour, particularly at the north. The size, shape and location of this feature were very reminiscent of the central feature with sterile fills in S4.

External features included a linear feature [3228] (5.05m × 0.26–0.38m × 0.32m) which extended northwest of the outer ditch [254] between S6 and S41. This was a narrow linear ditch, of a type seen at other structures on this site, for example at S4 and S9. It contained 24 pottery sherds and gravel-rich fills. It may represent a drainage channel, although it shared its alignment with several postholes running off to the northwest and may, therefore, have been accompanied by a fence.

Artefacts: In addition to the sherds from the Early Neolithic 'cup', 10 barrel-shaped vessels were identified along with sherds from a further six vessels and 221 sherds and fragments of varying fabric.

Radiocarbon dates: N/A

Notes: N/A

Structure:	7
Illustration:	2.7
Shape:	Oval
Measurements:	10m × 7.9m
Location:	At the northern end of the road F100, south of S9 and east of S43.
Outer ditch segments:	n=2

There were three concentrations of charcoal in the southwest of the ditch suggesting that the building, or at least parts of it, had been partially burnt. The first formed the remains of one or more burnt wooden planks broken into several pieces. This represented the only direct evidence on the site for the use of planks in the construction of buildings during the main phase of occupation. Their location – where the ditch intersected with the entrance feature – suggests that these timbers belonged to a porch covering the entrance. The other two charcoal concentrations, located against the outer edge of the ditch, were the remains of a series of burnt vertical timbers, several of which were still partially intact, and the burnt material in between them is presumed to represent the remains of the much smaller sails that ran horizontally between the timbers. A fourth deposit, comprising charcoal, ash and burnt soil, in the north of the ditch may represent the remains of an inner line of wattle which had collapsed inwards when the structure was burnt.

Outer postring:	n=14
Inner ditch:	n=0
Inner postring:	n=0
Entrance:	SSE

The sunken entrance [3768] (*c.* 4.5m maximum width × 4.3m maximum length) was located to the SSE. This entrance was unusual compared to the

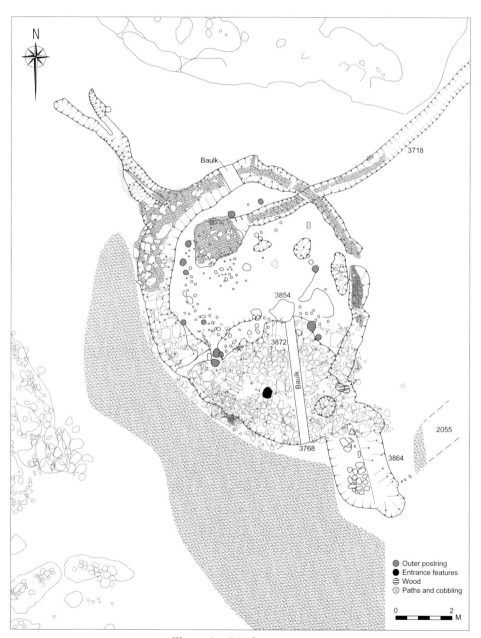

Illustration 2.7: Structure 7

typical design of the entrances during the main occupation phase (narrow, long, and covered by a porch). Beneath the upper fill was a charcoal layer which covered a single course of flattish stones and patches of cobble and a piece of burnt timber. An earlier entrance [3864] (4.7m length, with an original length of *c.* 8m, × 1.8m width) was of more typical design, being both narrower and longer than its successor. The roadway F100 was laid across this area after this original entrance was deliberately backfilled, thus consolidating the new entrance. A similar phenomenon was recorded at S4, where the drainage channel [377] was blocked off and covered over by the road surface, and the structure was then remodelled.

Additional features:	An area to the north of the entrance survived to a greater height than the rest of the internal surface. A possible hearth [3854] (0.83m × 0.7m × 0.35m) with patches of oxidised clay on the base and sides and two associated stakeholes was cut into this area. A pit [3872] (0.33m × 0.22m × 0.08m) with a well-compacted fill including stones, charcoal and two pottery sherds, may represent a previous hearth or a deliberately filled-in rubbish pit. A curving band of stakeholes was concentric with the northern edge of the entrance features and possibly formed a dividing screen. Other internal stakeholes concentric with the postring were observed and probably result from wattle screens and their replacements placed around the inside of the structure.

A cobbled, WSW–ENE pathway [2055] (5.5m length × 1.8m width), positioned east of the structure, was damaged in the area where it connected with the entrance(s), but it appeared to line up with the eastern side of the earlier entrance feature [3864]. It is not clear which entrance the pathway served, perhaps both.

S7 was truncated by an enigmatic later feature [3718] which ran southwest–northeast and which terminated in a pit in the northwest interior of S7; its function and date are unknown but the use of fine cobbles along its base suggests that it is broadly contemporary with the settlement.

Artefacts:	The pottery from S7 represented two barrel-shaped vessels and one other vessel; 10 fragments and bodysherds of fine and medium fabric were also identified.
Radiocarbon dates:	N/A
Notes:	N/A

Structure:	**8**
Illustration:	2.8
Shape:	Sub-circular
Measurements:	11m × 8m
Location:	Southwest of S1.
Outer ditch segments:	n=5
	All contained stones which overlay a layer of cobbles. One of the segments [3954] contained a stone mould (88.3mm × 22.3mm × 38mm) which was one of four discovered on the site and appeared to have been made from steatite and be of Middle Bronze Age type.
Outer postring:	n=21
	Almost all contained charcoal flecks and packing stones in their fills. The fill of [4104] comprised a black, charcoal-rich material with oxidised, sandy clay. A sample from this derived a radiocarbon date of 1601–1415 BC (UB-6240).

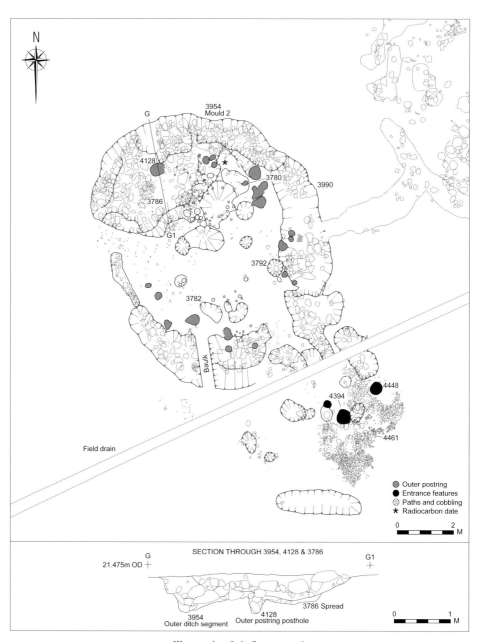

Illustration 2.8: Structure 8

Inner ditch:	n=0
Inner postring:	n=0
Entrance:	SE

This was a large cobbled area [4461] (4.1m length × 3.1m width). A total of 42 prehistoric pottery sherds were collected from the deposit above the cobble layer. Various pits and postholes were associated, most notably postholes [4448] (0.44m diameter × 0.4m depth) and [4394] (0.58m × 0.56m × 0.45m) which represent an opposing pair of posts for the entrance doorway.

Additional features: Many of the internal features in the northwestern quadrant of the structure were located under an irregularly shaped deposit [3786] (4.15m × 2.57m × 0.5m) consisting of stones, charcoal patches and areas of oxidisation in two distinct layers. The primary layer sealed patches of cobble stones and charcoal flecks and represents possible habitation layers or floor material within the structure. A total of 35 prehistoric pottery sherds from various vessels were derived from this deposit. Of the many internal pits, two may have been used as hearths. The larger pit [3782] (0.89m × 0.47m × 0.41m) contained unidentifiable burnt bone fragments as well as prehistoric pottery sherds on top of a charcoal-rich soil with an ashy composition and heat-fractured stone fragments. A number of predominantly flat-sided, medium-sized stones were set into the inner sides of the feature, providing a lining. The second, sub-circular, possible hearth [3792] (0.65m × 0.6m × 0.41m) cut the outer ditch [3990]. The primary fill contained charcoal flecks, unidentifiable burnt bone fragments and 19 prehistoric pottery sherds. A small band of oxidised clay was identified along the base. An ash layer was recorded above this fill. The nature of the pit would certainly indicate that it may have functioned as a probable hearth; however, its location may suggest otherwise. A fourth internal feature of note was a large, shallow feature [3780] (1.6m × 1.35m × 0.27m) which was associated with 15 roughly equidistant stakeholes, positioned in a rough circle around it and representing a possible surrounding framework for the suspension of cooking wares over a third cooking/hearth site. The fill was composed of mid-brown-grey, friable sandy clay with a moderate amount of small to medium-sized, sub-rounded/angular stones with occasional flecks of charcoal scattered throughout the soil. Approximately 25 charred cereal grains were identified, many of them barley (probably all of them belonging to the naked variety), and either emmer or spelt wheat (*Triticum dicoccum* Schübl./*T. spelta* L.).

A total of 87 prehistoric pottery sherds (barrel-shaped V121) were derived from a charcoal-rich layer in external, sub-oval pit [4094] (1.99m × 1m × 0.39m), located close to the entrance. Large pits positioned adjacent to the entrance were a common phenomenon at the Corrstown settlement.

Artefacts: The pottery from S8 included barrel-shaped V121 along with a further five barrel-shaped vessels, another vessel, and 83 sherds/fragments not assigned to particular vessels of varying fabric.

Radiocarbon dates:	Postring posthole: 1601–1415 BC (UB-6240).
Notes:	N/A

Structure:	**9**
Illustration:	2.9

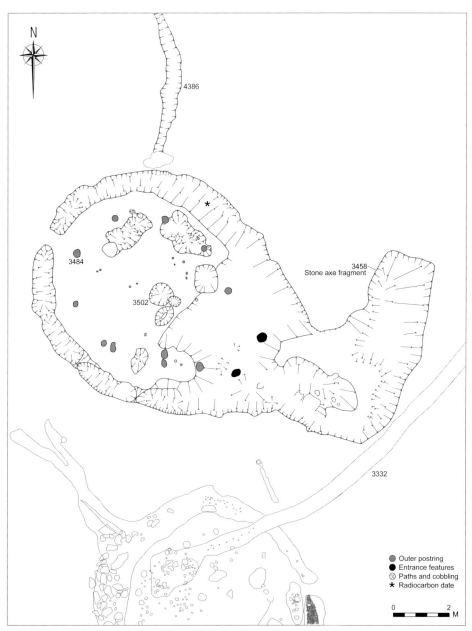

Illustration 2.9: Structure 9

Shape:	Sub-circular
Measurements:	10m × 8m
Location:	Directly north of S7; most northerly structure excavated.
Outer ditch segments:	n=8

A single course of or tightly packed stones at the base were laid on to three stones which ran across. Seventeen individual pieces of wood surviving in a carbonised form were found in the ditch fill and further pieces were discovered within the entrance fill. Many of these burnt timbers were discovered resting directly on top of the stone setting. Their presence indicates that the structure may have burnt down. One of these timbers was identified as alder (*Alnus glutinosa*) and radiocarbon dated to 1261–935 BC (Beta-190132).

Outer postring:	n=11

Many contained charcoal inclusions and one [3484] contained a prehistoric pottery sherd.

Inner ditch:	n=0
Inner postring:	n=0
Entrance:	SE

This entrance feature was unusual in several regards, while it still conformed to the general pattern of sunken entrance features observed during the main phase of occupation. As the entrance came out from the structure it continued for only 1m before turning 90° and heading off to the northeast for *c.* 3.6m. It turned abruptly to avoid crossing a curving linear boundary [3332], possibly a boundary ditch, which post-dated S7 and this deviation suggests that the ditch was contemporary with the occupation of S9. The entrance feature was 3.2m wide as it left the structure and between 2.4m and 2.8m wide after the 90° turn. There was no surviving evidence for doorposts or a porch. Twenty-six pieces of carbonised wood were recovered from various parts of this entrance feature. The centre of the base was paved with large flat stones, and the rest of the base was cobbled with small stones. The entrance feature also extended into the southeastern third of the structure's interior, in a similar, but more extensive, manner to the entrance of S6. Where the entrance crossed the internal threshold there was even a slight lowering of height and the base here was covered in fine cobbling rather than the usual large flat stones. A small raised pedestal was present and the overall unusual entrance arrangement meant that the interior would have been at two distinctly different heights. Sixty three sherds of pottery were recovered from this entrance feature as well as a stone axe fragment (26.5mm × 26mm × 7.5mm).

Additional features:	Internal features consisted of a variety of pits and postholes. A sub-circular pit [3502] (0.73m diameter × 0.17m depth), deliberately backfilled with stones and charcoal in a silty clay matrix, may represent a hearth which had been decommissioned before the destruction of the structure. A curvilinear feature [4386] (6.05m × 0.18–0.57m × 0.2m) ran from ditch [3454] at its most northerly point and, like similar linear features associated with other structures, it may represent a drainage channel.
Artefacts:	The pottery from S9 consisted of sherds from two barrel-shaped vessels, another thick-walled vessel and 45 sherds and fragments from fine and medium fabric unidentifiable vessels.

Radiocarbon dates:	N/A
Notes:	The 43 pieces of timber found in the fill of the ditch and entrance feature represent some of the best evidence recovered from this site regarding the nature of the buildings' superstructure and associated non-load bearing wall. The majority of the timbers appeared to be the fragmentary remains of small poles with diameters of *c*. 0.1m. These were arranged either perpendicular to the edges of the structure or parallel with them. The consistency of this arrangement indicates that it did not occur by chance. No attempt was made to rebuild the structure after it was destroyed by fire.

Structure:	**10**
Illustration:	2.10
Shape:	Circular
Measurements:	9.2m diameter
Location:	West of road F100, directly east of S11.
Outer ditch segments:	n=6
Outer postring:	n=?19
	It was not clear precisely how many postholes could be attributed to the postring.
Inner ditch:	n=?3
	Three inner ditch segments, two of which had cobbling in their base, may represent part of an earlier building phase.
Inner postring:	n=?19
	Nineteen of the internal postholes may have formed outer and inner postrings but modifications and rebuilds of the structure have obscured the extant evidence. Therefore, conclusively determining to which phase or to which postring (outer or inner) these postholes belonged was not possible, although a probable interpretation is portrayed in Illustration 2.10.
Entrance:	SE
	The southeast entrance was defined by two opposing postholes [2122] (0.53m × 0.42m × 0.28m) and [2124] (0.45m × 0.3m × 0.26m) set 0.7m apart at the southern end of a cobble patch [1960].
Additional features:	Further ditch segments extended internally from its west and eastern sides; these could not be defined as an inner ditch. Nineteen postholes were present but it was not possible to identify which of these belonged to an outer or an inner postring. Their arrangement – combined with the layout of the additional ditch segments and an external ditch segment – suggests that S10 had been considerably modified during the course of its occupation; indeed there may even be sufficient evidence to indicate the presence of two distinct structures.
	Two patches of cobbled surfaces were observed towards the south of the structure. Numerous internal stakeholes, with a particular concentration in the southeast quadrant, may be the remains of internal partitioning. An external ditch segment [2113A] (3.72m × 1.12m × 0.17m) contained a compact, cobbled surface and is similar to many other such segments on site.
Artefacts:	Only one vessel, a small barrel-shaped vessel with a round rim, could be identified from the pottery sherds associated with S10; two further bodysherds of coarse fabric were also identified.

Illustration 2.10: Structure 10

Radiocarbon dates:	N/A
Notes:	The positioning of ditch segment [1936], shared by S10 and S11, suggests that both structures were in use contemporaneously.

Structure:	**11**
Illustration:	2.11
Shape:	Sub-circular
Measurements:	8.8m × 6.4m
Location:	Immediately west of S10.
Outer ditch segments:	n=4
	Cobbled bases
Outer postring:	N/A
Inner ditch:	N/A
Inner postring:	n=6
Entrance:	SE
Additional features:	N/A
Artefacts:	One barrel-shaped vessel and five further fragments and sherds of fine and coarse fabric were discovered.
Radiocarbon dates:	N/A
Notes:	It seems likely that both S11 and S10 were being used simultaneously, as seems to have happened elsewhere on the site, such as the addition of S30 to the eastern side of S31, or the construction of S46 immediately south of S5.

Structure:	**12**
Illustration:	2.12
Shape:	Almost circular
Measurements:	8.4m × 8m
Location:	Between S2 and S16.
Outer ditch segments:	n=5
	Ditch segments were filled with stones and charcoal flecks and also contained almost 200 prehistoric pottery sherds.
Outer postring:	N/A
Inner ditch:	N/A
Inner postring:	n=10
	The majority contained packing stones and charcoal flecks.
Entrance:	SE
	Two pairs of postholes formed the threshold between the structure and the entrance and their pairing indicates that the entrance was modified at least once. An external cobbled path extended up to 5m was flanked by the remains of pits and postholes, suggesting the former presence of a porch.
Additional features:	Nine of the external features (which measured an average width of 1.34m, widening as the features continued southwards) formed a rough curvilinear shape around the west and southwest of the building which defined an open space between these features and the segmented outer ditch of S12.
Artefacts:	Pottery from S12 included a rimsherd and bodysherd from an Early Neolithic carinated bowl, as well as eight barrel-shaped vessels of varying sizes, and a further two vessels and a further 59 sherds and fragments too small or indistinct to be assigned to particular vessels.

1936

Outer postring
Entrance features
Paths and cobbling

0   2
           M

Illustration 2.11: Structure 11

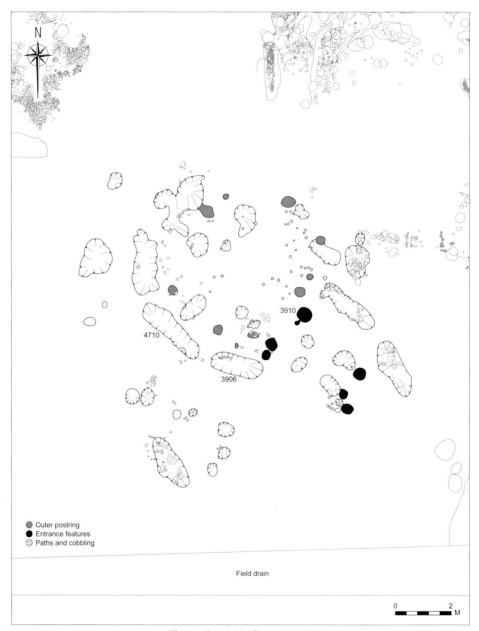

Illustration 2.12: Structure 12

Radiocarbon dates:	N/A
Notes:	N/A
Structure:	**13**
Illustration:	2.13
Shape:	Almost circular
Measurements:	11.2m × 11m
Location:	Central area of settlement, southwest of S15.
Outer ditch segments:	n=10

The fills of all 10 outer ditch segments were remarkably consistent and comprised dark sandy clay with occasional charcoal inclusions. Large stones were spread unevenly throughout the segments. A pit / posthole [6342] cut through the outer slope of segment [6268;8] and contained approximately 90 fairly well-preserved charred cereal grains; all were barley and both naked and hulled types were identified. Approximately 350 pottery sherds came from the fill of some of the outer ditch segments and just over 200 came from the fill of segment [6268;5] in two separate concentrations, one at either end of the feature. The largest concentration was found near the eastern end of the feature, just beyond the stone setting. It comprised the sides of a large, bucket-shaped vessel, which had been broken into three large pieces and then stacked one on top of the other. A smaller concentration was located at the western end of the feature. Although this was a more formless collection, it was found at a similar height and probably represents a considerable proportion of a vessel, as 37 separate sherds were recovered from a very small area.

Outer postring:	n=22

This postring was positioned on the bank between the outer and the inner ditch. Most of the postholes contained charcoal in their fills, as well as packing stones.

Inner ditch:	n=5

The fills of all five inner ditch segments were consistent and comprised a sandy silt with occasional charcoal among which 33 pottery sherds were recovered. The bases of some of these inner ditch segments were cobbled, while the bases of segments [6334;1] and [6334;2] at the north of the structure were covered in layers of large flat stone.

Inner postring:	n=29
Entrance:	SE

Two large opposed pits [6348] and [6456] which lay northwest–southeast and defined a channel between them with a width of 1.4m represented the principal components of the entrance. It is difficult to assign a structural function to these two features and they may simply be external pits flanking the entrance. Postholes in the area represent the remains of a porch. Combined, the features in this area form a pathway (4.2m length × 1.6m width) which had a small paved area at its southeast end. This entrance had clearly been remodelled on more than one occasion, and it is not clear which features were associated with any particular phase, or whether certain features, in particular the large pit [6348], were directly associated with the entrance at all.

Additional features:	An internal feature located immediately inside the entrance [6724] (0.8m × 0.6m × 0.12–0.19m) may represent a kiln. It was T-shaped and the northern

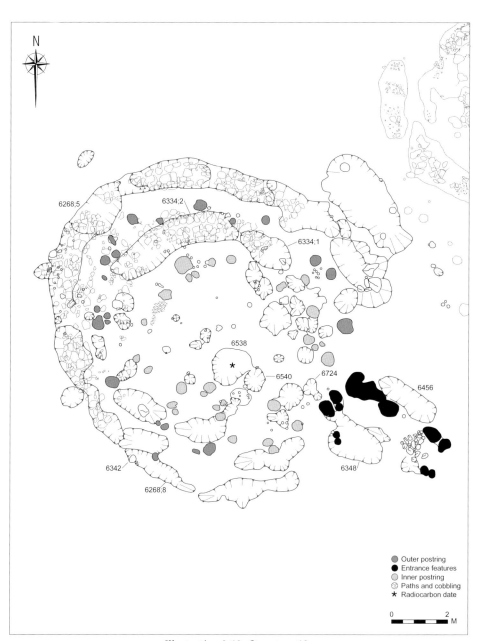

Illustration 2.13: Structure 13

part of the feature had a concave base and a general, bowl-like appearance. The southern section may have formed the flue; its fill contained a high proportion of charcoal. The top of the feature had been cobbled over. Two internal pits [6540] (0.76m diameter × 0.33m depth) and [6538] (1.5m × 1.26m × 0.35m) contained burnt stones and frequent charcoal inclusions in their fills. A sample from the fill of [6538] was radiocarbon dated to 1022–844 BC (UB-6245) and these features are considered to be later than the occupation phase of the S13 and may even post-date the occupation of the site.

Artefacts:	Two barrel-shaped vessels were obtained.
Radiocarbon dates:	N/A
Notes:	N/A

Structure:	**14**
Illustration:	2.14
Shape:	Sub-circular
Measurements:	9m × 8m
Location:	West of S13, east of S37.
Outer ditch segments:	n=5
	The fills in these segments consisted of silty clays with medium-sized and large stones, occasional charcoal flecks and flint fragments.
Outer postring:	n=16
	Many contained packing stones and charcoal occurred occasionally.
Inner ditch:	N/A
Inner postring:	N/A
Entrance:	SE
	The entrance was in the southeast of the structure and consisted of an elongated cut [1522] (3m length × 2.2m width) filled with stones. Two separate, opposing postholes [2690] (0.64m diameter × 0.54m depth) and [2732] (0.64m × 0.52m × 0.35m) were located at the opening of the structure, which could represent doorjambs.
Additional features:	A circular pit [1543] (0.6m diameter × 0.22m depth) was identified within the central area of the structure and appeared to have been used as a hearth. The base of the cut appears to have had small, rounded stones inlaid within it. The primary fill (0.12m depth) comprised a black, sandy clay with a high concentration of charcoal and oxidised clay. The secondary fill contained loose gravel, stones and occasional flint flakes. A shallow burnt spread [2676] (1.48m × 0.49m × 0.11m) was contained within a large shallow pit [2546]. Approximately 80 fairly well-preserved, charred grains of barley were observed in its fill and both naked and also hulled varieties were present.
	Several patches of cobbling were located around the immediate, external area of the structure, e.g. patch [1546] (8m × 6m × 0.11m).
Artefacts:	Three barrel-shaped vessels and a straight-sided vessel as well as eight sherds and fragments of fine and medium fabric were obtained.
Radiocarbon dates:	N/A
Notes:	N/A

Structure:	**15**
Illustration:	2.15
Shape:	Oval

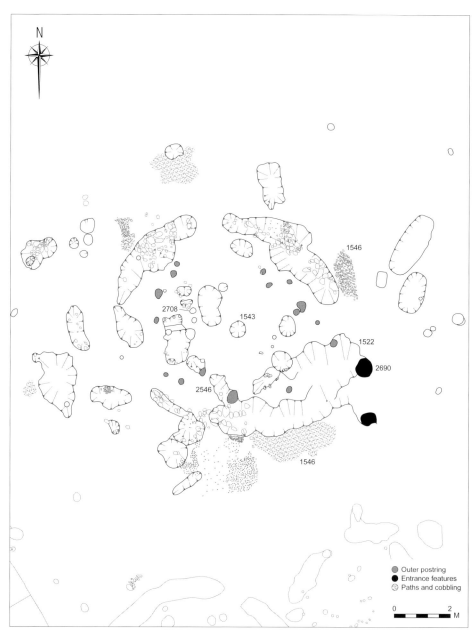

1546

2708

1543

1522

2690

2546

1546

Outer postring
Entrance features
Paths and cobbling

0   2
M

Illustration 2.14: Structure 14

Measurements:	9.4m × 7.8m
Location:	Centrally within the site, to the east of S13 and the south of S12.
Outer ditch segments:	n=5
	Each segment contained one fill which was similar throughout the circumference of the ditch and which consisted of brown sandy clay with frequent stones, clay patches, charcoal flecks, and flint fragments.
Outer postring:	n=29
	These were of various sizes and existed singly, e.g. [7052], and in clusters, of twos, e.g. [7328] and [7326], threes, e.g. [7154], [7154A] and [7182], and fours, e.g. [7100], [7162], [7098], and [7094]. This suggests that the structure had been rebuilt at least once but possibly twice, although only one phase contained an inner postring, as described below. Charcoal and flint fragments occurred frequently in the fills.
Inner ditch:	n=1
	The fill comprised mid-brown-black, loose, silty clay with moderate amounts of small and medium-sized stones, flint fragments and charcoal flecks.
Inner postring:	n=8
	Many contained flint fragments and charcoal inclusions. This inner postring was probably only used during a single building phase.
Entrance:	SE
	A long, sunken feature, the base of which was covered with fine cobbling [7126] (5m length × 2.2m width) comprised the entrance. The overlying fill was radiocarbon dated to 1410–1211 BC (UB-6378). This pathway was truncated by postholes and pits which may have formed a porch during a later phase of the building.
Additional features:	The excavation of the internal surface of the structure revealed an area surrounding the entranceway and eastern portion of the structure that had been covered with a compact layer of medium-sized and large, rounded and angular stones. This layer sealed a number of internal features. It is likely that the layer was intended to consolidate the strength of the floor with the addition of a rough cobbled floor surface. A similar process appears to have taken place towards the west of the structure, with the backfilling and levelling of two pit features.
	A sandy clay layer which served to level the interior was also identified within the structure. Part of this layer was covered with cobbles and may represent an extension of the entrance; another section was covered with a setting of several large stone slabs (0.6m × 0.5m) which may represent a later, stone floor surface.
	A possible central hearth [7175] (1.86m × 1.3m × 0.1m) contained charcoal flecks, fire-heated flint fragments, oxidised clay and stones. Six stakeholes were discovered in the base. An enigmatic curvilinear feature [7074] (8.15m length × 0.83m width) was cut by outer ditch segment [7080D] and cut through several internal features, although it appeared to pre-date the majority of S15's features. It is possible that [7074], with its stony fill and earlier date, may represent an unfinished structure, akin to S50.
Artefacts:	Two barrel-shaped vessels and 10 bodysherds and fragments of medium fabric.
Radiocarbon dates:	Posthole between the inner and outer postrings: 359–95 BC (UB-6242). Entrance feature: 1410–1211 BC (UB-6378).

Illustration 2.15: Structure 15

Notes:	A small, post-built structure was located immediately southwest of the house and consisted of 10 load-bearing postholes and several internal postholes and stakeholes. This may have been an annex possibly serving as an additional storage area or as an animal shelter or it may have been related to the internal posthole with the Iron Age date and therefore may represent a rectangular, Iron Age structure (projected dimensions 5m by 4m).

Structure:	**16**
Illustration:	2.16
Shape:	Oval/sub-rectangular
Measurements:	9m × 8m
Location:	This was partly overlain by or overlay S74 to the east.
Outer ditch segments:	n=3
	No traces of cobbling or stone settings were observed in the fills of these ditch segments.
Outer postring:	n=3
Inner ditch:	N/A
Inner postring:	N/A
Entrance:	SE
	No clear evidence was discerned although possible entrance feature (four postholes and two pits) were noted at the southeast.
Additional features:	There is evidence for three separate structures within the extant features, although the remains are too fragmented to warrant ascribing separate structure numbers. In addition to the features outlined above which appear to have comprised the latest phase of occupation, there is a further succession of outer ditch segments along the western side of S16 which seem to belong to an earlier building. The eastern edge of ditch segment [4760B] was adjacent to segment [4760A] of S16 but there was no evidence for truncation in either feature. A further segmented outer ditch with associated postholes can be observed in the interior of S16 and this represents the third structure in this locality.
Artefacts:	Six barrel-shaped vessels, a seventh vessel, and seven sherds and fragments of medium fabric and one bodysherd and one fragment of coarse fabric were discovered.
Radiocarbon dates:	N/A
Notes:	As with S74 the remains here are fragmented due to the presence of three separate rebuilds on the same spot.

Structure:	**17**
Illustration:	2.17
Shape:	Sub-circular
Measurements:	10.4m × 9.6m
Location:	South of road, north of S60, 10m east of S16.
Outer ditch segments:	n=6
	Four cobbled patches were discovered around the structure and some of these may represent the heavily truncated remains of further outer ditch segments. Two radiocarbon dates of 1429–1268 BC (UB-6381) and 1413–1213 BC (UBA-16611) (latter date by Chrono as part of Ginn's research; charcoal: hazel) were obtained from outer ditch segment [4118].
Outer postring:	n=18

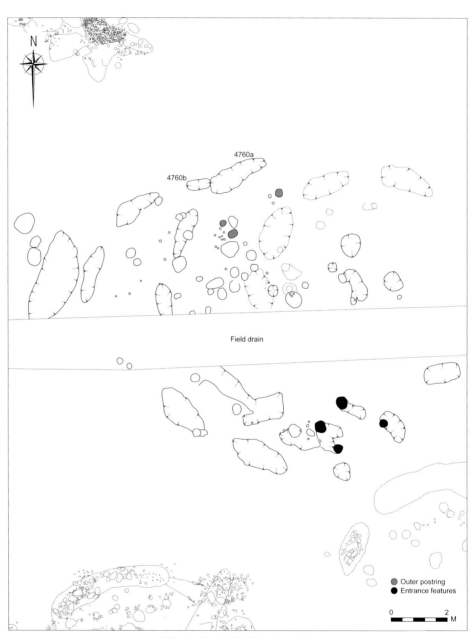

Illustration 2.16: Structure 16

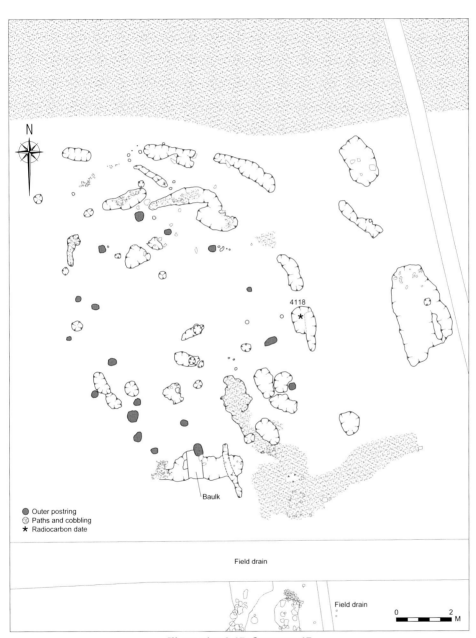

4118

Outer postring
Paths and cobbling
★ Radiocarbon date

Baulk

Field drain

Field drain

0   2
          M

Illustration 2.17: Structure 17

Inner ditch:	n=0
Inner postring:	n=0
Entrance:	SSE
	A cobbled spread with a narrow cobbled pathway running externally to the east was identified.
Additional features:	An arc of linear features was present around the outside of the structure at the north and northeast. This could represent the remains of an addition or extension, as seen at other Corrstown structures; although the trajectory of some of these linear features, and the lack of any similar features closer to the outer ditch segments, may indicate that this arc is later in date than the main occupation phase of the structure. It could therefore belong to an entirely different structure that used any number of the features within and around S17.
Artefacts:	Finds consisted of seven barrel-shaped vessels, a further vessel, and 49 sherds and fragments of varying fabric.
Radiocarbon dates:	Outer ditch segment: 1429–1268 BC (UB-6381); second date of 1413–1213 BC (UBA-16611) also obtained (by Chrono as part of Ginn's research).
Notes:	N/A

Structure:	**18**
Illustration:	2.18
Shape:	Almost circular
Measurements:	11.6m × 11.4m
Location:	Eastern edge of settlement, southeast of road F100.
Outer ditch segments:	n=1
	Continuous slot-trench, truncated by modern piped field drain.
Outer postring:	n=15
Inner ditch:	n=0
Inner postring:	n=0
Entrance:	SSE
	The only gap in the slot-trench could have lain beneath the field drain and therefore the entrance must have been located in the south or SSW of the structure. The field drain had obscured all evidence of the entrance; however, at the southeast the slot-trench swung around by 90° for a short stretch and then returned to its original direction, but *c.* 0.65m inside its former course. This area had a dense concentration of stone within it. The ditch then turned 90° again, was marginally truncated by the field ditch [742], became gradually shallower, and ran east–west for *c.* 2.1m before stopping at a shallow terminal on the same line as the internal postring described above. At the southwest, the ditch maintained its line, running up to the field ditch. If it had continued for another 2m on this line, it would have come in front of the other terminal, in effect creating an overlapping, and therefore concealed, entrance. This would have been entered from the SSW, a slightly different direction to most of the structures on the site. Presumably this was still out of the direction of the prevailing wind, and this arrangement would provide a rather elegant alternative to the extended porches seen elsewhere on the site.
Additional features:	N/A
Artefacts:	N/A
Radiocarbon dates:	N/A

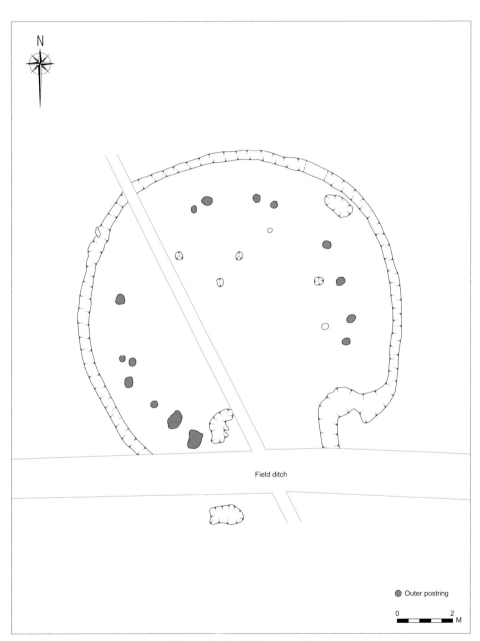

N

Field ditch

● Outer postring

0   2 M

Illustration 2.18: Structure 18

Notes:	S18 has several parallels across the site, with S33, S49 and S64 also displaying similar narrow and deep slot-trenches. These structures are all located along the fringes of the settlement complex. The closest parallel beyond the site comes from Co. Tipperary, where at The Lisheen Mine, Killoran 8, Houses A and B (Beta-117553, 1860–1845 or 1775–1430 BC, Early Bronze Age or Middle Bronze Age (Gowen *et al.* 2005)) bear striking similarity in form to S18, displaying similar slot-trench and entrance configuration.

Structure:	**19**
Illustration:	2.19
Shape:	Circular
Measurements:	10m diameter
Location:	Northeast of S20.
Outer ditch segments:	n=7
	Two segments had cobbled bases. Segment [5114] contained fragments of burnt bone from a large mammal.
Outer postring:	n=22
	Some of these postholes were clustered in groups of two, especially towards the back of the structure, e.g. [6006] and [6008], and [6002] and [5998]. This indicates that parts of the structure were strengthened or modified on one occasion or that the structure was rebuilt with certain postholes reused. Many contained charcoal flecks and packing stones. Occasional prehistoric pottery sherds were recovered from the fills but one posthole [6020] contained 36 such sherds. Four whole cereal grains (two were barley) and several small fragments were preserved in posthole [6010]; a charcoal sample from [6010] returned a radiocarbon date of 1665–1497 BC (UB-6247).
Inner ditch:	n=6
	Cobbled patches observed in base of [6024].
Inner postring:	n=13
Entrance:	SSE
	Cobbled pathway.
Additional features:	The house was enclosed by a large C-shaped ditch dug 2–3m beyond the outer ditch segments ditch (enclosing an area 17.6m × 17.2m) which extended around the northern half of the house. This feature was unique on the site and while its function was unclear, its fills, especially around the northeast, suggested manufacturing activity, as did the feature [4812] which connected to its northern side. These fills included a number of alternating layers of thin, charcoal-rich material and orangeish red burnt silt or ash. A modern field drain [5120] ran through the structure and truncated many of the features. There were many internal features, including pits, stakeholes and postholes.
Artefacts:	Sixteen barrel-shaped vessels, a further four vessels and 106 sherds and fragments of varying fabric were associated.
Radiocarbon dates:	Outer postring posthole: 1665–1497 BC (UB-6247). Internal posthole: 1614–1452 BC (UB-6246).
Notes:	The structure was also cut through by the extremely long curvilinear feature [5120] which ran across most of the site. This had a shallow U-shaped profile similar to [3332] which ran through S7 and close to S9. This feature also cut through S59 and S52, and although large sections of it were excavated no dateable artefacts or samples were recovered. While

Illustration 2.19: Structure 19

not precisely dated, this feature was consistently stratigraphically later than the Middle Bronze Age houses it passed through and earlier than the early modern east–west field boundaries. It may have belonged to a late phase of the settlement, as is suggested for [3332], or perhaps is associated with the early medieval activity on the site.

Structure:	**20**
Illustration:	2.20
Shape:	Circular
Measurements:	8.29m diameter
Location:	Southwest of S19.
Outer ditch segments:	n=3
	A posthole was discovered between two of the segments and a cobbled base was observed in some segments.
Outer postring:	n=1
Inner ditch:	n=2
	A patch of cobbling was noted along the base of [5080] which was covered with larger stones and four prehistoric pottery sherds.
Inner postring:	N/A
Entrance:	SE
	No formal features associated with an entrance were identified. However, an irregular-shaped cobbled area [6154] (6.5m length × 1.2m width) was identified at the southern edge of the structure and most likely represents a cobbled pathway thereby indicating where the entrance would have been. The cobble from the probable entranceway joined with a linear path lying northeast–southwest which was associated with S19, suggesting that the two structures may have been contemporary.
Additional features:	N/A
Artefacts:	One vessel and two fragments of medium fabric.
Radiocarbon dates:	N/A
Notes:	In common with a number of the other smaller buildings on the site, there is a confusing lack of postholes associated with this structure. The outer postring was largely incomplete and there were no traces of an inner postring.
Structure:	**21**
Illustration:	2.21
Shape:	Circular
Measurements:	7.43m diameter
Location:	Between S22 and S56.
Outer ditch segments:	n=2
	The segments each contained a layer of tightly compacted stones and were filled with material containing moderate quantities of stone and occasional charcoal flecks. The eastern segment was cut by several postholes and stakeholes and the western segment widened at the entranceway.
Outer postring:	n=8
	Charcoal flecks, flint fragments and small stones occurred with moderate frequency in the posthole fills.
Inner ditch:	N/A
Inner postring:	N/A
Entrance:	SE

Illustration 2.20: Structure 20

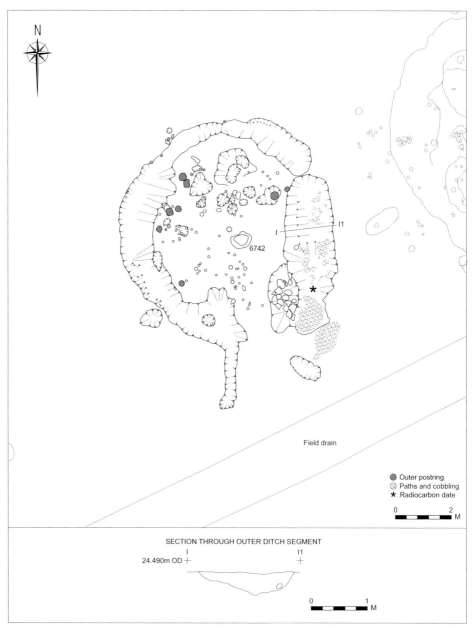

N

6742

I   I1

*

Field drain

● Outer postring
◎ Paths and cobbling
★ Radiocarbon date

0   2
▬▬▬▬▬ M

SECTION THROUGH OUTER DITCH SEGMENT
              I   I1
24.490m OD +   +

0   1
▬▬▬▬▬ M

Illustration 2.21: Structure 21

	Compact stone surface in shallow cut feature.
Additional features:	A sub-oval pit [6742] was located towards the centre of the structure. A layer of concentrated, oxidised clay at the base indicated *in situ* burning and that this pit was used as a hearth. Above this layer of reddened clay was a secondary fill of charcoal-rich, sandy clay.
Artefacts:	The remains of two vessels, one flat rimmed and one barrel shaped, and a further 14 sherds and fragments not assigned to a particular vessel were found.
Radiocarbon dates:	Outer ditch segment: 1531–1409 BC (UB-6379).
Notes:	N/A

Structure:	**22**
Illustration:	2.22
Shape:	Sub-circular
Measurements:	7.7m × 7.14m
Location:	Between S21 and S23.
Outer ditch segments:	n=3
	Three separate ditch segments formed the perimeter.
Outer postring:	n=10
Inner ditch:	N/A
Inner postring:	n=4
Entrance:	SE
	A series of postholes and pits appeared to form a porch; some of these features contained stones in their bases, suggesting that the entrance had been cobbled.
Additional features:	Further internal postholes, stakeholes and pits may have been related to the two postrings.
Artefacts:	These comprised a bodysherd from an Early Neolithic carinated bowl, a complete base of a barrel-shaped Middle Bronze Age vessel, along with further sherds of that vessel, and a further three sherds and fragments of medium and coarse fabric.
Radiocarbon dates:	N/A
Notes:	N/A

Structure:	**23**
Illustration:	2.23
Shape:	Circular
Measurements:	11.14m × 11m
Location:	Truncated by S75 and S39.
Outer ditch segments:	n=4
	The outer ditch segments contained large stones in their fills and unidentifiable burnt bone was derived from one of the segments.
Outer postring:	n=9
Inner ditch:	N/A
Inner postring:	n=6
Entrance:	SE
	Cobbled area accompanied by several postholes, cut by S75.
Additional features:	Six internal pits.
Artefacts:	Two barrel-shaped vessels, and a further 17 sherds and fragments of medium fabric.

Illustration 2.22: Structure 22

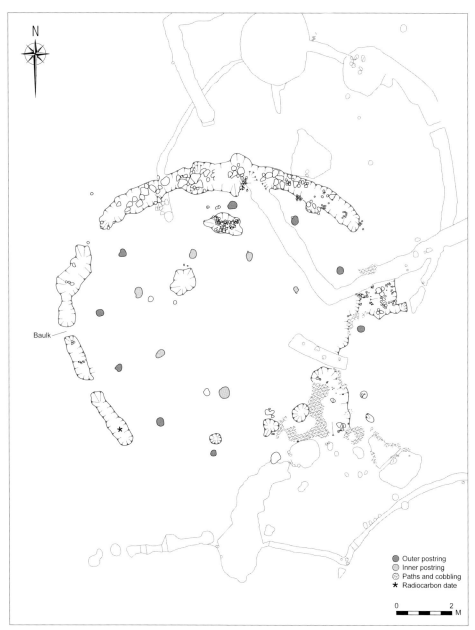

N

Baulk

Outer postring
Inner postring
Paths and cobbling
★ Radiocarbon date

0   2
▮▮▮▮▮▮ M

Illustration 2.23: Structure 23

Radiocarbon dates:	Outer ditch segment: 1408–1213 BC (UB-6249); second date of 1260–1055 BC (UBA-16610) also obtained (by Chrono as part of Ginn's research; charcoal: hazel).
Notes:	N/A

Structure:	**24**
Illustration:	2.24
Shape:	N/A
Measurements:	N/A
Location:	Cut through S75.
Outer ditch segments:	n=2
	Slot-trench segments.
Outer postring:	N/A
Inner ditch:	N/A
Inner postring:	N/A
Entrance:	N/A
Additional features:	Two pits located beyond the western terminal of slot-trench [7464].
Artefacts:	Three bodysherds from one Middle Bronze Age.
Radiocarbon dates:	N/A
Notes:	S24 may have been part of two conjoined structures that were either unfinished or have not survived in a fully comprehensible form. S24 may also represent an enclosure; certainly, its function is difficult to determine from its archaeological footprint.

Structure:	**25**
Illustration:	2.25
Shape:	Sub-circular
Measurements:	10.9m × 10m
Location:	Respecting S24 and S70.
Outer ditch segments:	n=3
	The outer ditch [8112] was almost continuous and enclosed the structure. It existed in three segments [8112], [8112a] and [8112b] and was cut to a maximum depth of 0.76m. The fill contained moderate amounts of small stones, frequent amounts of large stones and occasional flint fragments.
Outer postring:	n=11
	Most of these postholes contained charcoal and flint fragments in their fills and many also had packing stones.
Inner ditch:	N/A
Inner postring:	n=6
	Many contained charcoal flecks, flint fragments and small stones.
Entrance:	SE
	This entrance was two phased. A shallow depression [8110B] contained a fill with charcoal flecks and flint fragments and was partially lined with a compact layer of small stones. This sunken entranceway was replaced with an upper layer of stone which formed a short, cobbled pathway [8110] and which extended into the interior of the structure. The entranceway was truncated in several places by a modern piped field drain [8116]. Two postholes [8304] and [8302] may have acted as doorjambs.

7464

Field drain

0   2
            M

Illustration 2.24: Structure 24

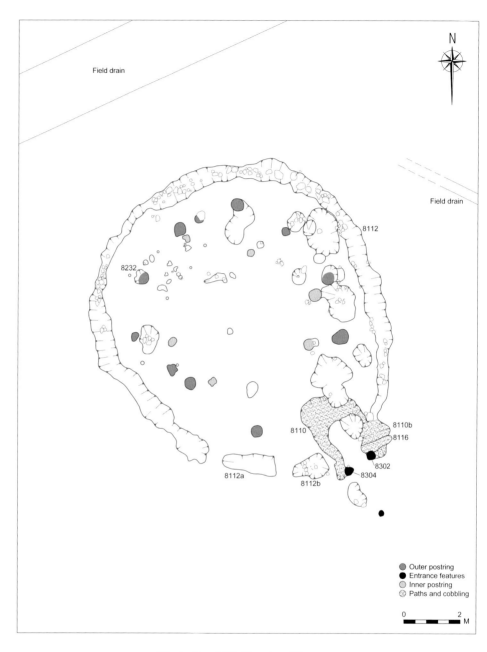

Illustration 2.25: Structure 25

Additional features:	Of the internal features one small posthole was of particular interest: [8232] contained *c.* 450 moderately preserved, charred cereal grains, all of which were of barley. It is possible that this deposit was mis-associated or incorrectly recorded on site as it seems unlikely that so many cereal grains would be found within one stakehole.
Artefacts:	N/A
Radiocarbon dates:	N/A
Notes:	Perhaps the occurrence of so much charred cereal indicates a functional difference between it and its neighbouring domestic structures.

Structure:	**26**
Illustration:	2.26
Shape:	W-shaped
Measurements:	N/A
Location:	North of S73 and northeast of S68.
Outer ditch segments:	N/A
Outer postring:	N/A
Inner ditch:	N/A
Inner postring:	N/A
Entrance:	N/A
Additional features:	The curvilinear ditch [7006] (18m × 0.45m × 0.2m) appeared as a double arc which formed a 'W' shape. The base was undulating and narrow. Stone packing and occasional Bronze Age pottery sherds were recovered from the silty clay fill. The ditch was truncated along the western edge by a number of intercutting pit features. These pits were relatively shallow and contained flint fragments, decayed stone nodules and small stones. The fills of the pit features contained no substantial packing material, which would suggest that upright posts were not placed within the cuts, and no posthole cuts were recorded in any of the pit features.
	Although 11 postholes were identified in the region, none could be attributed to an outer postring. The postholes were positioned randomly and their location did not suggest that they were intended to support a house structure of any description. It is more likely that these postholes were intended as a wind-break to provide shelter for a work area or marked the location of pieces of furniture or equipment.
	A number of additional isolated features, including pits, postholes and a compact stone spread [7548] were identified within the excavated area. However, their relative isolation means they can add little information on the intended use of the area. As with S24 this may have been part of two conjoined structures that were either unfinished or have not survived in fully comprehensible form, some form of enclosure, or a specific arrangement of another type which is not easily interpreted by its archaeological footprint.
Artefacts:	Three barrel-shaped vessels, a further straight-sided vessel and 44 sherds and fragments too small or indistinct to be assigned to particular vessels were recovered.
Radiocarbon dates:	N/A
Notes:	The surviving features consisted of an elongated curvilinear ditch, large pit features, postholes, and a number of additional linear gullies. No

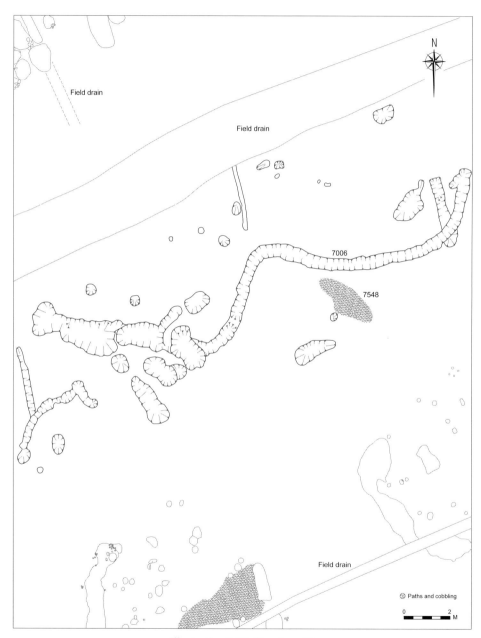

Illustration 2.26: Structure 26

entrance could be identified and the dimensions of the structure were not discernable. It is not likely to represent a dwelling.

The vicinity surrounding the features was extensively truncated by a modern field boundary, which ran east–west across the site. It is possible that this has destroyed key relationships that would help explain the intended use of these postholes.

Of particular interest regarding this enigmatic structure is the association of the pottery. The sherds from this structure showed evidence for a greater degree of weathering, indicating that they were exposed to the elements for a longer period of time. Many of these were derived from the fill of the ditch indicating that whatever its function, it was most likely contemporary with the site, and that it was treated in the same manner as the outer ditches associated with the structures.

Structure:	**27**
Illustration:	2.27
Shape:	Incomplete/badly truncated
Measurements:	N/A
Location:	Centre of site, between S55 and S60.
Outer ditch segments:	n=2
Outer postring:	N/A
Inner ditch:	N/A
Inner postring:	N/A
Entrance:	SE
	A shallow depression with four opposing postholes and an irregular cobbled area forming a path made up the entrance area.
Additional features:	The remains of a compacted, clay floor surface covered the entire internal area; it extended beyond the building through the entrance gap, as far as the outer ditch of S60. The internal features were cut into this floor. An oval-shaped pit, located towards the centre of the structure, may represent a hearth. A charcoal-rich, silty clay with a high percentage of small stones comprised the primary fill and the secondary fill consisted of reddish-orange, friable, oxidised, sandy clay with a moderate amount of pebbles. It is perhaps more probable that this represents a dump for hearth material due to its inverted sequence, or that two discrete burning episodes, the second more intense than the first, were present.
Artefacts:	Six barrel-shaped vessels and a further 18 sherds and fragments were associated.
Radiocarbon dates:	N/A
Notes:	It was not possible to identify which postholes may have belonged to an outer postring or to identify an inner ditch or an inner postring. The relationship between S27 and its eastern neighbour S60 is unclear, although they appear to have been separated by a gap 2m wide. This gap was devoid of features except a small stakehole and patches of cobble.

Structure:	**28**
Illustration:	2.28
Shape:	Circular
Measurements:	6.2m diameter
Location:	West of S19, southeast of S29 and north of S56 and S57.

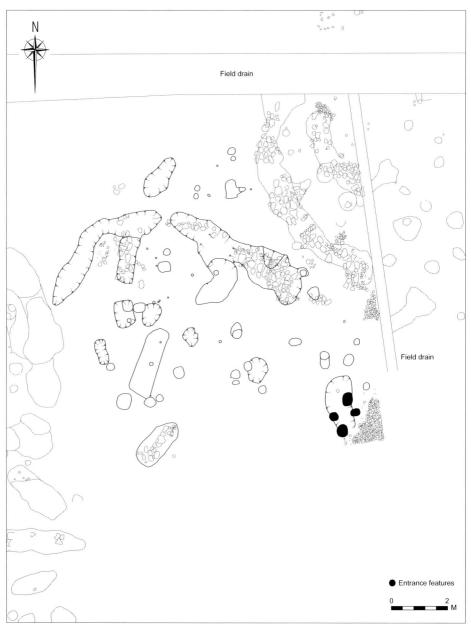

Illustration 2.27: Structure 27

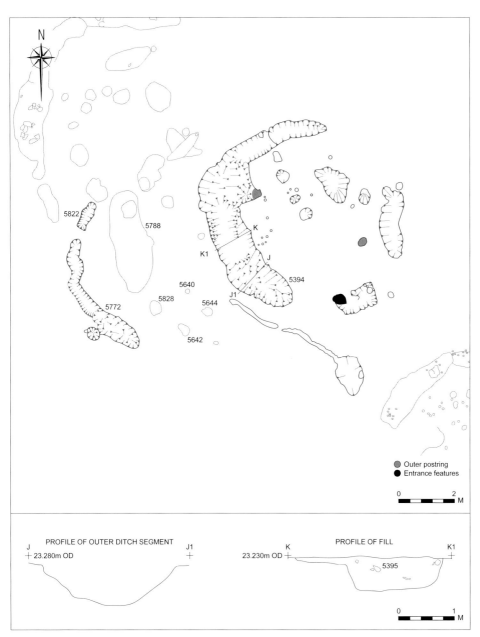

N

5822

5788

5640

5828

5772

5644

5642

5394

K

K1

J

J1

● Outer postring
● Entrance features

0   2
                      M

PROFILE OF OUTER DITCH SEGMENT
J
+ 23.280m OD   J1
                                       +

PROFILE OF FILL
K   K1
23.230m OD +   +
                    5395

0   1
                      M

Illustration 2.28: Structure 28

Outer ditch segments:	n=3
	The fills of these segments contained moderate concentrations of large stones with scattered charcoal flecks and pebbles. The base had patches of packed cobble.
Outer postring:	n=2
Inner ditch:	N/A
Inner postring:	N/A
Entrance:	SE
	An irregular-shaped feature was associated with two postholes and an entrance path which may have extended eastwards for at least 2.23m from the building was associated with seven truncated, external postholes in the vicinity.
Additional features:	Many external features were located on the western side of S28. Some of these were on the same alignment as the outer ditch of S28 and may represent an annex or extension. It is more likely that these features could have formed a separate structure; however, as this is not certain they have not been assigned a different structure number. The western perimeter of this structure was defined by the feature [5822] and curvilinear feature [5772]. Four postholes at the southeast [5828], [5640], [5642], and [5644] appear to mark the entrance. If this structure pre-dated S29 then its eastern side could have been removed during the excavation of the outer ditch segment [5394] of S29. Alternatively, the building may have abutted the western wall of S29 and not required additional foundations. It is clear that this structure could not have been used at the same time as S29, because the entrance of S29 [5788] extended right through the interior area.
Artefacts:	Twelve barrel-shaped vessels, a further four vessels and 33 sherds and fragments were mostly derived from the outer ditch segments.
Radiocarbon dates:	N/A
Notes:	The relationship between S28 and S29 is unfortunately unknown as no features truncated each other. It is unlikely that the two structures were occupied contemporaneously, as the trajectory of the outer ditch segments of S29 obstructs that of S28.
Structure:	**29**
Illustration:	2.29
Shape:	Circular or oval
Measurements:	8m terminal to terminal
Location:	Northwest of S28, south of S55.
Outer ditch segments:	n=4
	These segments all contained medium-sized and large stones as well as occasional charcoal flecks in a gravel-rich, dark, sandy clay fill.
Outer postring:	n=2
Inner ditch:	n=3
	These were filled with a silty clay containing small stones and charcoal flecks. Some of the internal postholes and pits which were situated on the same alignment may have been associated.
Inner postring:	N/A
Entrance:	S
	An elongated feature contained large stones and cobbled patches was associated with postholes.
Additional features:	N/A

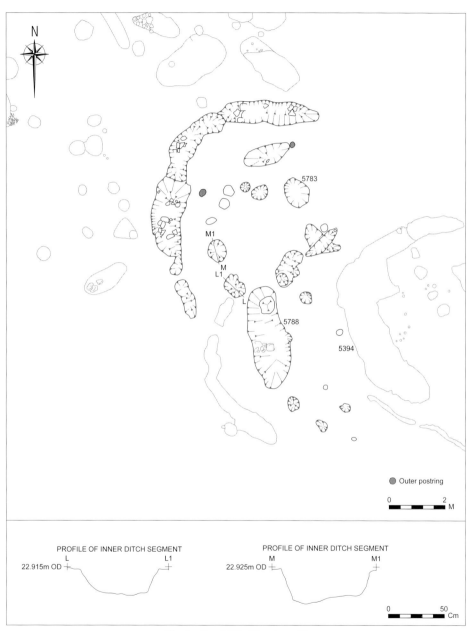

N

5783

M1

M

L1

L

5788

5394

● Outer postring

0   2
▬▬▬▬▬▬▬ M

PROFILE OF INNER DITCH SEGMENT

L   L1
22.915m OD

PROFILE OF INNER DITCH SEGMENT

M   M1
22.925m OD

0   50
▬▬▬▬▬▬▬ Cm

Illustration 2.29: Structure 29

Artefacts:	The remains of an Early Neolithic carinated bowl and three Middle Bronze Age barrel-shaped vessels.
Radiocarbon dates:	N/A
Notes:	The relationship between S29 and S28 is unfortunately unknown as no features truncated each other. It is unlikely that the two structures were occupied contemporaneously, as the trajectory of the outer ditch segments of S29 obstructs that of S28.

Structure:	**30**
Illustration:	2.30
Shape:	Oval
Measurements:	6.86m × 6m
Location:	South of S14, abutted S31.
Outer ditch segments:	n=6
	These segments were filled with dark sandy clay containing occasional charcoal and small quantities of flint and small stones. In the fill of [9004] 16 charred cereal grains were recovered; all of the identifiable examples were of barley.
Outer postring:	n=3
	The three extant internal postholes do not form an arc in the structure's interior and these postholes may not represent the remains of a postring.
Inner ditch:	N/A
Inner postring:	N/A
Entrance:	SE
	This comprised three irregular features into which several postholes were cut.
Additional features:	N/A
Artefacts:	N/A
Radiocarbon dates:	Internal pit: 1416–1265 BC (UB-6234).
Notes:	There are two valid interpretations for S30 and its relationship with neighbouring S31. Firstly, S30 may have been linked to S31, either as an ancillary building or as an annex and the two were contemporary. S30 may also have had a further compartment to the east, where an arrangement of features in a sub-rectangular pattern suggests the presence of a further structure (not assigned an individual structure number). Alternatively, S30 can be interpreted as a small, free-standing building which pre- or post-dated S31. Neither hypothesis is supported by conclusive evidence. Interestingly, S31 may have been built up against the eastern side of S33, see below, and it is possible that there were three conjoined structures aligned in an east–west row, each with its own southern-facing entrance. In light of this, it is worth pointing out the diminishing size of these structures from west to east.

Structure:	**31**
Illustration:	2.31
Shape:	Circular
Measurements:	7.71m diameter
Location:	East of S34, S33 and west of S30.
Outer ditch segments:	n=4
	A single course of medium-sized and large stones had been set in the

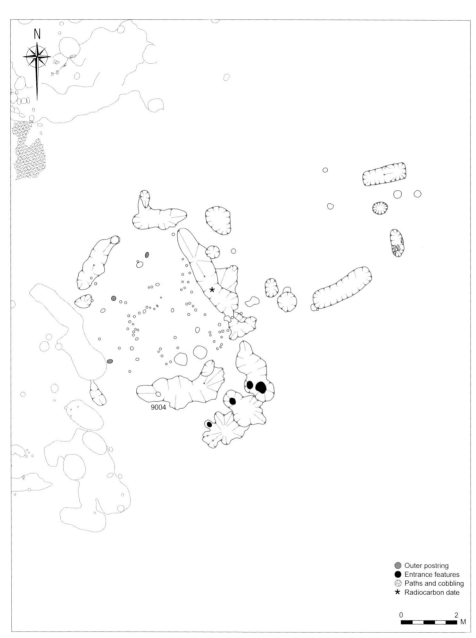

Illustration 2.30: Structure 30

Outer postring
Entrance features
Paths and cobbling
★ Radiocarbon date

9004

0 2 M

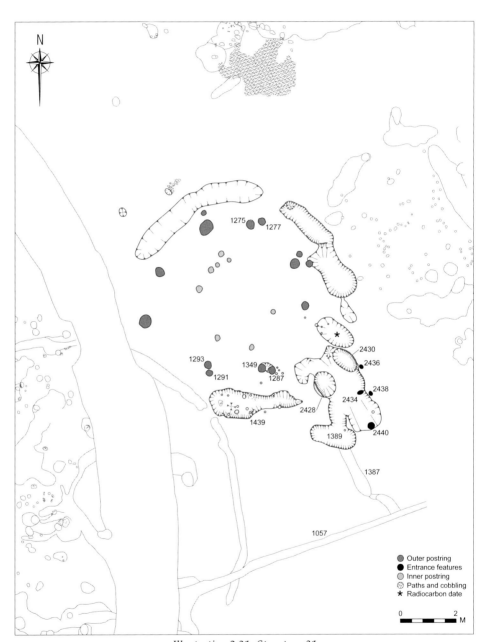

Illustration 2.31: Structure 31

	base of the ditch and in places overlay patches of cobble. Stakeholes were located in the base of segment [1439].
Outer postring:	n=14
	Some of these postholes were arranged in clusters of two, e.g. [1287] and [1349], and [1291] and [1293], and [1275] and [1277]. This clustering suggests that the structure had been rebuilt on one occasion. The clusters and the larger, individual postholes were arranged *c.* 1.8m apart. Many of the postholes contained packing stones and [1269] had nine prehistoric pottery sherds in its fill.
Inner ditch:	N/A
Inner postring:	n=8
	These were all circular and both smaller and shallower than those in the outer postring, which suggested that they did not fulfil a structural role but perhaps provided support for a screen or internal partition. The inner postring appears not to have been replaced and so was probably only used during one of the building's two phases.
Entrance:	SE
	This was a sunken, sub-rectangular feature; the northwest corner extended to form an L-shaped feature. The base was cobbled in the south area but contained larger, flat stones in its other areas. This layer of stone concealed two oval pits [2428] and [2430]. Four postholes were identified on the eastern side of the entrance feature: [2434], [2436], [2438], and [2440].
	At the south, the entrance feature connected to a narrow, north–south, linear feature, [1387] (3m length). It connected with the east–west, linear feature [1057] which ran through, and to the east of, S33. The exact nature of the relationship between this linear [1387] and the entrance feature could not be determined as the point where they joined had been cut through by the later sub-rectangular pit [1389].
Additional features:	The only other internal features consisted of a stakehole cluster to the south of the structure. The central area was devoid of features.
Artefacts:	Four barrel-shaped vessels and a further two vessels.
Radiocarbon dates:	Pit between entrance and eastern ditch segment (location suggests unlikely to have been used during the occupation of the structure): 1497–1318 BC (UB-6236). A second date from this context (charcoal: alder) was obtained (by Chrono as part of Ginn's research); it was early medieval in date: AD 653–766 (UBA-16613). The pit therefore contains both Bronze Age and later material and cannot be used as part of the chronology for the site.
Notes:	As described above this building may have been abutted by S30 on its east and butted up against S33. The relationship between it and S33 was not clear, but ditch segment [1439] appeared to stop immediately before the slot-trench of S33 and the incomplete perimeter around the east of the structure may indicate that it was conjoined with the wall of S33. Unfortunately, the missing eastern perimeter may have been removed by the early medieval enclosure, a situation which makes a definitive sequence elusive.
Structure:	**32**
Illustration:	2.32
Shape:	N/A

Illustration 2.32: Structure 32

Measurements:	Too truncated to determine dimensions; only west side of structure remained
Location:	East of S64.
Outer ditch segments:	n=4
	These ditches formed an arc around the western and northwestern sections of the structure. The segments enclosed an area with a maximum diameter of 8.15m. They each contained one fill of sandy clay with flint fragments and large packing stones.
Outer postring:	n=2
Inner ditch:	N/A
Inner postring:	N/A
Entrance:	N/A
Additional features:	N/A
Artefacts:	N/A
Radiocarbon dates:	N/A
Notes:	Only the west side of the structure remained and it consisted of four segments of outer ditch and two outer postring postholes. No inner ditch and no inner postring were present. There was no extant evidence for the entrance.

Structure:	**33**
Illustration:	2.33
Shape:	Almost circular
Measurements:	12.57m × 11.71m
Location:	East of the souterrain, cut by the southeast circuit of an early medieval enclosure/rath (see Appendix II); it also cut across the southwestern edge of S31 and the southern half of S34.
Outer ditch segments:	n=1
	A slot-trench enclosed an area 12.38m in diameter. Its fill was a dark sandy clay with high concentrations of medium-sized and large stones as well as two prehistoric pottery sherds.
Outer postring:	n=4
	Some of the other internal postholes may have been part of this postring but it is not possible to accurately determine which ones.
Inner ditch:	N/A
Inner postring:	N/A
Entrance:	SE
	This was an irregular cobbled area with 15 sherds of prehistoric pottery and two postholes associated.
Additional features:	The internal features in this area consisted of postholes, stakeholes and pits. It was difficult to discern which of the features in this area belonged to S33 rather than to the early medieval enclosure / rath or to S34. Many of the features contained charcoal flecks and inclusions in their fills and some contained deposits or patches of red, oxidised material. However, only one feature, pit [1609], may have been a hearth. It contained red, oxidised, sandy clay, a charcoal-rich middle layer, and heat-shattered stones in its fills. Similar material was discovered in irregular-shaped pit [1409] which returned a radiocarbon date of 1490–1305 BC (UB-6235). An internal spread which covered many of the internal features [1307] and was located to the west of the ditch of the early medieval enclosure /

Illustration 2.33: Structure 33

rath comprised a brownish-black, sandy clay with stones and moderate charcoal inclusions. A radiocarbon date of 1261–1022 BC (UB-6233) was returned for this feature. A second date (charcoal: alder) was derived (by Chrono as part of Ginn's research) from this context: 1260–1055 BC (UBA-16609).

Artefacts:	The remains of an out-turned round rimmed Early Neolithic carinated bowl, as well as four barrel-shaped Middle Bronze Age vessels, a further four vessels, and 45 sherds and fragments of fine and medium fabric were found.
Radiocarbon dates:	Internal pit: 1490–1305 BC (UB-6235).
	Internal spread: 1261–1022 BC (UB-6233) and 1260–1055 BC (UBA-16609).
Notes:	Some of the external features may have formed an annex or extension to S33. However, they may also have been part of S34 and have been described below. The slot-trench construction of this structure is similar in form to the enclosing slot-trenches of S18, S49 and S64.

Structure:	**34**
Illustration:	2.34
Shape:	Unknown
Measurements:	Unknown
Location:	Adjacent to the north side of S33.
Outer ditch segments:	n=1
	This contained charcoal flecks, stones and pebbles in its fill and had many stakeholes cut into its base. This feature in particular could be an extension to S33, as it respects the slot-trench [1005]; however, it may also form a structural component of an earlier structure, obscured by S33, as it is of different construction to the slot-trench form of S33.
Outer postring:	n=6
Inner ditch:	N/A
Inner postring:	N/A
Entrance:	Unknown
Additional features:	N/A
Artefacts:	N/A
Radiocarbon dates:	N/A
Notes:	The extant features in this area consisted of a high concentration of ditch segments, pits, postholes, and stakeholes. Establishing relationships between the features and assigning them to individual structures was not always possible. It seems probable, but not certain, that S34 (represented by two outer ditch segments, several stakeholes and a postring of six postholes) was a separate structure and not an annex of S33.

Structure:	**35**
Illustration:	2.35
Shape:	Unknown
Measurements:	Unknown
Location:	North of the early medieval enclosure/rath.
Outer ditch segments:	n=5
	The fill of [2592] contained a small patch of charcoal and oxidized clay as well as 17 sherds of prehistoric pottery. Other fills covered a compact, cobbled surface and contained up to seven similar pottery sherds.

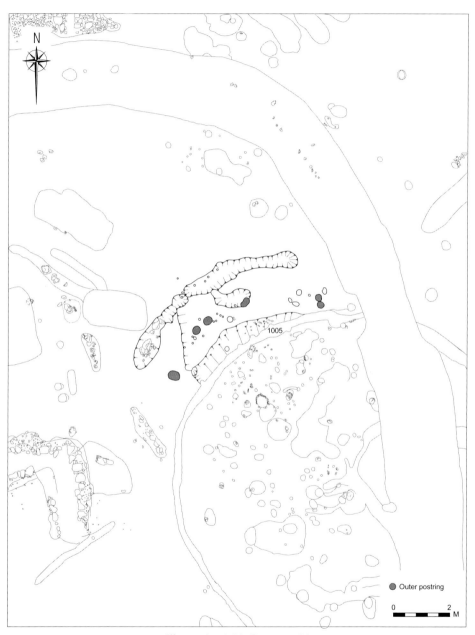

Illustration 2.34: Structure 34

Illustration 2.35: Structure 35

Outer postring:	n=5
Inner ditch:	N/A
Inner postring:	N/A
Entrance:	E
	No entrance features were discernable; however, it appears that the entrance would have connected with the cobbled path situated to the east. A circular stone setting [2738] (0.81m length × 0.67m width) was located in this direction.
Additional features:	A total of 19 sub-rounded stones were placed in a tightly packed formation with the majority angled inwards, towards each other. The outermost stones were slightly raised in height above the inner stones. Many of the stone edges were flush against adjacent stones and a medium-brown deposit filled any gaps that were present. It may represent an external hearth or it may have been associated with the entrance.
Artefacts:	One barrel-shaped vessel, a further three vessels, and 17 sherds and fragments of medium and coarse fabric.
Radiocarbon dates:	N/A
Notes:	Some of the features may have belonged to S37; however, it proved difficult to distinguish one structure from the other, even though some intercutting of features was evident. It is not clear whether this set of features represents a domestic building or even a walled structure at all. However, it was clearly an important area and a considerable amount of work went into creating these features, in particular the fine stone work.

Structure:	**36**
Illustration:	2.36
Shape:	Unknown
Measurements:	It was not possible to discern the dimensions of the possible structure, but features were recorded in a concentration approximately 10m from northeast–southwest and 8m from northwest–southeast.
Location:	South of S61 and S62.
Outer ditch segments:	N/A
Outer postring:	n=8
	Eight possible postholes were recorded which shared many characteristics with structurally supportive postholes identified from the roundhouses on site.
Inner ditch:	N/A
Inner postring:	N/A
Entrance:	S
	A large area of cobbling [6821] (4.4m length × 0.7m width) was identified at the south of this structure. It is comparable to that identified in entrance features associated with numerous roundhouses across the site, although it was not situated within a cut feature but lay directly on the top of the subsoil. It was very similar in construction and design, consisting of many small tightly compacted round stones. The location of the cobbled surface in relation to the group of postholes and pits was also significant in that it was placed along the southernmost area of the group and respected all the features around it. Many examples from elsewhere on site indicate that the location of large cobble spreads was associated with entrances and they were found within the southern or southeastern quadrants of

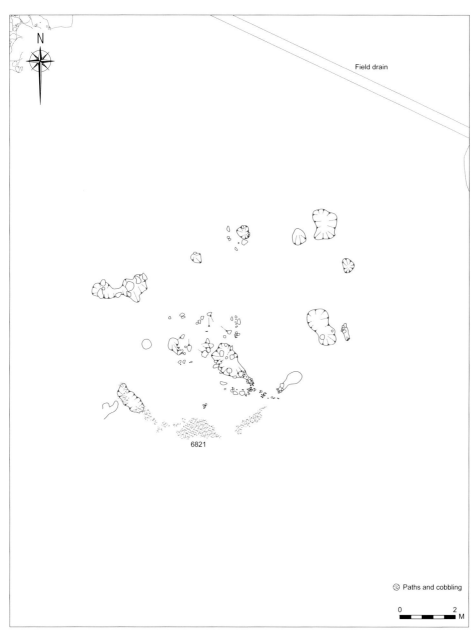

Field drain

6821

Paths and cobbling

0   2
M

Illustration 2.36: Structure 36

the constructions. It is possible that this cobbling denotes the base of a sunken entrance feature that had been almost totally ploughed away.

Additional features:	N/A
Artefacts:	N/A
Radiocarbon dates:	N/A
Notes:	Cobbled areas, pits and postholes suggest that S36 was a simple Type 1 roundhouse that had been particularly badly disturbed by later activity. However, as the extant evidence is limited a positive conclusion cannot be reached, and it is possible that these features do not relate to an actual roundhouse but are simply a small group of features relating to an area in which a particular activity occurred. Similar groups of features are present towards the perimeter of the site including S72, a group to the east of S17 and the group to the east of S14.

Structure:	**37**
Illustration:	2.37
Shape:	Almost circular
Measurements:	10.29m × 10m
Location:	North of early medieval enclosure / rath.
Outer ditch segments:	n=4
	Prehistoric pottery sherds (23 in total) were recovered from these fills.
Outer postring:	n=5
Inner ditch:	n=1
Inner postring:	N/A
Entrance:	E
	The cobbled area with associated pits and postholes was truncated by a series of later pits and features.
Additional features:	Approximately 30 complete charred cereal grains were recovered from the fill of internal pit [1139] (1.08m × 0.98m × 0.62m) and, where identifiable, were of barley and emmer wheat, in similar proportions.
	Located to the west of the structure were 45 external features which comprised a mixture of pits, postholes and stakeholes. They were concentrated within the area west of S37 and south of S35 and all respected the outer wall of the western outer ditch segments of S37. Some of the postholes may have represented an annex attached on to the western side of the structure. One of the elongated features [2262] (1.15m × 0.55m × 0.23m) contained some heat-fractured stones and charcoal, indicating a possible hearth function or, at the least, a rubbish pit for hearth-derived waste. Material from [2262] was radiocarbon dated to 1440–1293 BC (UB-6238) and to 1384–1212 BC (UBA-16612) (latter date by Chrono as part of Ginn's research; charcoal: alder).
Artefacts:	These included the remains of 15 barrel-shaped vessels, a further five vessels, and 57 sherds and fragments of varying fabric too small or indistinct to be assigned to particular vessels. Some of the sherds do not represent any identifiable prehistoric pottery type. The fabric is hard and dense with few noticeable inclusions visible. The well-fired sherds have an orange exterior and interior surface with a grey core and range from 7.3mm to 13.1mm in thickness. Carbonised residue is present on most of the exterior surfaces. The quality of the fabric and the curvature of some of the sherds suggest the possibility that they represent the outer casing

Illustration 2.37: Structure 37

of a mould or moulds. However, it is also and perhaps more likely that the sherds represent up to two unglazed medieval vessels.

Radiocarbon dates: External pit: possible hearth: 1440–1293 BC (UB-6238) and to 1384–1212 BC (UBA-16612) (latter date by Chrono as part of Ginn's research).

Notes: The remains of a coarse gravel path (8m × 3.1m × 0.07m) lay between the terminals of two outer ditch segments on the northern side of the structure. It extended northwards outside the structure and also continued into the central internal area of the building. A total of 54 prehistoric pottery sherds were derived from this gravel area as well as a well-ground, miniature stone axe (122.5mm × 67mm × 28.5mm), which was probably made in the Neolithic period, with little evidence of wear. Three postholes [2562], [2528] and [2564] (averaged 0.29m diameter × 0.44m depth) were cut within the path, all of similar size and form. This gravel spread and the irregular sunken feature possibly represent a surface or path between S37 and S35, located to the immediate north. An additional ditch segment [2498] (4.84m × 1.11m × 0.33m) situated to the east of the structure, immediately beyond the line formed by the outer ditch segments, might have formed part of an extension, a wind-break, or structural repair in this area.

Structure: **38**
Illustration: 2.38
Shape: Oval
Measurements: 11.14m × 10.86m
Location: Western fringe, northeast of S47 and northwest of S54.
Outer ditch segments: n=4–7
The fill in each of these segments contained stones, including packing stones, and charcoal, and patches of cobbling were noted.
Outer postring: n=12
Inner ditch: N/A
Inner postring: N/A
Entrance: SE
Three postholes may mark the position of a possible doorway or entrance 0.85–0.95m wide. This was flanked by an extensive cobbled path, which extended around the east, southeast and south of the house.
Additional features: A cobbled area [2768] (19.8m length × 10.5m width) was located outside S38 along the southern, eastern and northeastern edge of the building and continued in a southerly direction towards the northern edge of S47. Some disturbance was evident, the result of the east–west field ditch [742], which cut directly through the middle of the cobbled surface. A total of 177 fragments of coarseware prehistoric pottery were recovered from the cobbled area along with a stone mould (56mm × 25 mm × 12.5mm).
A small, curvilinear alignment of four separate features [3446A], [3444], [3442], and [3440] extended northwest from the northern tip of the structure which may mark the position of a wind-break or enclosure/pen wall associated with the main building.
Artefacts: The remains of 21 barrel-shaped vessels (including one large example with an estimated rim diameter of 20cm) and a further eight vessels as

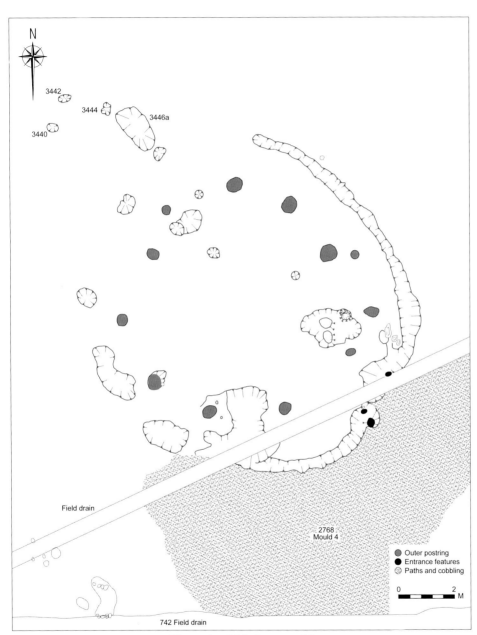

Illustration 2.38: Structure 38

well as 138 sherds and fragments too small or indistinct to be assigned to particular vessels were identified with S38.

Radiocarbon dates:	N/A
Notes:	N/A

Structure:	**39**
Illustration:	2.39
Shape:	Oval
Measurements:	10.29m × 9.71m
Location:	Truncated by S23 and the early medieval structure.
Outer ditch segments:	n=2
	Slot-trench in two segments.
Outer postring:	n=2
	Two postholes were identified that may have belonged to an outer postring, [7644], and [7640], but given the lack of other such features needed to complete the circuit, it is quite possible that these, along with stakehole [7642], belong to the early medieval period.
Inner ditch:	N/A
Inner postring:	N/A
Entrance:	N/A
Additional features:	Two large pits cut these slot-trenches: [8292] (1.83m length × 1.71m width) and [8164] (2.85m length × 2.51m width). The latter contained large quantities of charred grain. A small linear [8164A] (1.08m length × 0.51m width) was cut by [8164] and also cut the slot-trenches. It is believed that these features related to the early medieval structure and are described in more detail in Appendix II.
	A large sub-triangular pit located in the centre of the structure [7640A] (1.77m × 1.6m) was probably contemporary with the structure as its western tip had been cut by one of S23's ditch segments.
Artefacts:	N/A
Radiocarbon dates:	N/A
Notes:	N/A

Structure:	**40**
Illustration:	2.40
Shape:	Oval
Measurements:	10.6m × 8m
Location:	Northwest edge, on steeply sloping ground between S41 and S43.
Outer ditch segments:	n=4
	A 'dog-leg' bend existed and it is possible that this southward-heading section represents the ditch returning towards the entrance, and the remaining westward section represents an enclosure or ancillary structure of some form, contemporary with or pre-dating S40.
	Large stones were discovered in the base of the outer ditch in most sections, while the stone in the northern section resembled more the paved areas which were usually associated with the entrance features in the site and no edge to the ditch was identified in this area. No remains of a ditch survived on the western side. It is possible that, due to the nature of the sloping ground, prior to construction an artificial terrace was created in the area, by removing soil from upslope and dumping it

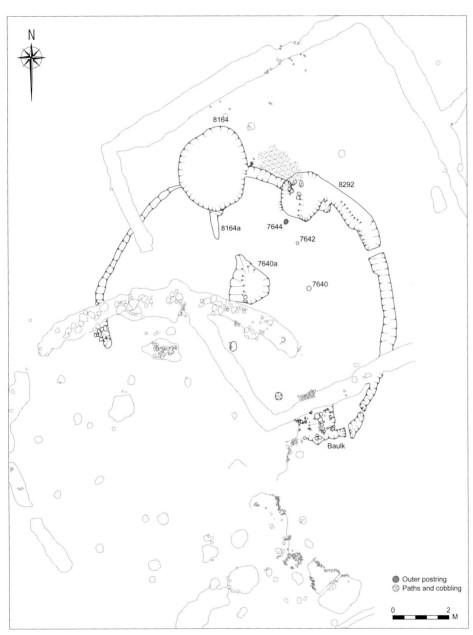

Illustration 2.39: Structure 39

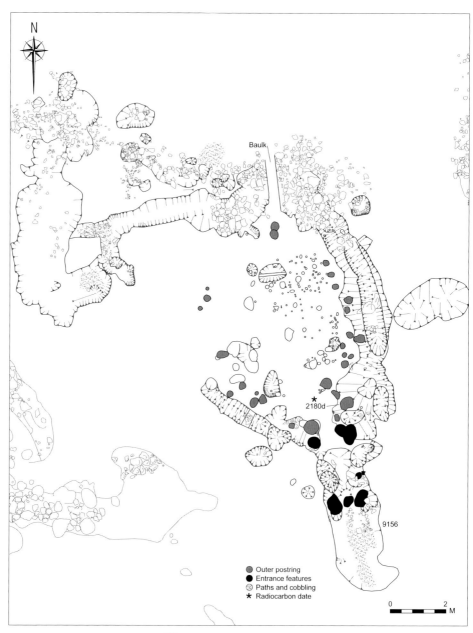

N

Baulk

★
2180d

9156

● Outer postring
● Entrance features
⊗ Paths and cobbling
★ Radiocarbon date

0   2
M

Illustration 2.40: Structure 40

	in a level platform down slope. A western ditch located in this material would have been removed if the material was eroded away.
Outer postring:	n=28
	The majority of these were located within 1m of the inner edge of the ditch segments, although a small number were cut into the inner edge of the ditch segments. Two radiocarbon dates of 1410–1215 BC (UB-6241) and 1374–1130 BC (UBA-16614) were derived from the fill of [2180d] (latter date by Chrono as part of Ginn's research; charcoal: alder).
Inner ditch:	N/A
Inner postring:	N/A
Entrance:	S
	The entrance comprised a large, sub-rectangular feature [9156] (6m × 1.7–1.9m × 0.3m) with its long axis north–south, which was filled with cobble and paving. A series of seven postholes and pits was arranged as pairs of features along the long sides which represent the remains of a porch. A single pit was located in the centre of the feature. The southern end of the entrance feature turned sharply to the east and this change in direction would align the final section of the entrance with the hypothetical trackway connecting to the major roadway (F100).
Additional features:	Internal features consisted of small postholes and domestic pits.
Artefacts:	The remains of three pottery vessels were associated with S40, one of which was barrel shaped.
Radiocarbon dates:	Outer postring posthole: 1410–1215 BC (UB-6241) and 1374–1130 BC (UBA-16614) (latter date by Chrono as part of Ginn's research).
Notes:	The western side, where the land sloped considerably, was badly damaged and much of the evidence was no longer extant.
Structure:	**41**
Illustration:	2.41
Shape:	Oval
Measurements:	9.14m × 8m
Location:	Northwest corner on steeply sloping ground west of S40.
Outer ditch segments:	n=2
	A bank of re-deposited subsoil had been placed along the centre of the base of the ditch, close to the entrance, splitting it into two approximately equally sized sections. The western section of the ditch had been recut.
Outer postring:	n=7
Inner ditch:	N/A
Inner postring:	N/A
Entrance:	E
	A large sunken entrance feature [9155] (10m × 1.08–1.6m × 0.38m) was one of the longest entrance features on site. Towards its eastern end it widened to form a large, triangular area (5.3m length) which, in effect, split the entrance into two sections heading in different directions. One section continued along the original alignment to connect with the proposed trackway running to the south of S40, S11 and S10, eventually connecting to the major road surface (F100). The other section headed to the north for *c*. 3m before fading out. It is suggested that this led to a path that skirted the west of S41 and connected with the sunken pathway [2886]. A layer of large, flattish stones was found beneath the fill of the

Illustration 2.41: Structure 41

entrance feature and these were tightly packed to produce a pavement. This paving layer rested upon a thick layer of cobbles.

Six postholes were found within the entrance feature, four of which were sealed beneath the layer of large stones. Postholes [1886] and [2152], which were significantly smaller and were not covered by the layer of large stones, were sited along the north edge of the entrance, between the structure and the group of four large postholes. It is therefore suggested that at an early stage the building had a medium-sized sunken entrance with a cobbled base. This entrance was covered by a porch that was supported by four large postholes at the eastern end. Subsequently, the entrance was greatly enlarged, the porch was removed and the area it formerly covered was paved with large flat stones. The two smaller postholes close to the building may have supported a wind-break or may mark the location of the remodelled structure's door.

Additional features:	Internal pits occupied the ground on the inside of the ditch segment. The ground surface here was a little lowered, forming a shallow shelf on the inside of the ditch and all of the features were found on this shelf or, in a few cases, cutting the inner lip of the ditch. Many more internal postholes and pits were located in the interior of the structure and such a large number of features in such a limited area suggest that more than one episode of rebuilding or repair had been undertaken to the dwelling.
Artefacts:	Remains of five barrel-shaped vessels and one further vessel were identified with S41 along with 27 sherds and fragments of fine and medium fabric.
Radiocarbon dates:	N/A
Notes:	The western half of the structure was entirely missing which may have resulted from modern disturbance as the adjacent area had clearly been dug away and backfilled with rubble. It is also possible that, as with S40, this structure could have been built on a raised terrace to provide level building ground in this steeply sloping area of the site; this terrace could have been subsequently ploughed away, or simply eroded, to leave the extant incomplete house plan.

Structure:	**42**
Illustration:	2.42
Shape:	Oval
Measurements:	9.14m × 8.86m
Location:	Northeast edge with road F100 to the east and immediately west of, and partly overlapping, S3
Outer ditch segments:	n=6
	These formed an elliptical enclosed area with an internal dimension of 9.7m by 7.2m. Two fills were removed from the segments, the upper of which contained charcoal, flint flakes and 22 sherds of prehistoric pottery in total. The primary fill was rich in stone and consisted of cobbling covered with larger packing stones of various dimensions.
Outer postring:	n=2
Inner ditch:	n=3
	Cobble lined and associated with a further five large postholes/pits.
Inner postring:	N/A
Entrance:	E

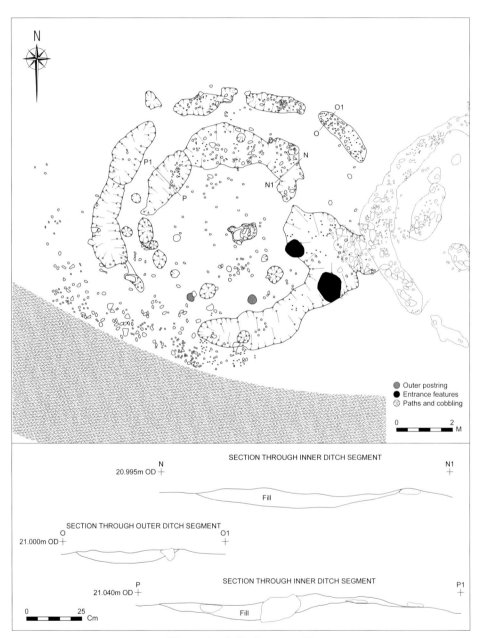

Illustration 2.42: Structure 42

A sub-rectangular-shaped cut covered by fine cobbling was subsequently overlain with a layer of larger stones. One posthole may represent a doorjamb.

Additional features:	N/A
Artefacts:	The remains of five barrel-shaped vessels and a further 26 fragments and sherds were associated.
Radiocarbon dates:	N/A
Notes:	The precise relationship between S42 and S3 is unknown as, during excavation, this area was constantly waterlogged. It is possible that S42 post-dated S3, but it is also possible that the two structures were contemporary and associated, at least for part of their occupation. The southwestern part of S42 is disturbed and it is possible that after S3 was constructed, the entrance was altered from the east to the southwest where it would exit on to the road.

Structure:	**43**
Illustration:	2.43
Shape:	Sub-circular
Measurements:	12m × 10m
Location:	Northern edge of the settlement, to the east of S40, north of S10 and S11 and west of road F100.
Outer ditch segments:	n=4
	All ditch segments contained medium-sized and large stones which formed the base of a stone foundation. The southern section of the larger segment [2198] contained part of a stone paving, consisting of very large, flat stones, extending from the entrance feature [3796] to the southeast.
Outer postring:	n=21
	Several of the postholes, e.g. [2828] and [2924]; [3336] and [2904]; and [3248] and [3152] formed close set pairs suggesting that the building was of two separate phases. A further five large postholes / pits may have been associated.
Inner ditch:	n=1
	This ran from the north of the structure around to the west and contained large stones at its base. These stones may have been the base of a stone foundation, but these single segments of internal ditch are not properly understood in terms of their structural role. Single segments of internal ditches in this location, opposed to the entrance feature, were recorded in several structures at the north of the settlement, including S2, S3, S6, and possibly S42.
Inner postring:	n=3
Entrance:	SE
	There were also two discernable phases to the entrance [3796]. The first was represented by a sub-circular, cobble-filled cut (3m × 2.86m × 0.23m). Various associated postholes formed the remains of a porch. At some stage the decision was made to lay the major road surface past the east of this structure and the larger stones used to form the road were laid on the original entrance. A second entrance cut (3.2m × 2.8m × 0.17m) was then created, thus connecting the structure to the road, and the porch was removed. It is not known whether the modification to the entrance to S43 was accompanied by alterations of the rest of the structure. However, the

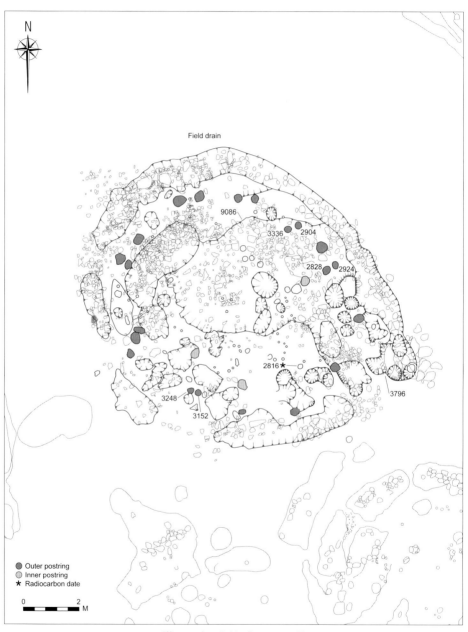

Illustration 2.43: Structure 43

modification of the entrance presumably occurred at the same time as the major rebuilding of S4 (see above), and the sealing of its linear drainage channel, [377], over which the road surface was also laid.

Additional features:	Internal features consisted of pits, postholes and stakeholes. Charcoal from one of the postholes [2816] (0.18m diameter × 0.19m depth) was radiocarbon dated to 1497–1320 BC (UB-6239). A large and irregularly shaped hollow [9086] occupied much of the building's interior. It was filled with a mixture of large stones and sterile sandy clay, suggesting that whatever its origin it was deliberately backfilled in order to permit one of the phases of construction. It is possible that the hollow was created through erosion during the first building phase and was consolidated prior to the commencement of the second phase. A similar hollow was observed at S9.
Artefacts:	Two barrel-shaped vessels as well as 17 sherds and fragments were recovered.
Radiocarbon dates:	Internal posthole: 1497–1320 BC (UB-6239).
Notes:	N/A

Structure:	**44**
Illustration:	2.44
Shape:	Unknown
Measurements:	12m terminal–terminal of the outer ditch segments
Location:	Truncated by outer enclosure of S19.
Outer ditch segments:	n=4
	None contained stone settings.
Outer postring:	n=4
Inner ditch:	N/A
Inner postring:	N/A
Entrance:	SSE
Additional features:	N/A
Artefacts:	N/A
Radiocarbon dates:	N/A
Notes:	This structure was identified during post-excavation analysis; a lack of features in the north suggests that it may have been an enclosure. Some of the features may be associated with S19, the outer enclosure ditch of which truncated S44.

Structure:	**45**
Illustration:	2.45
Shape:	Sub-circular
Measurements:	9.1m × 8.4m
Location:	East of S5, north of S1, west of road F100, south of S10.
Outer ditch segments:	n=5
	The fills of these segments contained pottery and flint and had cobbled bases. Neither postholes nor stakeholes were cut into the segments.
Outer postring:	n=9
Inner ditch:	n=3
	Three ditch segments, two of which contained patches of cobbling, and an additional two areas of cobbling comprised the inner ditch remains.
Inner postring:	n=3
	These postholes are thought to have functioned in a similar way to the

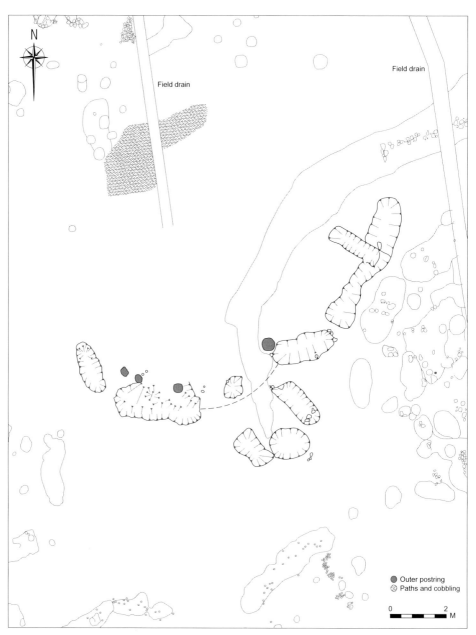

Illustration 2.44: Structure 44

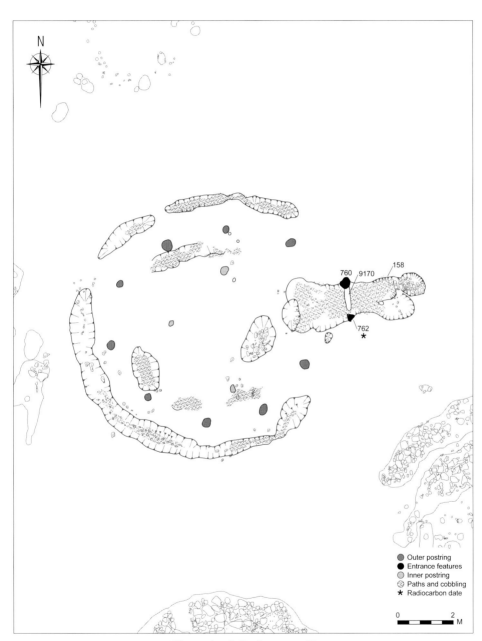

Illustration 2.45: Structure 45

inner postrings seen elsewhere, although it is unlikely they could have supported a ring beam.

Entrance:	E

The finely cobbled linear path [158] (*c.* 7.94m × 0.96–1.76m × 0.2–0.4m) lying west–east, began in the interior, extended out through a doorway defined by opposing postholes and was connected by a clay threshold feature positioned across the width of the path. It continued on for several metres outside of the structure. It faced east, in order to gain direct access on to the adjacent road F100 and also to respect S1, which was situated to the immediate southeast. The western end of the entrance feature sloped gently downwards from the house interior, while the north and southern sides were steeply sloped or nearly vertical. The sides turned in sharply 2.3m from the eastern end to form a constriction 0.96m by 0.4m. The sides then gradually curved back out to regain their former width, before ending at a rounded terminal. The base of the entrance feature was cobbled with small pebbles, and large, flattish stones were laid in one or two courses in the 4m nearest the eastern end. Adjacent postholes [760] and [762] represented the doorjambs which, positioned out from the outer postring, suggest the presence of a projecting doorway, or a small porch. A radiocarbon date of 1415–1264 BC (UB-6248) was obtained from the fill of [762]. Between these two postholes, running north–south, was a small clay bank [9170] (0.92m length × 0.14m width) which was raised above the base of the entrance by up to 0.16m and consisted of greenish-brown, hard-packed clay and marked the threshold. This was a unique feature within the structures excavated at Corrstown although it displays similarities with a possible threshold at the nearby Bronze Age settlement of Cappagh Beg, Portstewart, Co. Londonderry (Appendix IIII).

Additional features:	N/A
Artefacts:	The remains of two barrel-shaped vessels and one further vessel were associated with S45 along with seven fragments and sherds.
Radiocarbon dates:	Entrance posthole: 1415–1264 BC (UB-6248).
Notes:	N/A
Structure:	**46**
Illustration:	2.46
Shape:	Almost circular
Measurements:	7.4m × 7m
Location:	South of S5.
Outer ditch segments:	n=7
Outer postring:	n=5
Inner ditch:	N/A
Inner postring:	N/A
Entrance:	SE

The entrance comprised a linear feature and four shallow pits. Many of these features, most notably the linear [3662], hindered, rather than facilitated access via the entrance and, therefore, they may not all have been contemporary.

Additional features:	N/A
Artefacts:	The remains of three vessels, including two barrel shaped, were associated with S46.

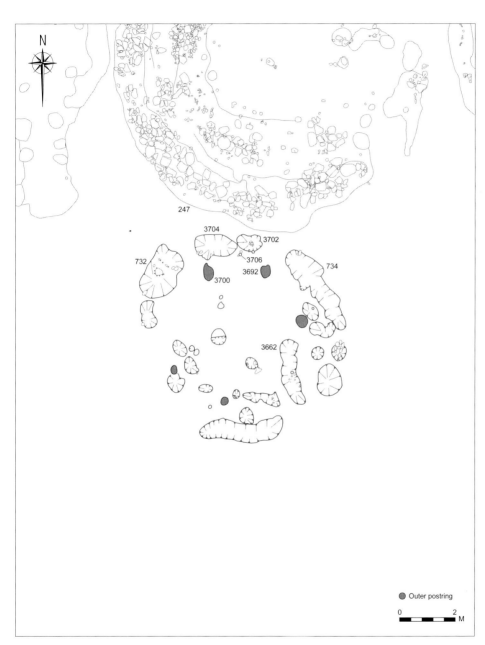

Illustration 2.46: Structure 46

Radiocarbon dates:	N/A
Notes:	Compared to the size of the other structures on site S46 is relatively small and may not have fulfilled an occupational function but may instead have been used for storage or as an ancillary building related to adjacent S5.

Structure:	**47**
Illustration:	2.47
Shape:	Sub-circular
Measurements:	8m × 7m
Location:	Centre-west of settlement, southwest of S38.
Outer ditch segments:	n=4
	These ran around the east and south of the structure but not the north and west. The segments contained large quantities of stone in their bases. Nineteen sherds of prehistoric pottery were recovered from the fill of [3416] and two radiocarbon dates of 1502–1322 BC (UB-6382) and 1432–1312 BC (UBA-16608) (latter date by Chrono as part of Ginn's research; charcoal: alder) were also obtained from this ditch segment.
Outer postring:	n=11
	Packing stones and charcoal inclusions occurred frequently. Posthole [3384] contained a few scattered unidentifiable burnt bone fragments in its fill. No postholes were recorded around the southwest of the structure and these may have been removed by the later field drains or simply eroded away on this steeply sloping ground. It is therefore almost certain that the outer postring originally consisted of several more postholes.
Inner ditch:	N/A
Inner postring:	N/A
Entrance:	E
	An entrance to the structure [3396] (5.5m length × 2.7m width) was located at the east which led onto the large sunken cobbled feature [2768] that also ran past S38. The entrance was filled with a dense layer of large flat stones. No postholes were associated with this entrance and it is unlikely that this building had a porch.
Additional features:	N/A
Artefacts:	The remains of two vessels, one of which was barrel shaped were found.
Radiocarbon dates:	Outer ditch fill: 1502–1322 BC (UB-6382) and 1432–1312 BC (UBA-16608) (latter date by Chrono as part of Ginn's research).
Notes:	The structure was cut by both a large field ditch [742] and also by a smaller field drain [334] which extended across the site southeast–northwest and northeast–southwest, respectively, converging and cutting one another at the western side of S47. The disturbance caused by these later features cut through and removed many structural features associated with the house, making accurate reconstruction and measurement difficult.

Structure:	**48**
Illustration:	2.48
Shape:	Circular
Measurements:	8.3m diameter
Location:	Northwest edge of settlement, north of S38 and southwest of S6.

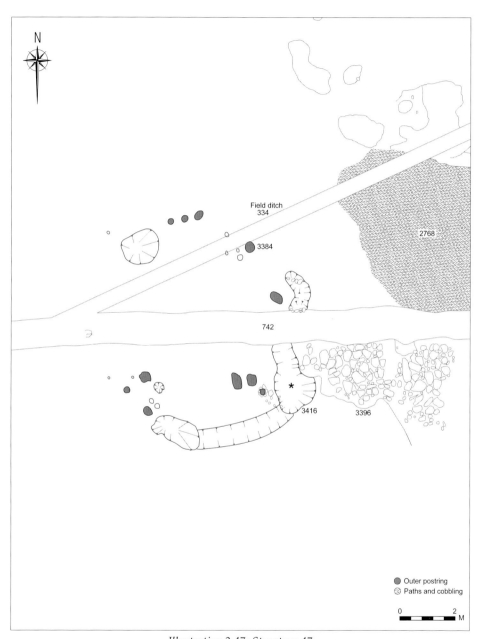

Illustration 2.47: Structure 47

Illustration 2.48: Structure 48

Outer ditch segments:	n=1
	This extended along the southern part of the structure and consisted of a concave base and small patch of cobble.
Outer postring:	n=31
	Approximately one third of these contained packing stones which distorted their shape and overall dimensions. Charcoal was recovered from the fill of the majority. Most of these postholes occurred in clusters of two or three, e.g. [3596] and [3602] and also [3900], [3896] and [3898], thus suggesting that at least two phases of substantial rebuilding had occurred.
Inner ditch:	N/A
Inner postring:	N/A
Entrance:	E
	There was no cut for an entrance feature, as with other structures, and instead the entrance was represented by nine postholes and several other associated features that led to an elaborate cobbled surface. This surface [3576a] (8.8m length × 1.3m width) was located immediately south of the structure and continued around the southeast corner. As it continued towards the northeast, it became more extensive and incorporated a larger surface area and met the entrance feature of S6.
	Nine postholes were associated. These do not seem to have formed a porch as they do not demonstrate the widely spaced pairing seen elsewhere on the site. It is more likely that they represent two or more successive wind-breaks, consisting of a sturdy fence supported by three to five stout posts.
Additional features:	N/A
Artefacts:	The remains of four vessels, two of which were barrel shaped, were associated with S48, as well as 11 sherds and fragments.
Radiocarbon dates:	N/A
Notes:	The remaining components of the structure had most likely been ploughed out.
Structure:	**49**
Illustration:	2.49
Shape:	Almost circular
Measurements:	9.2m × 9m
Location:	Eastern edge of settlement, southeast of S18, northeast of S26.
Outer ditch segments:	n=1
	A slot-trench was filled with occasional charcoal flecks and frequent large stones. Three postholes cut the slot-trench along the western side.
Outer postring:	n=10
	This was placed at a consistent distance away from the slot-trench and was equally spaced apart from a cluster of three postholes at the northwest.
Inner ditch:	N/A
Inner postring:	N/A
Entrance:	Unknown; it presumably lay to the south or southeast and had been removed by the field ditch.
Additional features:	N/A
Artefacts:	N/A
Radiocarbon dates:	N/A
Notes:	S49 was cut along its southern side by a field ditch.

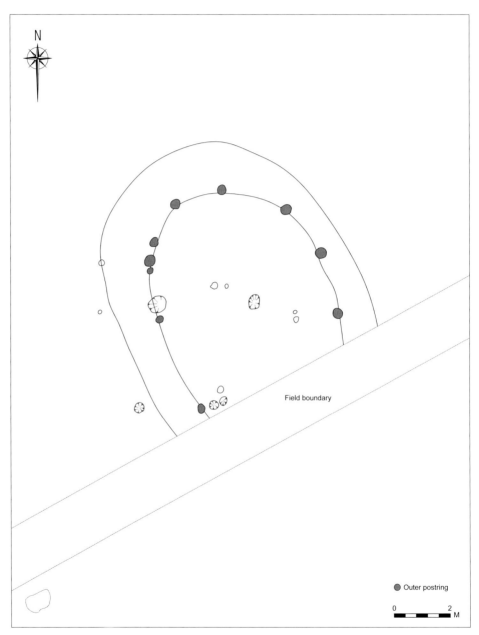

Illustration 2.49: Structure 49

Structure:	**50**
Illustration:	2.50
Shape:	Oval
Measurements:	12m diameter (internal)
Location:	East of S4.
Outer ditch segments:	n=1

The uninterrupted outer ditch was *c.* 15.2m long. During excavation, the outer edge of ditch [4000] was identified as a slight step on the inner edge of S52's outer ditch segment [3914]. The northern portion of S50's ditch segment contained neat cobbles and the southern section cut through a small cobbled path that pre-dated the major road surface F100.

Outer postring:	N/A
Inner ditch:	N/A
Inner postring:	N/A
Entrance:	N/A
Additional features:	

A series of postholes and pits was associated with the ditch but the precise function was not determinable. The posthole [4790] which was located underneath the intersection between the ditches of S50 and S52 was particularly large. It had a distinct V-shaped profile and its small rounded base was 0.7m below the top of the adjacent subsoil. A narrow, east–west linear feature [4062] (2.8m × 0.28–0.34m × 0.2m) was located in the eastern interior of S50 and ran from the edge of S52's outer ditch [3914]. It was not clear what the purpose of this feature was, or to which structure, if any, it belonged. It may have acted as a drain or fence associated with S52, or it may have been a partition within S50.

Artefacts:	N/A
Radiocarbon dates:	N/A
Notes:	

It is uncertain if the outer ditch segment functioned in the same way as it did at other structures. It is possible that this structure was never completed, or that the outer ditch served as a wind-break. The lack of associated features, notably postring postholes and features in the gap between S52 and S4, also suggests this possibility. There are several similar features on the site, principally the apparently incomplete double arcs of S24 and S26 and a curious curvilinear arrangement of features on the northwest side of the S19 house which pre-date S19's enclosing ditch.

However, although the precise function of S50 is unclear, it is apparent that S50 must have been constructed after the first phase of S4 as the small cobbled path which pre-dated the major road surface F100 and which served the early phases of S4 was cut by the outer ditch segment of S50.

Structure:	**51**
Illustration:	2.51
Shape:	Sub-circular
Measurements:	9.5m × 9m
Location:	Eastern edge of site, to the east of S52/S50.
Outer ditch segments:	n=3

The fills of these segments contained moderate charcoal inclusions and medium-sized and large stones, which did not obviously form walls or cobbled bases.

Outer postring:	There were many internal postholes that could have been part of an outer

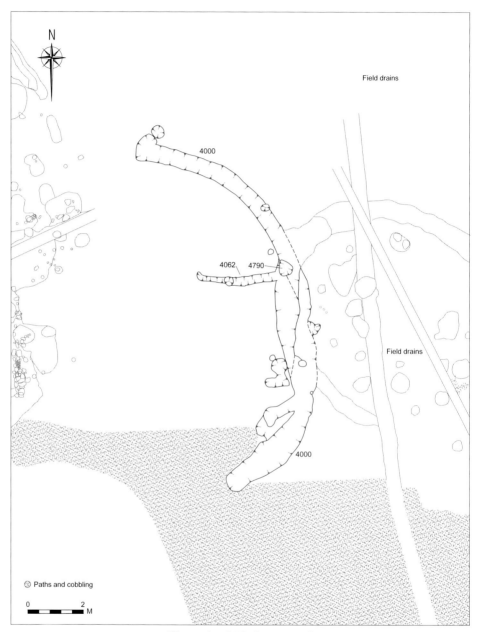

Illustration 2.50: Structure 50

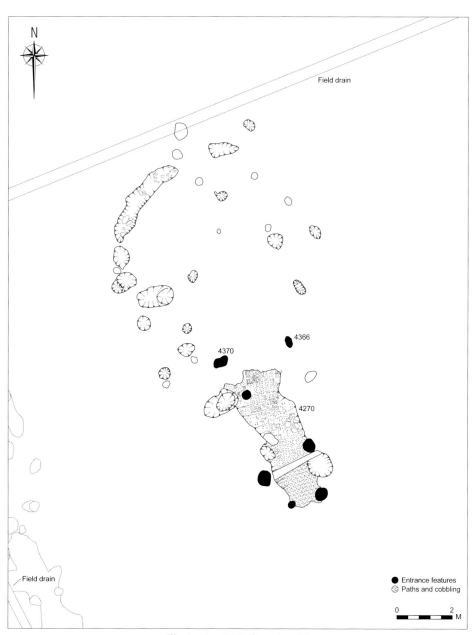

Illustration 2.51: Structure 51

postring; however, accurately determining this was not possible with the extant evidence.

Inner ditch:	N/A
Inner postring:	N/A
Entrance:	SSE

The large, sub-rectangular sunken entrance [4270] measured 5.3m by 0.78–1.35m by 0.28m. The base of the feature was covered in a particularly fine and well-laid cobble, comprising small, rounded stones. The fill above this was rich in charcoal and contained 34 sherds of prehistoric pottery. The arrangement of pairs of postholes and pits on either side of the southern half of the sunken pathway suggests that a porch covered the entire approach. The threshold between the entrance and the structure appeared to be marked by two opposing postholes [4370] (0.53m × 0.33m × 0.31m) and [4366] (0.4m × 0.22m × 0.43m). An isolated posthole was located at the northwest of the entrance and this was clearly a secondary feature as it was cut through the cobbles which had been displaced around the northern side. The extended cobbled path led towards, but was not connected to, road F100 to its south.

Additional features:	N/A
Artefacts:	The pottery associated with S51 included the remains of an Early Neolithic carinated bowl, along with five Middle Bronze Age vessels, including one barrel-shaped vessel, and a further 18 sherds and fragments.
Radiocarbon dates:	N/A
Notes:	S50–S52 form a neat row and have the appearance of a single phase of well-planned organization. This is in stark contrast to other areas on the site where successive structures have been built up against each other, e.g. S30, S31 and S33, and where buildings have had their design modified to fit into spaces left between pre-existing structures, e.g. S45.

Structure:	**52**
Illustration:	2.52
Shape:	Circular
Measurements:	9.8m × 8m
Location:	East of S51, west of S4, north of road F100.
Outer ditch segments:	n=5

Two to three courses of medium-sized and large stones represented material from a wall which had collapsed. The original height of the stone wall is not known, and it may have continued as a turf wall after a few more courses of stone. It is worth noting that only a single large posthole [4790] and a single small posthole [5806] were located in the base of this ditch, and both had been covered over by the wall. The wall therefore did not have a structural timber component, and the roof must have simply rested upon it, with its main load being carried by the internal posts.

Outer postring:	n=9
Inner ditch:	N/A
Inner postring:	N/A
Entrance:	SSE

This consisted of a large sub-rectangular cut [3918] (4.5m × 1.7m × 0.39m). At its southern end, the feature turned to the west at 90°, extending *c*. 20m and connecting with the cobbled trackway running between S4,

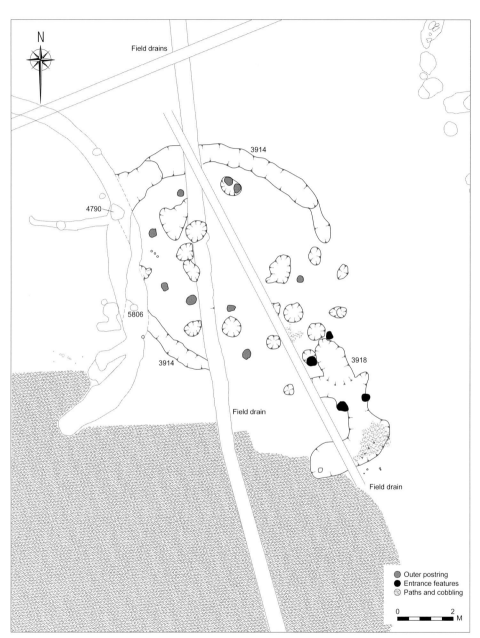

Illustration 2.52: Structure 52

S52 and S51. The sides of the entrance feature were cobbled, but the base was not, presumably a result of wear during the structure's use. A layer of large flat stones had been laid in the entrance and these covered the surviving portions of cobble. Twenty-two sherds of prehistoric pottery were recovered from the entrance cut. Two sets of opposing postholes were associated with the entrance.

Additional features:	Nearby pits may have post-dated the main occupation phase of the structure.
Artefacts:	The associated pottery remains comprised seven vessels, including four barrel-shaped vessels, and 37 sherds and fragments.
Radiocarbon dates:	N/A
Notes:	S52 cut the outer ditch segment of S50. S52 may have been associated with S51 and S4, both of which shared the same cobbled pathway.

Structure:	**53**
Illustration:	2.53
Shape:	Sub-circular
Measurements:	9m × 8m
Location:	Centre-west within the site, south of S54.
Outer ditch segments:	n=5
	Cobbling was observed in the base of the fifth segment, while the bases of segments [4644] and [4606] were covered in a layer of large flattish stones. Charcoal and a high concentration of stones characterised the fills of all segments.
Outer postring:	n=18
	Many of these occurred in clusters of three, e.g. [4608], [4696] and [4610]; [4564], [4566], and [4568]; [4574], [4584] and [4588]; and [4613], [4650] and [4614]. This suggests that the structure was completely rebuilt on two occasions.
Inner ditch:	n=1
	Feature [4898] (2.68m × 1.54m × 0.09m) may represent a segment of inner ditch; however, it may also have been associated with S54. Unfortunately, the field drain [742] ran through the area where the two adjacent structures met, and it is impossible to positively assign [4898] to either structure.
Inner postring:	N/A
Entrance:	SSE
	Patchy cobbling and a sub-circular pit were recorded within the possible entrance feature and contained a small piece of unidentifiable burnt bone in its primary fill along with 75 prehistoric pottery sherds.
Additional features:	An irregular, semi-circular, shallow gully [4620] (5.5m × 0.12m × 0.03m) was identified to the east of the entrance. A large stakehole [4804] was located at the southern end, and a smaller stakehole [4806] was located at the northern end. This arrangement appears to represent the foundation of a flimsy structure attached to the side of S53. Unfortunately, no evidence was recovered that could be used to determine the function of this small appendage, although it was certainly not a residential space. The feature is probably best interpreted as an animal pen, although other explanations cannot be ruled out.
Artefacts:	The pottery associated with S53 included the remains of an Early Neolithic carinated bowl with an out-turned rim, and six Middle Bronze

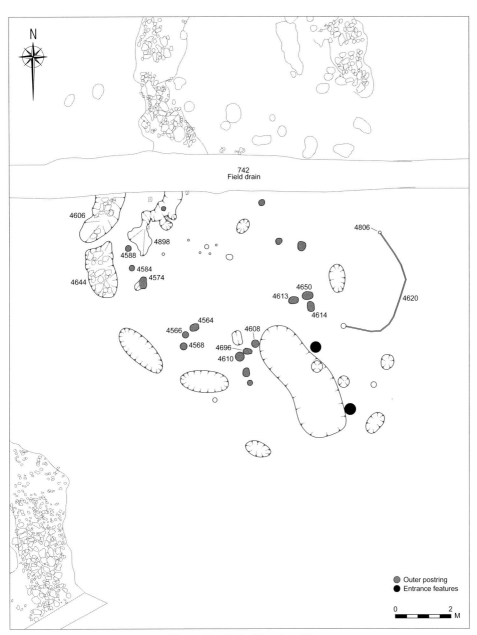

Illustration 2.53: Structure 53

	Age vessels, including two barrel-shaped vessels, and 30 sherds and fragments.
Radiocarbon dates:	N/A
Notes:	It is possible that S53 and S54 were contemporary structures, and they may have been conjoined. The important interface between these structures, which would probably have clarified this supposition, was cut through by modern field ditch [742]. Both structures had their own external entrance, and there is no reason to suggest that they had an interconnecting doorway, as no other example of such an arrangement can be cited within the settlement.

Structure:	**54**
Illustration:	2.54
Shape:	Oval
Measurements:	8.2m × 8m
Location:	North of S53, southeast of S38.
Outer ditch segments:	n=4
	These segments defined the eastern and western sides; no ditch segments were noted at the north or south of the structure. The fills of these segments contained a dense layer of medium-sized and large stones. A concentration of 267 prehistoric pottery sherds was recovered from the fill of [4396A]. Sixteen stakeholes were discovered along the base of [4396A] and [4396B]. The arrangement of these stakeholes suggests that they held stakes that were part of the outer wall, possibly a timber fence retaining a turf wall standing on the stone settings. Between the ditch sections [4396] and [4538] was a medium-sized pit [4594] (0.86m × 0.5m × 0.18m). The purpose of this feature is unknown but a similar arrangement of a pit in the middle of a wide gap between two outer ditch segments is clearly paralleled by the entrance to S5, and on the western side of S6.
Outer postring:	n=13
	Several of these were clustered in groups of two, e.g. [4468] and [4472], and [4534] and [4462], and [4742] and [4744], and [4790] and [4464], which suggests one phase of considerable modification/rebuild of the postring.
Inner ditch:	N/A
Inner postring:	N/A
Entrance:	SE
	No definite evidence of an entrance was forthcoming; however, a large gap at the southeast was associated with a number of small pits and this may mark its location, given the trend in the majority of the buildings.
Additional features:	N/A
Artefacts:	Associated pottery consisted of the remains of 10 barrel-shaped vessels, a further nine vessels, and 178 sherds and fragments too small or indistinct to be assigned to any particular vessels.
Radiocarbon dates:	N/A
Notes:	Due to its proximity to S53, its small size, its simplicity of design, it is highly likely that S54 was an annex to S53. Unfortunately, the area where the two structures would have intersected had been cut through by a large modern field boundary [742] and any opportunity to examine directly the relationship between the two structures had been lost.

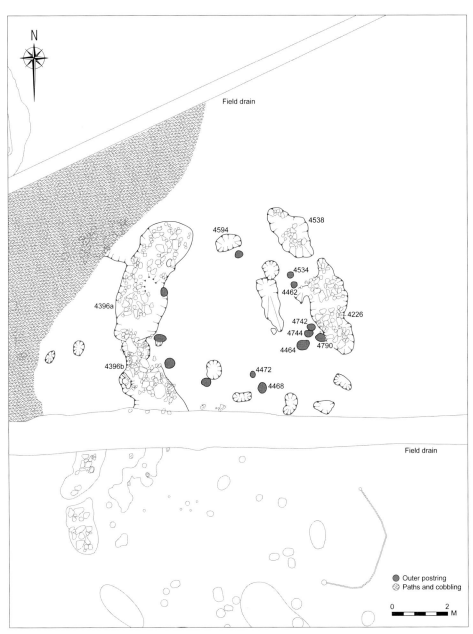

Illustration 2.54: Structure 54

Structure:	**55**
Illustration:	2.55
Shape:	Sub-circular
Measurements:	10m × 8.6m
Location:	Centre of site, east of S15, west of S27.
Outer ditch segments:	n=7
	All of the segments contained charcoal and large stones in their fills but only three contained stones which represented the remains of a stone foundation.
Outer postring:	n=18
	All of these postholes were clustered in groups of two, e.g. [5204] and [5238], and [5192] and [5194], indicating that the postring had been completely replaced on one occasion.
Inner ditch:	N/A
Inner postring:	N/A
Entrance:	SE
	The entrance feature [5138] contained 28 prehistoric pottery sherds in a deliberately backfilled stony matrix. A line of three postholes was arranged on the same alignment as the entrance feature [5138], in the narrow space between that feature and the doorway. These three postholes may have been entirely unconnected, and this structure did not have a porched entrance, but they may have held posts supporting a wind-break or a fence, protecting the entrance against wind coming from the southwest.
Additional features:	One of the 20 interior features pit [5274] (0.51m diameter × 0.43m depth) contained unidentifiable burnt bone fragments.
Artefacts:	The remains of nine vessels, including only one barrel-shaped vessel, were associated with S55, along with 44 sherds and fragments.
Radiocarbon dates:	N/A
Notes:	Many of the features of S55 appeared to have been deliberately backfilled, e.g. two of the entrance postholes and the drain to the southwest of the entrance, and the outer ditch segments appear to have had the majority of their stone robbed, possibly for re-use in another structure. This may indicate that the structure was abandoned while the rest of the settlement was still occupied.
Structure:	**56**
Illustration:	2.56
Shape:	Sub-circular
Measurements:	9.8m × 8.4m
Location:	S56 lay between S20 to the east and S21 to the west and was truncated on its southern side by a field boundary ditch.
Outer ditch segments:	n=4
	These ran from the northwest through to the southwest side of the structure.
Outer postring:	n=13
Inner ditch:	N/A
Inner postring:	N/A
Entrance:	S
	This irregularly shaped feature [5040] measured 4.5m × 3.49m × 0.23m.
Additional features:	There were many internal features, including pits, postholes, stakeholes,

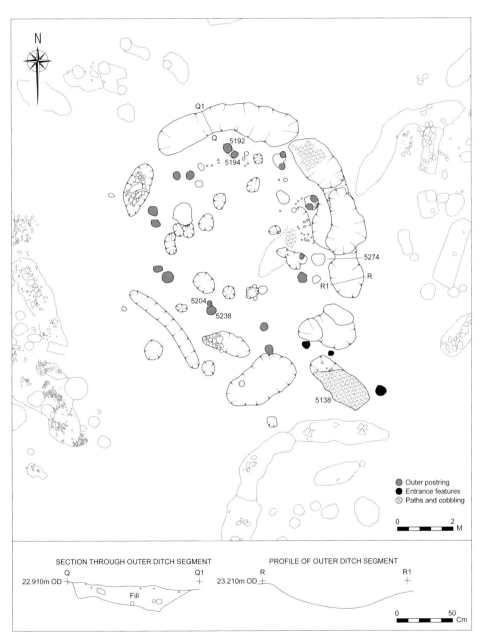

Illustration 2.55: Structure 55

Illustration 2.56: Structure 56

and one area of internal cobbling [5066] (1.7m × 1.05m × 0.12m). As with many entrances in the Corrstown settlement, this cobbling extended into the interior of the structure and it appeared to have been two phased. The base of the feature contained a cobbled layer and 12 prehistoric pottery sherds, which was then covered by a fill with a high concentration of tightly packed, large stones, along with 73 prehistoric pottery sherds. Eight features, including pits and two postholes which possibly represent doorjambs, were cut into this entrance feature. The entrance was also cut by a large field ditch (1.7m width × 1.5m depth), which extended across the site east–west. A patch of interrupted cobbled stones [5040a] (2.2m length × 0.41m width) lay to the south of this ditch and indicates that the entrance was once much longer.

Artefacts:	The remains of 13 vessels, including five barrel-shaped vessels, were associated with S56, along with 48 sherds and fragments.
Radiocarbon dates:	N/A
Notes:	S56 overlapped with the foundation of S57, located to the north, and it was not always possible to accurately determine which features belonged to which structure. The chronological relationship between S56 and S57 was not determined, although they clearly could not have been used simultaneously.

Structure:	**57**
Illustration:	2.57
Shape:	Sub-circular
Measurements:	7m × 6.4m
Location:	Northeast of, and partially within, the remains of S56.
Outer ditch segments:	n=5
	These ditch segments defined a circular area with a gap at the east. The segments had cobbled bases and numerous prehistoric pottery sherds were contained in the overlying fill.
Outer postring:	n=7
	They contained charcoal flecks and stones, including packing stones. As S57 overlapped the northeastern part of S56 it was difficult to discern which internal features belonged to which structure.
Inner ditch:	N/A
Inner postring:	N/A
Entrance:	SE
	A large pit to the southeast of the structure may represent the remains of the entrance feature [5034] (2.18m × 1.56m × 0.32m). It was typical of entrance features within the settlement, having a layer of large flat stones on its base. A small quantity of prehistoric pottery sherds was found in the overlying fills.
Additional features:	N/A
Artefacts:	The remains of two vessels, including one barrel-shaped vessel, as well as 11 fragments and sherds of fine and medium fabric were associated with S57.
Radiocarbon dates:	N/A
Notes:	As mentioned above, the chronological relationship between S56 and S57 could not be established but the structures could not have stood simultaneously.

Illustration 2.57: Structure 57

Structure:	**58**
Illustration:	2.58
Shape:	Oval
Measurements:	10.8m × 9.3m
Location:	West of S59.
Outer ditch segments:	n=7

A single fill containing a high concentration of tightly packed medium-sized and large stones on top of a cobbled base was removed from each of the segments, except [5378] where a charcoal-rich, ash spread with unidentifiable burnt bone fragments, 40 sherds of prehistoric pottery and an area of red, oxidised clay and heat-fractured stones lay above the stony, primary fill. Approximately 100 charred cereal grains, mostly naked barley were recovered from this fill. The northern edge of this segment was truncated by a modern, west–east field drain [5542].

Outer postring: n=20

Each contained a single fill, many of which had charcoal flecks and packing stones. Some of these postholes, e.g. [5560] and [5548], were arranged in pairs which suggested that the postring had been considerably re-strengthened on at least one occasion. Approximately 80 charred cereal grains, most of which were naked barley and some cereal grain fragments were recovered from the fill of posthole [5844].

Inner ditch: n=4

Like the outer ditch segments, these features contained cobbled bases and stony fills.

Inner postring: N/A

Entrance: SSE

This comprised a set of opposing postholes and an extensive cobbled surface [6336] (7.36m length × 2.5m width) from which 76 pottery sherds were recovered. One of the features associated with the cobbled pathway was posthole [6298] from which a radiocarbon date of 1511–1406 BC (UB-6243) was derived.

Additional features: Of the internal features stakehole [5466] was of particular interest as it contained approximately 150 charred cereal grains (mostly barley) alongside a single grain of rye (*Secale cereale* L.)) in a charcoal-rich, sandy clay fill. (It is possible that the context of these grains was incorrectly recorded during excavation and that they actually derive from the adjacent pit located to the south of the stakehole.)

Artefacts: The pottery associated with S58 comprised the remains of 13 barrel-shaped vessels and a further six vessels as well as 138 sherds and fragments too small or indistinct to assign to any particular vessel.

Radiocarbon dates: Entrance posthole: 1511–1406 BC (UB-6243).

Notes: N/A

Structure:	**59**
Illustration:	2.59
Shape:	Circular
Measurements:	9.2m diameter
Location:	South of S72, east of S58, northwest of S67, and southwest of S68.
Outer ditch segments:	n=8

Cobbled bases were overlain with a layer of tightly packed larger stones.

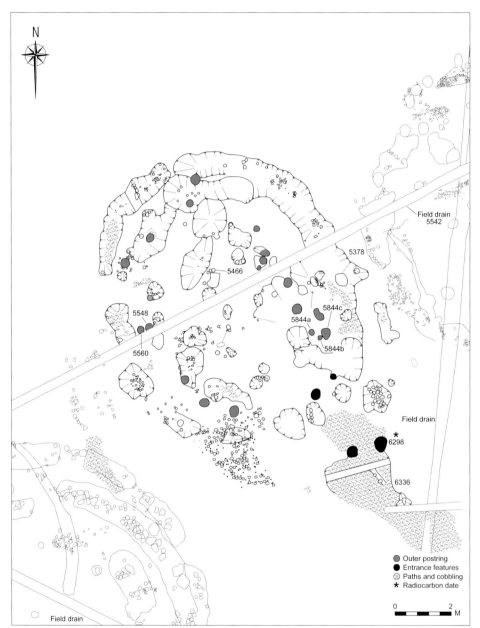

Illustration 2.58: Structure 58

Illustration 2.59: Structure 59

An intermittent cobbled patch was identified 0.33m southeast of the southern end of the outer ditch [5590] and may represent the truncated base of another outer ditch segment.

Outer postring:	n=12

Some of these postholes, notably [5628], [5630] and [5872], were grouped together, indicating that several phases of modification and re-strengthening had occurred.

Inner ditch:	N/A
Inner postring:	N/A
Entrance:	SSE

This was sunken with a cobbled base. Unfortunately, this entrance was disturbed by the modern field drain [6286]. The cobbling extended beyond the southern end of the sunken feature (5.2m × 2.6m × 0.21m) and 30 prehistoric pottery sherds were recovered from its surface. It did not appear that this entrance was covered by a porch as only a single definite posthole was associated with it. Several large pits of unknown function had been placed in this area.

Additional features:	Two cobbled patches were observed in the interior of the building and may represent the remains of a floor surface.

There were many external features, especially postholes located close to the north of the structure, along the outer ditch segments. This group may represent an external feature or may be from an earlier phase of the structure.

Artefacts:	The pottery associated with S59 comprised the remains of 14 vessels, including six barrel-shaped vessels, one of which had an estimated rim diameter of 23cm. A further 71 sherds and fragments of varying fabrics were also identified.
Radiocarbon dates:	N/A
Notes:	N/A

Structure:	**60**
Illustration:	2.60
Shape:	Sub-circular
Measurements:	11m × 8m
Location:	East of S27, south of S17; the structure was cut along its northern side by a large southeast–northwest modern field drain removing the northern-most part of the building.
Outer ditch segments:	n=1

A single, large ditch segment along the western side contained tightly packed, large stones which were overlain with a charcoal-rich soil. Two postholes cut the ditch segment along its outer edge. At the east of the structure the irregular oval-shaped feature [5710] may have been a second segment of outer ditch but is best interpreted as an external pit.

Outer postring:	n=8
Inner ditch:	n=1

The tightly packed stones on its base contained 10 prehistoric pottery sherds. Two pits cut the inner ditch.

Inner postring:	N/A
Entrance:	SSE

Three sets of opposing postholes indicated that the entrance had been

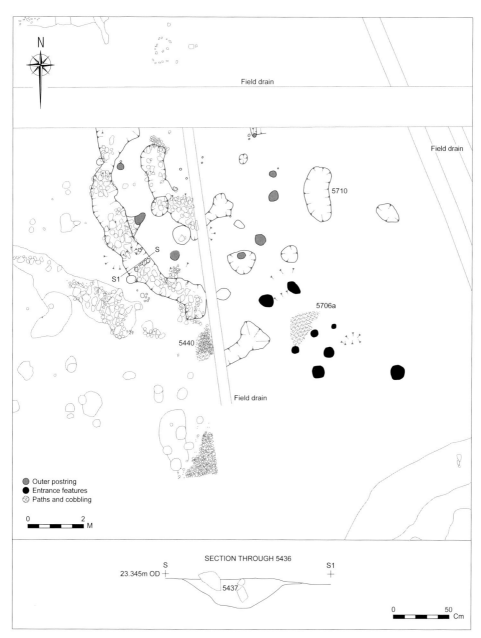

Illustration 2.60: Structure 60

porched. The doorway was 0.6m wide. Between these postholes was a
patch of cobbling [5706A] composed of small, tightly packed, rounded
stones. Another cobble patch [5440] situated to the west may have been
associated with a path or working area.

Additional features:	N/A
Artefacts:	The remains of four vessels, including three barrel shaped, and a further 10 sherds and fragments of medium fabric were associated with S61.
Radiocarbon dates:	N/A
Notes:	N/A

Structure:	**61**
Illustration:	2.61
Shape:	Almost circular
Measurements:	8.4m × 8.2m
Location:	Close to the southern edge of the site, to the west of S62 and southeast of S69.
Outer ditch segments:	n=5
	These segments contained patches of cobbling at their base, which had been covered over by a stony fill.
Outer postring:	n=1
	There was one posthole and this was located in the right position to suggest that it may have formed part of an outer postring. However, no further postholes were identified and this lack of postholes suggests that the structure may simply have been open and unroofed, or that the roof was supported entirely by a wall which stood in or adjacent to the outer ditch segments.
Inner ditch:	N/A
Inner postring:	N/A
Entrance:	SSE
	A cobbled was area overlain with a paved area. Two postholes were located outside the entrance feature and suggest that this structure may have had a very small porch.
Additional features:	A large, irregular feature [6426] (3.6m × 2.2m × 0.11m) was backfilled with stone to allow for the construction of S61. It may have been a natural depression which needed to be filled before S61 was built or it may have been an earlier feature that was filled in to create an even floor surface within the interior of the structure.
	A narrow linear feature [6340] ran southwards from the western side of the structure. Its purpose was unclear, although it may have been a drain. After this feature was filled in, whether naturally or deliberately was unclear, its fill was covered by patches of medium-sized stone.
Artefacts:	N/A
Radiocarbon dates:	N/A
Notes:	S61 is representative of a small group of structures located at the south of the site, a group that includes S62 and S67. This group is characterised by small dimensions, simple plan and low numbers of postholes, although they still share architectural design features with the other, larger structures on site. These structures are of similar size and design to some of the annexes attached to the sides of larger structures, such as S5's annex, S46. This resemblance may indicate that all these structures

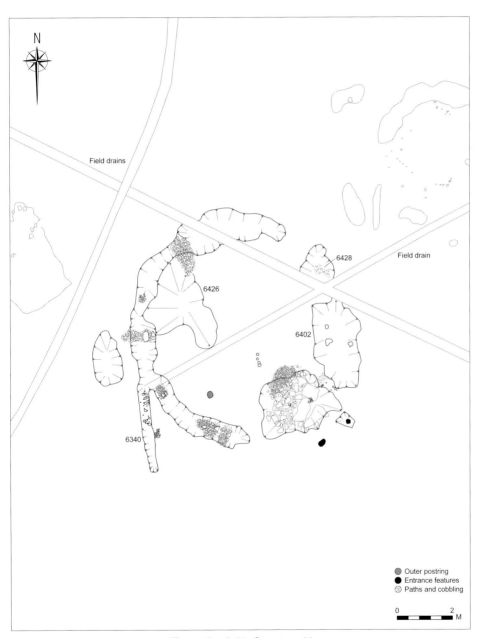

Illustration 2.61: Structure 61

were probably used primarily for storage as they are considerably smaller than the other structures on site.

Structure:	**62**
Illustration:	2.62
Shape:	Circular / oval
Measurements:	7.4m × 6.5m
Location:	Southern end of the site, northeast of S61.
Outer ditch segments:	n=2
	These segments ran around half of the structure from the northwest to the southeast and none were present around the rest of the perimeter.
Outer postring:	n=1
Inner ditch:	N/A
Inner postring:	N/A
Entrance:	S
	No discernable entrance was identified, although the postholes which cut the eastern, outer ditch segment could represent part of an entrance structure.
Additional features:	The most prominent feature within the structure was the large block of fine cobbling [6328], which covered the northwest quarter of the structure's interior. The rest of the structure may have originally been cobbled, which may have been removed by ploughing, but if the recorded distribution reflects the original distribution of the cobbling, then it must be assumed that this quarter of the structure was in some way different from the rest.
Artefacts:	The remains of three vessels were associated with S62.
Radiocarbon dates:	N/A
Notes:	S62 is one of a group of similar structures, consisting of S61 and S67, located in this area of the settlement. This group is also similar to the annexes of several of the larger structures, including S46 of S5 and S11 of S10. All these structures share similar dimensions, low numbers of postholes and simplicity of design, yet the architectural features are similar to the other, larger structures on site and therefore this group cannot be considered as a separate house type.

Structure:	**63**
Illustration:	2.63
Shape:	Oval
Measurements:	11m × 9.4m
Location:	Southern end of the site.
Outer ditch segments:	n=6
	Medium-sized and large stones were present in their fills. These segments were similar to the slot-trenches of other structures; yet they were not totally dissimilar to the outer ditches of the majority of structures in the complex.
Outer postring:	n=9
	Two sets pairs of postholes were noted: [6756d] and [6862], and [6850d] and [6850c].
Inner ditch:	N/A
Inner postring:	N/A

N

6328

Field drain

● Outer postring
⊗ Paths and cobbling

0   2
M

Illustration 2.62: Structure 62

Illustration 2.63: Structure 63

Entrance:	S

It was not possible to identify the entrance from the extant remains. However, the gap between the outer ditch segments [6646] and [6832] at the south of the structure is the most likely location.

Additional features: Four postholes were arranged as a small square to the north of the central area of the structure. These postholes may not have played a structural role, but may have supported some piece of equipment or furniture within the structure. It is also possible that they were not contemporary with S63 and the association may be, therefore, fortuitous. If so, then the four postholes would represent a small, freestanding, four-post structure constructed either before or after S63.

Artefacts: N/A

Radiocarbon dates: N/A

Notes: Two modern field drains bearing ceramic pipes, which had cut through various segments of the outer ditch, crossed the structure.

The form of the building was very similar to S64 and the other continuous slot-trench structures, S18 and S49, apart from the segmented nature of the outer ditch. The possibility that the outer ditch of S63 had originally been continuous but had been partially truncated was considered, but this explanation would have required the base of the original continuous outer ditch to undulate, a feature not observed in the other continuous slot-trench structures. Because of this, the discontinuous nature of the outer ditch is considered to be an original feature of the design. The sparse number of internal features is another aspect that makes this structure particularly similar to the continuous slot-trench structures.

Structure:	**64**
Illustration:	2.64
Shape:	Oval/circular
Measurements:	10.4m × 9.1m
Location:	Southeastern edge of the site, to the west of S32 and southeast of S65/ S71.
Outer ditch segments:	n=1

The slot-trench [6430] was reasonably close to being a true circle, and the width of the slot-trench was fairly consistent, between 0.4–0.6m. Around the southeast the slot-trench became noticeably wider with a width of up to 1m. It had a U-shaped profile with vertical and near-vertical sides all around, except for the inside edge around the wider southeast section, which was sloping. The base of the slot-trench was slightly concave throughout the circuit. The slot-trench was excavated to a maximum depth of, typically, between 0.2–0.3m. The slot-trench contained a stony fill with packing-stones and charcoal. It is possible that, like S18, this slot-trench had held a continuous wooden palisade.

Outer postring:	n=5
Inner ditch:	N/A
Inner postring:	N/A
Entrance:	SSE

Although no obvious entrance feature was located as a break in this slot-trench or as an adjacent set of features, a cobbled trackway [9044], [9045] and [9046] ran past the south of the structure, linking up with the wider and deeper southeastern section of the slot-trench, which was

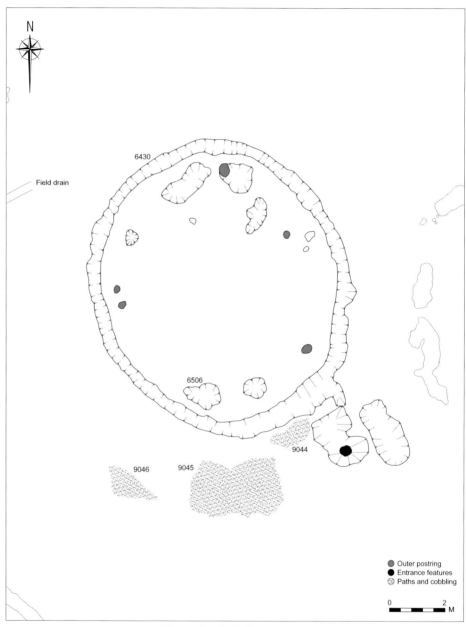

Illustration 2.64: Structure 64

presumably the location of the structure's entrance. An irregularity in the outer edge of the slot-trench was located in this area, in the form of a small projection, 0.9m × 0.4m, which ran away to the south. This projection may have defined the eastern side of the entrance.

Additional features:	N/A
Artefacts:	The remains of four pottery vessels were identified with this structure.
Radiocarbon dates:	N/A
Notes:	S64 was located on sloping ground where the ground at the eastern side of the structure was up to 0.31m higher than at the western side. There had been no attempt in digging the slot-trench to counteract this slope by deepening the eastern side. S64 has several parallels across the site. S18, S33 and S49 also displayed similar narrow and deep perimeter wall-slots and all were located along the fringes of the settlement complex.

Structure:	**65**
Illustration:	2.65
Shape:	Oval
Measurements:	8.3m × 6.6m
Location:	Northwest of S64, overlapping southern side of S71.
Outer ditch segments:	n=4
	These contained stones and charcoal in their silty clay fills.
Outer postring:	n=6
Inner ditch:	N/A
Inner postring:	N/A
Entrance:	S
	The entrance comprised a cobbled [6604] surface. A sample from the cobbled fill returned a Middle Bronze Age radiocarbon date of 1499–1324 BC (UB-6244). Several pits and postholes were also associated with this entrance.
Additional features:	Much of the interior was covered in cobbling and in places this extended to the exterior. It would appear that S65 post-dated these areas and they are likely to have been associated with a stone pathway that existed between structures prior to the construction of S65.
Artefacts:	The remains of four pottery vessels and a further eight fragments of fine and medium fabric were associated with S65.
Radiocarbon dates:	Entrance feature: 1499–1324 BC (UB-6244).
Notes:	The relationship between S65 and S71 was not definitively proven during excavation. Unlike S56 and S57, these buildings could have stood at the same time, as is the case with S53 and S54. However, while it is appealing to think of these as a pair of conjoined buildings, one may have succeeded the other, each then being a small isolated structure. Unfortunately, the ground plans, as excavated, do not indicate the presence of an interconnecting doorway, nor conversely do they disprove the existence of such a feature.

Structure:	**66**
Illustration:	2.66
Shape:	Unknown
Measurements:	8.8m × 8m
Location:	East of site, northeast of S32, heavily truncated along its eastern side.

Illustration 2.65: Structure 65

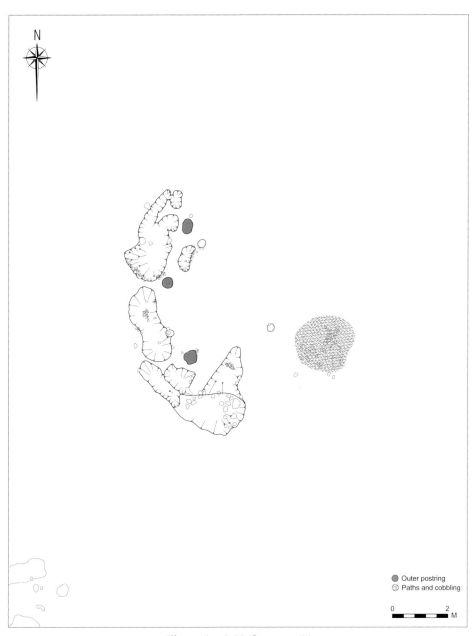

N

● Outer postring
⊘ Paths and cobbling

0   2
              M

Illustration 2.66: Structure 66

Outer ditch segments:	n=4
	The base of some of these segments contained a fragmented layer of small cobbles. Larger stones in a silty clay covered this layer.
Outer postring:	n=3
	Packing stones, flint and charcoal were contained within the fills.
Inner ditch:	N/A
Inner postring:	N/A
Entrance:	SSE
	This small sunken feature contained a layer of large flat stones on its base.
Additional features:	N/A
Artefacts:	N/A
Radiocarbon dates:	N/A
Notes:	The eastern side of this building had been removed apparently during an earlier period of construction activity, probably when the houses to the east were built. The surviving parts of the building suggest that it may originally have been a medium-sized building defined by a segmented ditch.

Structure:	**67**
Illustration:	2.67
Shape:	Circular
Measurements:	6.8m diameter
Location:	Close to and respecting S68 and S59.
Outer ditch segments:	n=3
	All were lined with stones and filled with larger stones, pebbles, charcoal flecks, and flint fragments.
Outer postring:	n=3
Inner ditch:	N/A
Inner postring:	N/A
Entrance:	S
	An elongated cut with a heavily compacted gravel surface formed the entrance to S67. Two opposing postholes located at the southern end of this feature may have represented doorjambs. A further small cobbled area was identified to the south of the extant entrance and may have been part of a pathway leading to the entrance.
Additional features:	N/A
Artefacts:	N/A
Radiocarbon dates:	N/A
Notes:	N/A

Structure:	**68**
Illustration:	2.68
Shape:	Oval
Measurements:	10m × 8m
Location:	North of S67.
Outer ditch segments:	n=5
	The fills of these ditch segments contained large, medium and small stones, and flint fragments. A cobbled base was noted in places.
Outer postring:	n=16
	The fills contained charcoal and small stones and occasional flint

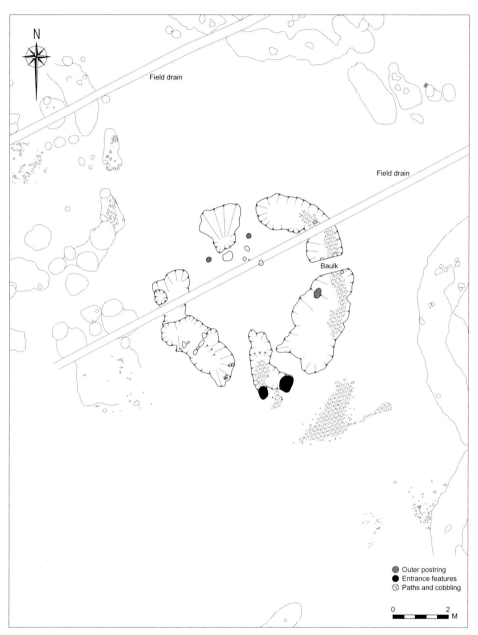

Field drain

Field drain

Baulk

⬤ Outer postring
⬤ Entrance features
⊛ Paths and cobbling

0   2
▬▬▬▬▬ M

Illustration 2.67: Structure 67

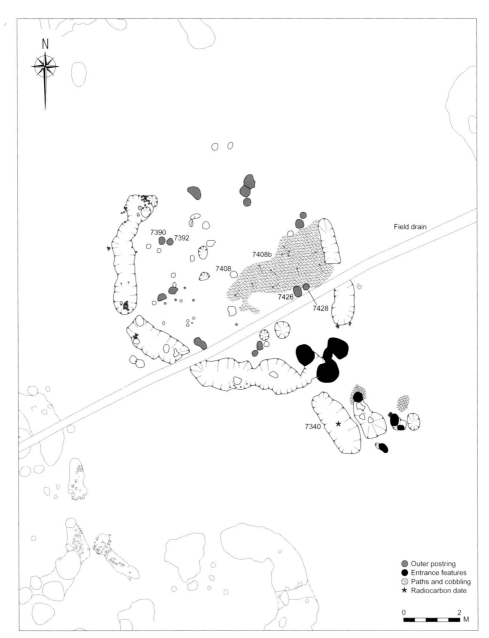

Illustration 2.68: Structure 68

fragments. The majority of these postholes were grouped in pairs e.g. [7426] and [7428] and [7390] and [7392], which suggests that the structure was completely rebuilt on one occasion, rather than merely strengthened at points of weakness.

Inner ditch:	N/A
Inner postring:	N/A
Entrance:	SSE

An area of compacted stones had an associated gully, pits and postholes. One of the pits [7340] contained charcoal flecks in its fill which returned a radiocarbon date of 1421–1265 BC (UB-6380). It is possible that the cut features may have supported a porch structure or wind-break.

Additional features: A centrally placed circular feature [7408] (0.22m × 0.2m × 0.04m) was too shallow to have been a posthole for a load-bearing post.
A compact stone surface [7408b] (*c.* 3.22m length × 2.25m width) – which may represent the floor surface or a possible work area – was located in the northeastern area of the structure.

Artefacts:	N/A
Radiocarbon dates:	Entrance pit: 1421–1265 BC (UB-6380).
Notes:	A modern field drain extended across this area of the site and cut some of the features.

Structure:	**69**
Illustration:	2.69
Shape:	Circular
Measurements:	11.2m × 11m
Location:	Southwest of S58 and overlapping with the stratigraphically earlier S76.
Outer ditch segments:	n=6

All contained layers of large stones on their bases and charcoal in the overlying fills. The fill of segment [8214] also contained flint, organic root material, decayed stone fragments, significant quantities of charcoal, oxidised clay, and *c.* 450 well-preserved charred cereal grains (naked barley) along with two fruits of black-bindweed (*Fallopia convolvulus*). The internal surface around the inside edge of the cut was packed with a layer of small stones and pebbles which extended *c.* 0.5m into the interior of the structure and partly surrounded the cut for the inner ditch segment [8218].

Outer postring:	n=5
Inner ditch:	n=1

It contained an incomplete layer of medium-sized and large stones on its base, and charcoal flecks, pieces of decayed stone, and flint fragments were present in the overlying fill.

Inner postring:	N/A
Entrance:	SE

A substantial elongated, slightly sunken entranceway continued as a stone pathway. This pathway (cut to a maximum depth of 0.08m) had a silty clay fill containing four prehistoric pottery sherds and approximately 300 well-preserved cereal grains, most of which were of barley, with the naked variety prevailing and a few hulled grains also present. Additionally, one fruit of black-bindweed was identified.

Additional features: S69 had a secondary outer ditch system of six segments. These were all of similar size and contained fill similar to the outer ditch segments. A

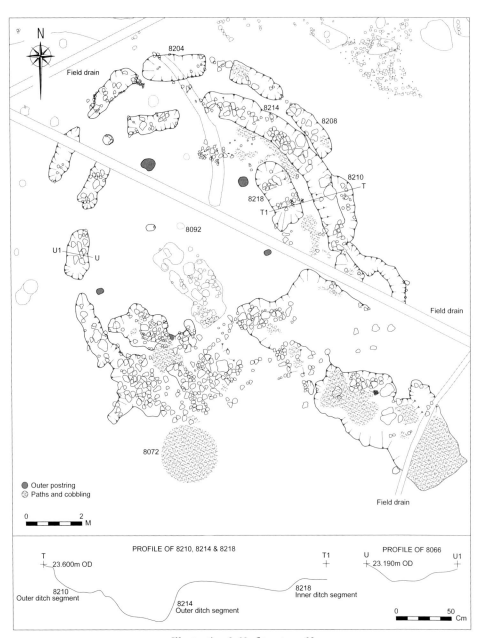

Illustration 2.69: Structure 69

base layer of cobbling was noted and large flat stones were recorded on the base of some of the segments. Four complete charred cereal grains and some cereal grain fragments were recovered from [8208]; three grains were barley. These features relate to a different building phase of the structure, which must have been built on a slightly different alignment. These segments may be associated with the cobble patches around the inner edge of outer ditch segment [8214], in which case they must post-date the main structural phase being described here.

The centrally located posthole [8092] (0.21m × 0.15m × 0.37m) may have been a support post; however, it may alternatively have represented part of the outer postring of S76.

A sub-circular external stone surface [8072] (2.4m length × 2.1m width) may have represented the remains of a work area.

Artefacts:	The remains of seven barrel-shaped vessels and one further vessel, as well as 52 sherds and fragments of varying fabric were associated with S69.
Radiocarbon dates:	N/A
Notes:	The enranceway was truncated by modern drain.

Structure:	**70**
Illustration:	2.70
Shape:	Sub-circular
Measurements:	10m × 8.4m
Location:	Close to and respecting S25; adjoined to S76.
Outer ditch segments:	n=2
	Both segments contained layers of large stones on their bases and were truncated along their inner edges by postholes of the outer postring. Fifteen whole charred cereal grains, as well as several cereal grain fragments were recovered from the fill of [7940]; naked barley comprised the majority of the grains and one grain of emmer wheat was also identified.
Outer postring:	n=11
	Charcoal flecks and flint fragments occurred occasionally in their fills.
Inner ditch:	N/A
Inner postring:	N/A
Entrance:	SSE
	A stone pathway and a cobbled surface formed the entrance. Underneath the pathway were several pits, including rectangular pit [7948]. This pit contained packing stones, flint, Bronze Age pottery sherds, and charcoal, some of which derived a radiocarbon date of 6461–6255 BC (UB-6250), within the Mesolithic period. This feature obviously pre-dated the entrance to S70. Two postholes may represent doorjambs leading into the interior of the structure while a further three postholes and a double posthole most likely represent the remains of a porch.
Additional features:	To the immediate north of the structure were four ditch segments. These may have belonged to an earlier phase of the structure built on a slightly different alignment. Their fills contained flint fragments and medium-sized stones. A centrally placed posthole / pit may have represented a hearth, although there was no evidence for *in situ* burning. Other internal postholes, stakeholes and pits represented evidence for further strengthening of the structure, for internal divisions and for domestic activity.
Artefacts:	The remains of four barrel-shaped vessels and a further two vessels

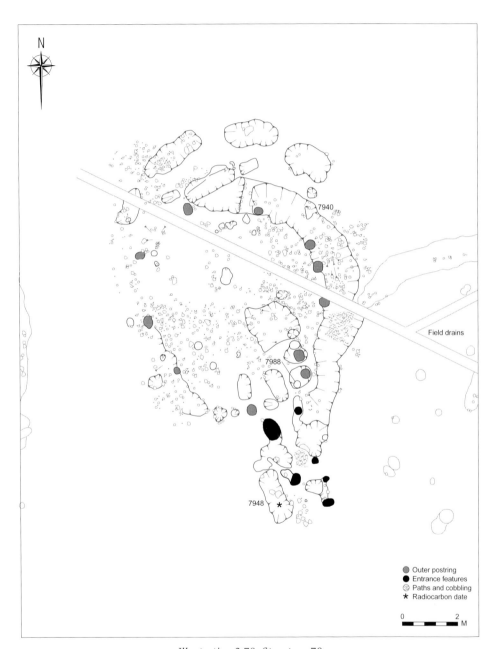

N

7940

Field drains

7988

7948 ★

Outer postring
Entrance features
Paths and cobbling
★ Radiocarbon date

0   2
▬▬▬▬▬ M

Illustration 2.70: Structure 70

were associated with S70, as well as 39 sherds and fragments of varying fabric.

Radiocarbon dates:	N/A
Notes:	N/A

Structure:	**71**
Illustration:	2.71
Shape:	Circular
Measurements:	9.2m diameter
Location:	Southeast of S67; truncated by S65.
Outer ditch segments:	n=5

The fills of these features contained prehistoric pottery sherds and flint fragments, while layers of large stones were located on their bases.

Outer postring:	n=3
Inner ditch:	n=1
Inner postring:	N/A
Entrance:	?S/SE

There was no direct evidence for the entrance; however, it may have been located towards the south/southeast of the structure where [6582] of S65 was located. The irregular feature [6569] may have been associated with an entrance feature, and the area of cobbling in the northeast corner of S65 may have been related to the entrance of S71.

Additional features:	N/A
Artefacts:	The remains of two large barrel-shaped vessels were associated with S71; the estimated rim diameters were 22cm and 21cm.
Radiocarbon dates:	N/A
Notes:	The chronological relationship between S71 and S65 was not established during the excavations. It is possible that the two structures were associated, either as two conjoined houses or, alternatively, one may have represented an annex or storehouse to the other. If this was the case, then the larger of the two, S71, was probably the residential building. However, as discussed above, either building may have post-dated the other.

Structure:	**72**
Illustration:	2.72
Shape:	Unknown
Measurements:	7.6m × 6.86m
Location:	Northwest of S59 and S58 and south of S20.
Outer ditch segments:	n=4

Small stones, charcoal and flint fragments were recovered from the fills of these segments but only one fill, that of segment [6956], contained any large stones which could represent the collapsed remains of a foundation for a wall.

Outer postring:	n=9
Inner ditch:	N/A
Inner postring:	N/A
Entrance:	SE

An entranceway was identified to the southeast of the structure, and consisted of a continuation of the east extent of the outer ditch segment [6940] and sub-circular pit [6938]. Both features were cut by the modern field

Field drain

Field drain

6569

● Outer postring
⊗ Paths and cobbling

0   2
▬▬▬▬▬ M

Illustration 2.71: Structure 71

Illustration 2.72: Structure 72

drain [7810]. A short, compact stone and pebble pathway was evident.

Additional features: N/A
Artefacts: The remains of one large barrel-shaped vessel (estimated rim diameter 19.5cm) and two fragments of fine fabric were associated with this structure.
Radiocarbon dates: N/A
Notes: Only the southern half of the structure remained extant and, unlike with S66, there was no obvious explanation as to why the northern half of the building was absent.

Structure: **73**
Illustration: 2.73
Shape: Oval
Measurements: 9.26m × 7.43m
Location: Southeast of S26 and northeast of S68.
Outer ditch segments: n=3
                              A similar fill was present in these ditch segments and comprised a silty clay with frequent charcoal flecks and prehistoric pottery sherds. Cobbling was noted in the fill of the second segment [7130]. None of the segments contained large stones.
Outer postring: n=10
                              Most contained occasional charcoal flecks and small stones.
Inner ditch: N/A
Inner postring: N/A
Entrance: SSE
                              A paved surface was present. A pair of large postholes was located on either side of the paving; these features may represent the doorjambs and foundation posts for a porch.
Additional features: A number of additional postholes was identified within the house structure which, while they cannot be assigned to a particular postring, may have acted as additional supports for those timbers or they may represent the remains of internal divisions. The internal surface of the structure also contained a number of stakeholes, positioned in groups. While it is unlikely that these features were intended for load-bearing use, it is probable that they represent the remains of internal features or temporary divisions.
Artefacts: The remains of two large barrel-shaped vessels (estimated rim diameters of 10.7cm and 22cm) and one further vessel were associated with the structure.
Radiocarbon dates: N/A
Notes: N/A

Structure: **74**
Illustration: 2.74
Shape: Oval
Measurements: 6.6m × 6m
Location: Cut or was cut by S16; truncated by field ditch [742].
Outer ditch segments: n=4
                              None of these segments contained stone settings.
Outer postring: n=5
Inner ditch: N/A
Inner postring: N/A

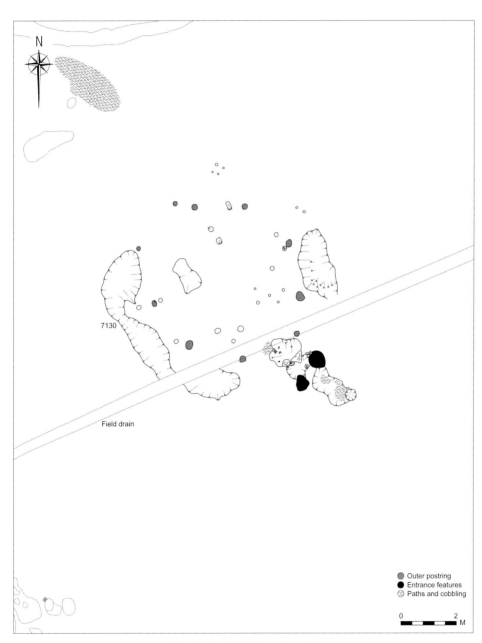

Illustration 2.73: Structure 73

742
Field drain

● Outer postring
○ Associated structural postholes
⊗ Paths and cobbling

Illustration 2.74: Structure 74

Entrance:	Unknown
Additional features:	N/A
Artefacts:	N/A
Radiocarbon dates:	N/A
Notes:	The presence of S74, an additional structure in this area, only became apparent during post-excavation analysis. It was difficult to discern which features belonged to S16 and which to S74 and where this has not been possible the features have been described in S16. However, it is apparent that at least four segments of outer ditch and five postholes of an outer postring must belong to a structure other than S16.
	Although not all the structural components of S74 can be identified, the remaining extant evidence would suggest that there was only one phase of construction / modification to this structure. The relationship between S74 and S16 is unknown.

Structure:	**75**
Illustration:	2.75
Shape:	Unknown
Measurements:	7.71m width, not possible to estimate length
Location:	Close to S23; cut through at the south by S24 and by the line of a modern field boundary.
Outer ditch segments:	n=3
	Three ditch segments formed the northern part of the structure. The ditch fills all contained frequent and large stones and occasional charcoal flecks and their bases were lined with smaller stones. Prehistoric pottery sherds were recovered from the fill of segment [7502].
Outer postring:	n=4
Inner ditch:	N/A
Inner postring:	N/A
Entrance:	Unknown
	The structure was too heavily truncated to be able to determine the precise location of the entrance.
Additional features:	N/A
Artefacts:	The associated pottery remains included sherds from one Early Neolithic carinated bowl and two Middle Bronze Age vessels as well as three sherds and fragments.
Radiocarbon dates:	N/A
Notes:	N/A

Structure:	**76**
Illustration:	2.76
Shape:	Circular
Measurements:	12m diameter
Location:	South of site, adjoined to S70, truncated by S69.
Outer ditch segments:	n=1
	Outer ditch segment [8196] contained one fill with moderate amounts of charcoal, small patches of burnt clay, pieces of decayed stone, and flint fragments. This segment had been cut through by the ditch segment of S69, [8204]. It extended 4.6m into the internal area of S69. Therefore, S76 was conclusively shown to have pre-dated S69.

7502

Field drain

Outer postring
Paths and cobbling

0   2
▬▬▬▭▬ M

Illustration 2.75: Structure 75

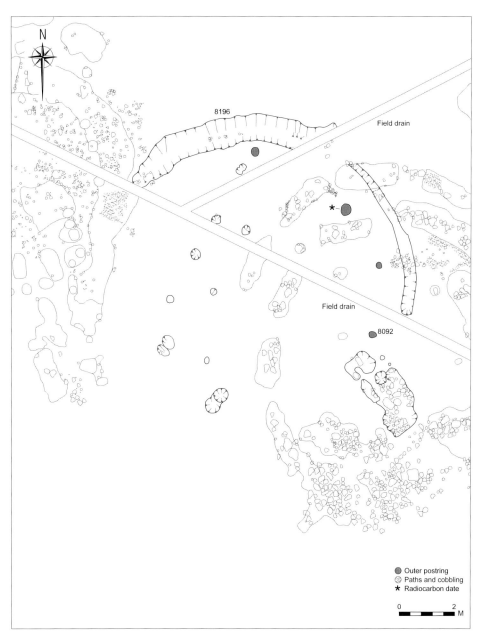

Illustration 2.76: Structure 76

Outer postring:	n=3–4
	Some of these were in the interior of S69, most notably centrally placed [8092], but given their positioning they are more likely to relate to S76. A sample from the fill of [8096] yielded a radiocarbon date of 1433–1312 BC (UB-6251).
Inner ditch:	N/A
Inner postring:	N/A
Entrance:	SE
	A layer of large flat stones covered its base and subsequent to the abandonment of S76, this feature would have been centrally located within S69.
Additional features:	N/A
Artefacts:	N/A
Radiocarbon dates:	Outer postring posthole: 1433–1312 BC (UB-6251).
Notes:	The western portion of the outer ditch marginally overlapped the eastern side of the outer ditch of S70, but not so much that both buildings could not have stood at the same time. It is possible that S76 formed an annex to S70, although they need not been contemporary. The east–southeast section of S76 appeared to have been truncated by S69.

2.4 The road (F100) and large path (F101)

A substantial cobbled roadway extended through the northeast part of the settlement complex, and survived for over 95m and was typically 10m wide. The Bronze Age houses were arranged on either side of it. The road was also associated with a network of smaller, lightly cobbled paths linking some of the adjacent houses to it. The road was slightly bevelled in profile with its upper surface composed of larger stones, rounded and sub-rounded in form. Two narrow trenches were excavated across the road surface to the west of S4. These trenches showed that the road comprised a mixture of stone with a little soil that was up to 0.1m thick. Artefact material was found in direct association with the road surface, particularly towards its northern end where Bronze Age pottery was recovered. A stone mould (see Chapter 3) was recovered from the cobbles near S4 and S52. A larger area of the road surface was subsequently removed immediately to the west of S4, where differential drainage suggested that a number of features were present beneath the surface. Below the road a mixture of pits, postholes and stakeholes survived, but no additional structures were identified.

There were many small cobble paths that ran across the site, mostly from the entrances to the road surface; however, there was one of these which was much larger than the others. This ran between S38 and S37 and was a large, sunken feature covered in fine cobble that measured 37m in length from the north to the south. It was much wider at the northern section, where it was up to 16m in width, and it narrowed rapidly southwards to a typical width of 4m. The relationship between the path and the adjoining buildings is complicated. S38 and S47 were clearly contemporary with this surface as their entrances connected directly to it, and indeed the perimeter of S38 defined the shape of the path in this area. S53 and S54 are located to the east of the path and certainly it appears that either they respect the path or that the path respects them. At the south the path runs through the areas occupied by S35 and S37 and in this case the path cannot have been in use at the same time as the buildings. At the northwest, the path extends through the narrow gap between S38 and S53 and reaches out into a large linear area that is devoid of structures and features.

This linear area has been interpreted as representing the location of a second large roadway, similar in scale to F100, but which was either never surfaced with stone, or represents an area where the stone has subsequently been removed through later activity, possibly ploughing. This possible roadway ran past several houses, including S6, S48, S38, and S54 which had cobbled areas associated with their entrances that most likely led out onto this roadway. Five other structures were in similar locations along the edge of this possible roadway, although no connecting cobbles were identified.

This network of paths and roadways was visibly maintained and replaced when necessary by the Corrstown occupants. The survival of such a network is uncommon on domestic sites and the Corrstown examples are therefore of considerable interest and importance (see Chapter 4).

Chapter 3

Material Culture and Environmental Analysis

There was an abundance of lithics and pottery sherds from the excavations: over 509kg of flint were recovered from secure contexts and a further 63kg from non-stratified contexts (in topsoil associated with individual structures) and over 9,000 sherds of prehistoric pottery (approximately 15.4% of these were derived from topsoil) were retrieved. Twelve ground and/or polished stone artefacts forming a particularly interesting assemblage were recovered from the site and consisted of four moulds, a palstave axe, a macehead, a miniature axe, and five large axe fragments. All of these artefacts – the lithics, the pottery and the stone – were made from locally derived material and suggest the presence of a thriving community, but do not provide any evidence of contact with other groups from other locations.

In direct contrast to the large quantities of lithic and pottery artefacts, there was a disappointing paucity of organic remains. Due to the sheer size of the settlement and the number of archaeological contexts, combined with the lack of organic preservation, the scope for palaeoecological and environmental studies was limited. A small amount of seed analysis was undertaken. Cereal remains were infrequent; however, some substantial deposits were identified. Some burnt timber survived, most notably stakes from the perimeter of S9, which was identified as alder. The wood species of other charcoal deposits were not identified due to a paucity of funding (although subsequent research by Lorna O'Donnell revealed the presence of further alder and hazel in the remaining charcoal samples).

This chapter includes the specialist reports obtained for the lithic, pottery and stone assemblage, as well as the results of the palaeoenvironmental analysis.

3.1 Lithics: Maria O'Hare

The large lithic collection derived from Corrstown represents a significant example of the poorly understood Middle Bronze Age Irish lithic industry. This type of material has only a short history of research in Ireland and in general very little is known about the nature, function and role that chipped stone technology played within the everyday life of domestic communities throughout the Bronze Age. The Corrstown assemblage closely conforms to patterns established through recent research into this type of material from Irish Bronze Age domestic contexts (Illustration 3.1) and also conforms to patterns established through comparative studies of similar lithic industries across a wide range of geographically dispersed regions (O'Hare 2005; O'Hare forthcoming). Most of the tools produced by the Corrstown inhabitants appeared to be ad hoc pieces of flint which had been produced in a highly expedient manner but which would have met the needs of a whole range of everyday tasks. The similarity between the Corrstown assemblage, other broadly contemporary Irish assemblages and those from further afield, strongly suggests that the Corrstown-type lithic assemblages are functional and widespread.

The lithic assemblage from the site was too large (approximately 16,500 pieces) for the analysis to be conducted in one single phase, or indeed to be anything other than

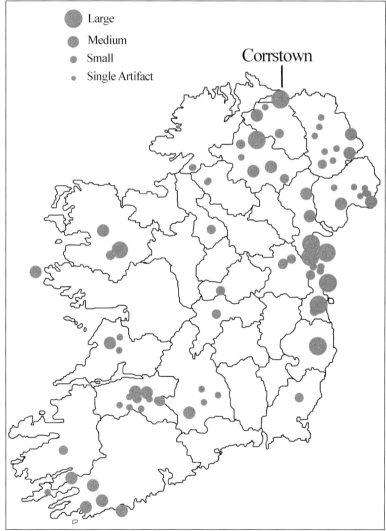

Illustration 3.1: Distribution map of Bronze Age lithic sites in Ireland post 1800 BC (Maria O'Hare)

representative, and therefore an estimated two-thirds of the total assemblage was assessed in two parts (first and second analysis). The assessments were compared statistically using Statistical Program for Social Sciences (SPSS: Version 13) and no significant variability was found between them. It was therefore assumed that the remaining estimated third of the lithic assemblage would also be predictably similar and would therefore not require further detailed investigation.

3.1.1 Raw materials

Flint is by far the predominant raw material identified within the assemblage and accounts for 99.4% of the entire collection. The remaining marginal materials include quartz and a few coarse stone artefacts which are discussed by Eoin Grogan within this chapter. The flint is predominantly fresh and of large cortical nodular type, frequently with large inclusions, although occasionally rolled beach pebbles were employed. As nodular flint is abundant within the vicinity of the Corrstown site, its procurement would have been a relatively simple activity. This mirrors the localized procurement strategy of the Bronze Age period in Ireland (O'Hare 2005; O'Hare forthcoming) and in turn reflects the emerging regionally diverse pattern of the use of highly localized sources of stone in the later prehistoric period (as highlighted by Healy 2004, 184).

3.1.2 Reduction strategy: bipolar-on-anvil technique

The reduction strategy employed in the Corrstown assemblage has its closest parallels with bipolar-on-anvil technique (also referred to as scalar technology, "smash-it-and-see" technology (Healy 2000, 13), and more commonly as split-pebble reduction within Irish literature), although there is evidence to suggest that some limited platform reduction also occurred. There is much confusion surrounding the identification of the bipolar-on-anvil technique, as noted by Shott who points out that 'there are nearly as many definitions of bipolar reduction as there are bipolar objects' (1989, 2). However, in essence the bipolar technique involves resting a nodule or block of flint on a hard stone (an anvil) and hitting it from above with a hammerstone at about 90°, producing 'relatively uncontrolled flake removals' (Knight 1993, 57). These cores and 'flake removals' are often described as chunks, fragments, and unmodified pieces within specialist reports. Illustration 3.2 demonstrates the basic stages of knapping employing bipolar reduction.

The technique appears to emerge as a component within platform-reduced assemblages of the Late Neolithic period in association with Grooved Ware material (author's observations). It has been identified as the sole reduction strategy within the earliest domestic assemblages of the Early Bronze Age and is observed throughout the Irish Bronze Age (O'Hare 2005; O'Hare forthcoming). The Irish Bronze Age bipolar lithic industry finds its closest parallel with the Scandinavian industries of the same period when compared to Knarrström's research (2001, 143, 139). However, when this reduction technique is interpreted in its broadest sense, similarities can be drawn not only from Sweden (*ibid*.) and Britain (Edmonds 1995, 185) but also from Eastern Europe and Jordan (Healy 2000, 13).

   Illustration 3.3 shows three bipolar cores from Irish Bronze Age sites, where their pointed form and opposite flattish platforms indicate that these have been 'anvilled' several times. This selection of bipolar cores highlights the remarkable morphological conformity of bipolar pieces as all three are of different raw materials (nodular flint, riverine flint and chert) and all three are derived from settlements which, combined, span the entire Irish Bronze Age period. Typically, bipolar cores and some thicker scalar flakes have a characteristic 'twist' present. This appears to have been caused by the energy of the simultaneous impact from the downward percussion and the upward impact of the anvil converging in the central part of the piece (Illustration 3.3 shows a slight twist at the pointed end of the bipolar core on the right). Illustration

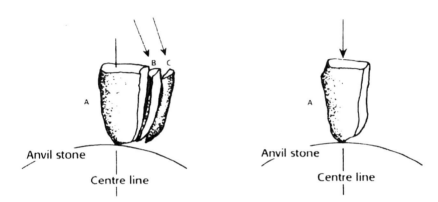

Illustration 3.2: Stages of knapping strategy via bipolar reduction suggested by the cores recovered from a Bronze Age settlement in Sweden (Knarrström 2001, fig. 51). Throughout this volume the term 'scalar flake' has been used to describe the products of this process (B and C in the illustration) and the term 'bipolar core' describes the remaining nodule or chunk of flint (A in the illustration). 'Pseudo-struck' flakes refer to flakes which have platform-struck attributes but which are technically unintentional product of bipolar reduction. Micro-debitage (<10mm) from bipolar reduction is similar to that from platform technology (Maria O'Hare)

Illustration 3.3: Three bipolar cores from Irish Bronze Age settlements dating from the Beaker/Early Bronze Age period (right); Middle Bronze Age (Corrstown left) and the Late Bronze Age (middle) (Maria O'Hare)

3.4 presents two scalar flakes and a thinner (more reduced) bipolar core with edges suitable for use as tools from Corrstown. These are compared with some examples from another bipolar reduced lithic collection relating to a very different region and time period (Illustration 3.5), again highlighting the morphological similarities of this expedient reduction technique.

The fundamental difference between platform and bipolar reduction technique is that the platform core types exhibit evidence of careful planning in terms of a preconceived

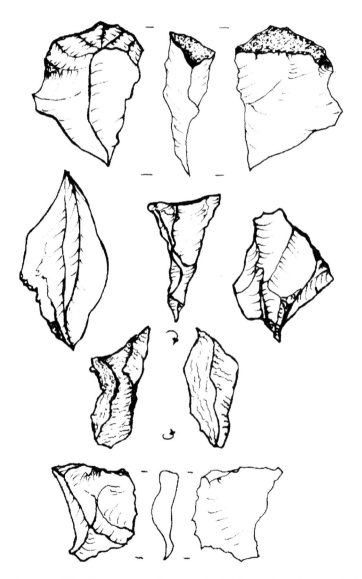

Illustration 3.4: A range of flint bipolar-on-anvil sharp-edged flakes and a thin pointed bipolar core from Corrstown (Maria O'Hare)

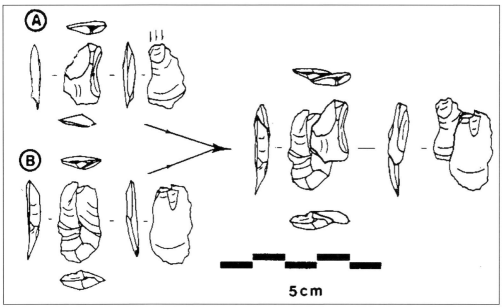

Illustration 3.5: A range of bipolar–on-anvil chert flakes and cores, some refitted, showing 90° impacts from Turtle Rock, Australia (right) (after Knight 1993, fig. 13) (Maria O'Hare)

outcome, in other words the type of tool desired will impact the way in which the core is struck. With the bipolar technique it is evident that after reduction the broken pieces are simply chosen for suitability to the task, as highlighted by Knight (1993, 65). Shott and Sillitoe have investigated the ethnographic evidence of bipolar industries and discovered that the resultant flakes are used only briefly and then discarded, resulting in a short or non-existent curation life – as opposed to that of retouched flakes. They have also ascertained that the resultant flakes are multifunctional, although their research demonstrated that typically each individual piece is restricted for its short usage to one material and one task (Shott and Sillitoe 2005, 653–4).

3.1.3 Primary assemblage: reduction

Of the sampled assemblage, where the technology could be ascertained, primary technology – in the form of bipolar cores, scalar flakes, micro-debitage, and pseudo-struck material (blades and flakes) – along with non-classifiable pieces, such as fragments, accounts for 93.2% (n=10,590 pieces).

Illustration 3.6 presents the proportional percentages of primary components within the assemblage. Over half (55.1%, n=5,881) of the primary assemblage from Corrstown was made up of bipolar cores, followed by a high proportion of scalar flakes (n=3,348) representing almost one-third (31.4%) of the primary technology. There were 289 (2.7%) micro-debitage pieces (<10mm). This high proportion of bipolar cores, scalar flakes and minimal proportion of micro-debitage is characteristic of other Irish Bronze Age assemblages examined by the author.

There were 1,072 (10%) pieces with *platform struck attributes* (pseudo-struck flakes). This is quite a high percentage for platform-type pieces compared to the proportion typically found within other bipolar-reduced assemblages belonging to the Irish Bronze Age. It is therefore possible that at least some of them may have actually been produced intentionally, using platform reduction on the freely available large nodular flint cores. The other category (Illustration 3.6) represents mainly blades and amorphous type cores. For example, there were 22 (0.2%) blades from the entire collection which reflects the low frequency of such technology within other bipolar reduced Irish Bronze Age assemblages. There were 52 amorphous cores, making up 0.5% of the total primary assemblage, and most of these had a single or a few deliberate flake removals, indicating fairly wasteful use of raw material. Although these platform cores represent a more ad hoc approach to knapping, these are fairly rare within other Irish Bronze Age assemblages and perhaps this lends further support to the premise that at least some platform reduction was employed at Corrstown during the Bronze Age period.

Illustration 3.7 demonstrates the dimensional ranges in 10mm intervals for bipolar cores and scalar flakes (conventional recording strategies cannot be employed due to

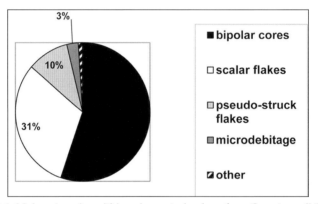

Illustration 3.6: Main categories within primary technology from Corrstown (Maria O'Hare)

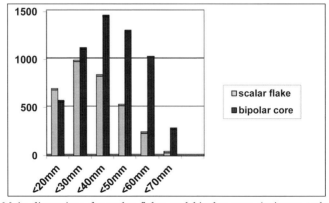

Illustration 3.7: Main dimensions for scalar flakes and bipolar cores (primary technology) within the Corrstown assemblage (Maria O'Hare)

the fact that bipolar pieces cannot be orientated like platform flakes and blades with distal and proximal ends). The scalar flakes basically show a bell-curve distribution with preferred dimensions of <30mm and likewise, bipolar cores show a similar distribution with preferred dimensions of <40mm.

3.1.4 Secondary production: tools

The tools from Corrstown accounted for 5.58% (n=634) of the sampled collection (Illustration 3.8). Tools produced by bipolar-on-anvil are not necessarily characterised by secondary retouching and are here defined as pieces of struck flint which appear as if they could have been employed for one or many different tasks. The non-formal attributes of such tools make it fairly difficult to firstly identify such pieces and secondly to use existing conventional classification systems. The main thrust of tool production and use within the Corrstown tool assemblage is represented by informal and ad hoc tools with utilized tools representing almost 60% (n=371) of the total identifiable classes: a typically high frequency for Bronze Age assemblages (O'Hare 2005; O'Hare forthcoming).

These selected tools appear to be just as valid as pre-determined platform produced tools and although the bipolar produced tools are frequently unmodified they were almost certainly employed for a range of functions such as scraping, sawing, boring, planning, engraving, drilling, shredding, and cutting. Naturally sharp thin edges created via bipolar reduction could be used in their unmodified forms for tasks such as scraping, piercing and cutting.

There were 33 roughly flaked pieces (5.2%) which do not fall into any particular category of tool. Scrapers represent just over one-third of the tool assemblage (35.3%, n=224) and the majority of these appeared to simply exploit the natural edge of the anvilled flake. A selection of different scrapers from the Corrstown collection are illustrated (Illustration 3.9).

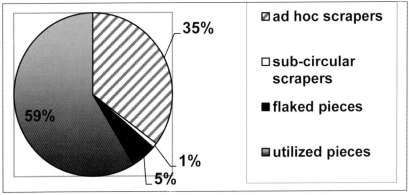

Illustration 3.8: Proportions of secondary technology components (tools) from Corrstown(Maria O'Hare)

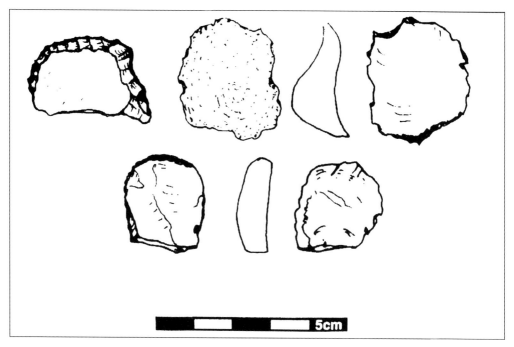

Illustration 3.9: Scrapers from Corrstown (Maria O'Hare)

3.1.5 Contexts for lithics

The majority of the analysed lithic concentrations (containing sufficient lithics to make a meaningful assessment) for which context information was available (n=6,124) was derived from the topsoil (n=2,223).

Table 3.1 shows the similar array of bipolar technology and tool components found throughout different contexts on the Corrstown site (further contexts are shown in Table 3.1). There is no discernable significant difference between the composition of the unstratified lithic concentrations from the topsoil and the stratified concentrations. Approximately 10% of each of the concentrations consisted of tools and of these ad hoc scrapers, bipolar core and scalar flakes dominate. This strongly indicates that although a large proportion of the Corrstown assemblage was unstratified, it is a still a fairly cohesive assemblage. Overall the assemblage reflects a surprisingly consistent and conservative approach to the production and the use of lithic technology within the Corrstown settlement during the later prehistoric period.

Contexts with relatively high concentrations of tools are highlighted in grey in Table 3.1. Several contexts associated with structures showed a fairly dense concentration of tools which may reflect task-specific areas within the Corrstown site. Although some contexts contained very few tools or did not produce any at all, most contained the typical array of primary reduction material in the form of bipolar core and scalar flakes (Table 3.1). The fill of an entrance feature of S45 [158] contained 150 pieces,

Fills derived from main contexts	Pseudo-struck Flakes %	Scalar flakes %	Blades %	Micro-Debitage %	Fragments %	Bipolar cores %	Amorphous Cores %	Utilizedpieces %	Retouched Pieces %	Ad hoc Scrapers %	Sub-circular Scrapers %	Total (N)
Topsoil [101]	3.7	29.0	0.22	2.7	0.31	51.5	0.0	5.3	0.0	4.3	0.0	2223
S45 Entrance feature [158]	4.0	31.3	0.0	2.0	0.0	41.3	0.0	18.0	0.0	3.3	0.0	150
S1Outer postring posthole [197]	9.7	40.0	0.5	0.0	0.0	42.5	0.0	3.7	0.0	2.7	0.0	216
S4 Outer ditch [235]	8.7	20.4	0.0	3.8	0.0	45.0	2.0	13.6	6.3	0.0	0.0	206
S5 Outer ditch segment[247]	8.0	28.0	1.3	0.6	0.0	69.0	0.7	13.0	4.3	3.3	0.0	303
S5 Inner ditch segment [249]	12.0	26.0	0.0	0.0	0.0	50.0	1.3	2.0	0.7	5.4	0.0	149
S6 Outer ditch segment [254]	12.0	29.0	0.0	0,0	0.0	56.0	0.7	2.0	0.0	0.0	0.0	148
S37 Posthole [2224]	10.5	29.1	0.4	0.0	0.15	53.0	0.0	3.1	0.4	3.0	0.3	686
S37 Entrance feature [2692]	43.0	0.0	0.0	0.0	0.0	57.0	0.0	0.0	0.0	0.0	0.0	91
S14 Posthole [2708]	15.0	17.0	1.2	0.0	0.0	67.0	0.0	0.0	0.0	0.0	0.0	84
S38 External cobbled area [2769]	21.0	28.6	0.08	0.0	0.0	45.0	0.4	3.4	0.0	1.2	0.0	497
S47 Outer ditch segment [3416]	0.3	37.0	0.0	25.1	2.5	33.0	0.0	2.0	0.0	0.0	0.0	354
S12 Outer ditch segment [3906]	0.0	54.1	0.0	25.0	0.0	0.0	0.0	10.4	0.0	8.3	2.0	48
S12 Entrance posthole [3910]	0.0	46.0	0.0	0.0	0.0	49.0	0.0	0.0	0.0	0.0	5.4	37
S52 Outer ditch segment [3914]	10.8	26.0	0.0	12.1	0.0	50.4	0.0	0.0	0/0	0.0	0.8	240
S8 Outer ditch segment [3990]	17.0	30.0	0.0.	0.0.	0.0.	53.0	0.0.	0.0.	0.0.	0.0.	0.0.	153
S2 Inner postsring posthole [4316]	18.0	46.0	0.0	4.0	0.0	28.4	2.0	2.0	0.0	0.0	0.0	102
S54 Outer ditch segment [4396A/B]	15.3	36.0	0.0	0.0	0.0	49.0	0.0	0.0	0.0	0.0	0.0	131
S54 Outer ditch segment [4226]	1.7	26.0	0.0	5.2	0.0	52.1	0.0	11.3	0.0	3.5	0.0	115
S29 Pit [5783]	25.5	25.0	0.0	0.0	0.0	49.0	0.7	0.0	0.0	0.0	0.0	137
S64 Pit [6506]	33.3	20.0	0.0	0.0	0.0	43.0	0.0	0.0	0.0	3.7	0.0	54

Table 3.1: Tabulation of the main lithic components within context (including [101] topsoil), from Corrstown – grey highlights the tool-rich contexts

of which over 21% were tools. Contexts from S54 (outer ditch [4226]), S5 (outer ditch [247] and inner ditch segment [249]), S4 (deposit [235]), and S1 (outer postring posthole [197]) (Table 3.1) also contained a relatively high frequency of tool types in their fills. S12, in particular, had discernable atypical tool densities associated with it. An outer ditch segment [3906] from S12 contained a significant number of tools including utilized pieces, ad hoc scrapers and a few sub-circular-type scrapers which were not identified with any frequency in the Corrstown assemblage (six in total were recovered) (Table 3.1). The assemblage from this particular context was also of interest as micro-debitage accounted for over a quarter of it, and over half of it consisted of scalar flakes. Pseudo-struck pieces and bipolar cores were also noteworthy by their absence. Another context of interest, an entrance posthole [3910], associated with S12 did have a significant representation of bipolar cores in its fill, along with scalar flakes, as well as sub-circular scrapers.

An assessment of a horizontal distribution of the lithic material indicated two main densities within Corrstown. One of these was in the southwest of the site, in the fill of an outer ditch segment [4710] associated with S12. This context contained a high density of tools and may represent a particular concentration of task-specific lithic material zoned within and around this structure. This, combined with the tool-rich collections relating to other structures, strongly suggests that some of these areas may have been production zones. The nature of the Corrstown tool assemblage is such that determining precisely what was produced in these possible working areas / production zones is not possible, but it is likely that hide or leather-working as well as food preparation would have occurred in these areas. Without use-wear analysis, it is not possible to make conclusive statements about what precise functions the Corrstown tools performed; however, it is likely that the lithic assemblage fulfilled the needs of a whole range of cutting, scraping, sawing and piercing tasks which would have formed part of the everyday life in and around Corrstown.

3.1.6 Conclusions

The 11,000 piece sampled assemblage represents an estimated two thirds of the total lithic assemblage from Corrstown. The analysis of the sample assemblage reveals very similar results to other Irish Bronze Age domestic assemblages and in turn these patterns reflect other broadly contemporaneous domestic collections from many different countries, from Jordan to Poland (Healy 2000, 13; 2004, 184). Similarities can also be seen in terms of the use of highly localized lithic material and the use of bipolar reduction, a strategy which is beginning to emerge as an archaeological chronological marker for the later prehistoric period within a wide range of other countries as previously indicated by Healy (2000, 13; 2004, 184). The results from the Corrstown analysis, combined with the author's analysis of other Irish Bronze Age sites, indicate that bipolar cores and scalar flakes are surprisingly conservative both in their morphology and metrical attributes. This suggests that the bipolar reduction strategy is perhaps more structured than previously believed. This in turn has aided the identification, recording, classification and interpretation of such material.

Another aspect of these expediently reduced assemblages is that the primary assemblages are dominated by bipolar cores and scalar flakes, and that micro-debitage, if present, is typically a marginal component, although it should be noted that this absence may relate to the recovery and sampling strategies. Blade technology is also typically sparse. Where platform technology is identifiable, it is typically not found with any notable frequency and most likely an unintentional by-product of bipolar reduction. Overall, it seems apparent that bipolar represented the predominant reduction strategy not only at Corrstown, but throughout the Irish Bronze Age (author's personal observation).

In terms of the tools produced by this reduction strategy, utilized pieces and scrapers (both formal and ad hoc types) dominate the domestic assemblages, with lesser quantities of flaked and more formal tools occasionally apparent. There is little chronological variation among the nature of the assemblages or in the proportion of the assemblage that these tools represent. The expedient nature of these tools does not appear to have impacted upon their utility; the utilized pieces produced via the bipolar reduction strategy were selected and employed without further modification. This was due to their suitable pointed, sharp and scraping edges which could have functioned as a variety of tools for a range of tasks, as evidenced by ethnographic research (e.g. Shott and Sillitoe 2005, 654) and use-wear analysis (e.g. Knarrström 2001). Bipolar-produced tools show remarkably consistent morphological and metrical attributes.

3.2 Pottery: Helen Roche and Eoin Grogan

The Corrstown assemblage consists of a small quantity of Early Neolithic pottery and the largest collection of Middle Bronze Age pottery found in Ireland to date. The extensive range of contexted Middle Bronze Age pottery associated with such a large settlement site creates an important opportunity to review the development, use and domestic disposal patterns of pottery during this period. In view of the dating programme at Corrstown it is also opportune to review the emergence of these plain, coarse vessels towards the end of the second millennium BC. A small assemblage of souterrain ware was found within the souterrain but not analysed (details on the early medieval features of the site are located in Appendix II).

A prehistoric assemblage of over 9,000 sherds representing a minimum of 492 vessels was found during the excavation. These consisted of nine Early Neolithic bowls and 483 Middle Bronze Age vessels and the above-mentioned small assemblage of souterrain ware. The extensive Middle Bronze Age assemblage is a critical resource in developing a clear understanding of the development and use patterns of material in a domestic context in this region and the suite of radiocarbon dates offers an opportunity, in conjunction with a number of other recent excavations, to produce a more extensive and integrated chronology for this material.

In general the pottery was well preserved and although a large number of sherds had evidence for weathering, generally shown by an erosion of the outer surface and the exposure of inclusions on the surface, this was largely minor weathering.

3.2.1 Early Neolithic bowls

A small group of 15 Early Neolithic sherds dating to *c.* 3900–3500 BC, representing eight carinated bowls and a single 'cup' was identified from features associated with Structures 4, 6, 12, 22, 29, 33, 51, 53, and 75 (Table 3.2). The carinated bowls (Vessels 34, 128, 185, 216, 234, 324, 337, and 456) with simple rounded out-turned rims and gently curving necks represent the earliest form of Neolithic pottery (Case 1961: 'Dunmurry-Ballymarlagh styles'; Sheridan 1995: 'classic' carinated bowls). This vessel type consists of a hemispherical bowl above which there is a distinct shoulder or carination and a generally curved neck and a simple, often slightly out-turned, rounded rim. Vessels of this type in Ireland usually have deep bowls with a neck to bowl height ratio of *c.* 1:2 although the ratio ranges from 1:1 to 1:4. They also have neutral or open profiles, i.e. where the neck diameter is equal to or less than that of the rim. Simple un-carinated 'cups' similar to Vessel 96 have been found sporadically throughout the country in association with carinated bowls.

The fabric varies in quality but is mainly thin-walled, hard and compact and sometimes brittle. The fabric is dark orange-brown to black in colour and ranges in thickness between 4.5mm and 10.0mm. Many sherds show evidence for weathering with inclusions occasionally protruding; however, smooth surfaces are present and evidence for burnishing is present on Vessels 128 and 216. The inclusions are mainly finely crushed quartzite generally less than 2.5mm long. Carbonised matter is present on the exterior surfaces of Vessel 96 and 216, the interior surface of Vessel 337 and both surfaces of Vessels 234, 324 and 456.

Similarly rimmed vessels with simple shoulders are found in ever-increasing numbers, mainly associated with rectangular houses throughout the country (Grogan 2004a, 103–114). Comparable bowls feature at Ballygalley, Ballymarlagh and Ballyutoag, Co. Antrim (Simpson 1996; Davies 1949; Herring 1937). This style is also present at Knowth, Co. Meath (Eogan and Roche 1997), Ballyglass, Co. Mayo (Roche forthcoming

STRUCTURE	VESSEL	RIM	SHOULDER	BODYSHERD	FRAGMENT
4	34		1		
6	96	2			
12	128	1		1	
22	185			1	
29	216			3	
33	234	1			
51	324				3
53	337	1			
75	456			1	
Total		5	1	6	3

Table 3.2: Location and total number of Early Neolithic sherds

a), Kerloge, Co. Wexford (Roche 2004), and at Lough Gur Circles J, K, L and Site 10 (Grogan and Eogan 1987, figs 15, 20, 27, 40–41, 67), and Site C (Ó Ríordáin 1954, fig. 11) in Co. Limerick.

The single 'cup' is an intermittent part of the repertoire of Early Neolithic assemblages with especially well-known examples coming from Lough Gur (Ó Ríordáin 1954, fig. 15; Grogan and Eogan 1987, fig. 32:2514–2518). The 'cups' are generally small and casually executed with a generally shallow profile. They tend to have simple rounded or pointed upright rims but are occasionally slightly in-turned. While some fine 'cups', similar to those from Corrstown, occur especially in the northeast, those from Lough Gur tend to be squat with relatively thick lower bodies. The fabric often has a sandy texture and tends to be thoroughly fired, due principally to the small size of the vessels. Rather than being coil-built these small 'cups' were simply kneaded into shape. The vessels are generally smaller than the carinated bowls and range in size from *c.* 5–9cm in maximum external diameter.

3.2.1.1 Discussion

The Corrstown Early Neolithic vessels have a wide variety of parallels on other Neolithic domestic sites, including those with characteristic Early Neolithic rectangular houses, and in funerary contexts in court tombs. The dispersed contextual nature of the sherds throughout the site suggests small-scale residual domestic activity that was disturbed during the main Middle Bronze Age phase of occupation. Early Neolithic houses were not identified but it is possible that later activity completely removed or masked such occupation, or that occupation was such that it would only be represented archaeologically by a scatter of pits, of which there are many undated examples across the site. Despite the lack of definite evidence for a house it is obvious that the carbonised pottery, in conjunction with the stone axe fragments (see below), represents residual domestic activity. Closely comparable material has come from house sites at Ballygalley, Ballyharry and Broughshane, Co. Antrim, Ballynagilly, Co. Tyrone (Simpson 1996, 123–32; Moore 2004, 144; ApSimon 1976, 15–38), Enagh and Thornhill, Co. Londonderry (McSparron 2003, 172–5; Logue 2003, 149–55), Inch, Co. Down, and Monanny, Co. Monaghan (Walsh 2005; Grogan and Roche 2006a). Examples further afield include Coolfore and Richardstown, Co. Louth (Ó Drisceoil 2003, 176–81; Byrnes 1999, 33), Tankardstown South (Gowen 1988; Gowen and Tarbett 1988), the earliest Neolithic phase at Knowth (Eogan and Roche 1997, 24–50), Corbally, Co. Kildare (Purcell 2002, 31–76), and Newtown, Co. Meath (Halpin 1995, 45–54), as well as Lough Gur Circles J, K, L, Site 10 and Site C (Grogan and Eogan 1987; Ó Ríordáin 1954).

Small 'cups' were initially recognised by Ó Ríordáin (1953, fig. 9.3; 1954, 327, 328–30, fig. 13) at Lough Gur and were subsequently described from other sites on the Knockadoon peninsula (Grogan and Eogan 1987). Un-carinated bowls have been found at a number of sites in the northern part of the country, for example, Ballyharry, Co. Antrim (Moore 2004, 144), Ballyutoag and Lyles Hill, Co. Antrim, and Ballymarlagh, Co. Armagh (see Sheridan 1995, fig. 2.4.3; Case 1961, figs 4.8, 4.10, 8.5), forming an intermittent part of the repertoire of Early Neolithic assemblages.

3.2.2 Middle Bronze Age assemblage

The bulk of the pottery assemblage is Middle Bronze Age in date and is currently the largest assemblage of this type of pottery found in Ireland (Illustration 3.10). Sherds were uncovered from the majority of houses although the quantity from each differed dramatically, ranging from as little as six sherds associated with S20 to 711 sherds associated with S4 (see Table 3.3). Although predominately undecorated (386 vessels), the form of the rims and the presence of cordons and other decorative motifs on 97 vessels (Tables 3.4–3.5) suggest that these vessels share their origin in the cordoned funerary urn tradition. However, the construction, the decorative treatment and of course the context of the Corrstown material in direct association with houses demonstrate that the pottery is domestic rather than funerary in function. The prolonged use of these vessels in a domestic context is demonstrated by the presence of carbonised residue on the majority of the vessels. Residue was present on the exterior surface of 140 vessels, on the interior surface of 75 vessels and on both surfaces of 190 vessels (Table 3.6). While generally similar in shape, decoration and the presence of cordons, the Corrstown vessels are thinner-walled and lack the typical broad cord decorative motifs found on the funerary variant. Cordoned urns are widely represented in burial contexts and constitute one of the latest special funerary wares in the Bronze Age (Grogan 2004b; Kavanagh 1976; Waddell 1995). A general date range of *c*. 1730–1500 BC is indicated for this type of pottery (Brindley 2007, 328), although the domestic variety had a longer currency and seems to have continued in use to *c*. 1200 BC (Grogan 2004b), a suggestion that is now reinforced by the suite of dates acquired from the Corrstown

Illustration 3.10: Coarseware from S13

STRUCTURES	NO. OF SHERDS	NO. OF VESSELS	STRUCTURES	NO. OF SHERDS	NO. OF VESSELS
Topsoil	1109				
Pit	54		S36	1	
S1	294	16	S37	196	20
S2	90	9	S38	226	29
S3	195	8	Souterrain	270	
S4	711	38	S40	29	3
S5	268	24	S41	42	6
S6	291	17	S42	66	5
S7	79	3	S43	25	2
S8	193	7	S45	26	3
S9	53	3	S46	15	3
S10	3	1	S47	18	2
S11	8	1	S48	35	4
S12	198	11	S50	1	1
S13	692	2	S51	37	6
S14	26	4	S52	56	7
S15	173	2	S53	94	7
			S54	264	19
S16	95	7	S55	86	9
S17	83	8	S56	119	13
S19	166	20	S57	33	2
S20	6	1	S58	265	19
S21	55	2	S59	161	14
S22	24	2			
S23	38	2	S60	15	4
S24	5	1			
S26	102	4	S62	4	3
S27	31	6	S64	5	4
S28	140	16	S65	29	4
			S69	114	8
			S70	146	6
S29	28	4	S71	27	2
			S72	51	1
S30	8	1	S73	20	3
			Early medieval structure	2	1
S31	21	6	S75	12	3
S33	83	9			
S34	1	1			
S35	26	4			

Table 3.3: Total number of sherds and vessels from structures

excavation as well as dates from Ballybrowney, Co. Cork, and Ballydrehid, Co. Tipperary (Cotter 2005; Roche and Grogan 2005a; McQuade 2005; Grogan and Roche 2007a). This assemblage is generally similar in form and fabric to the funerary type but is well made and finished and the decoration, where present, is more haphazardly applied. The rims can be rounded and unexpanded or with a straight or curved inward bevel. The vessels are usually tub or jar shaped and while S-shaped profiles are unusual, an example was identified on a domestic site at Ballinaspig More, Co. Cork (Danaher 2004; Grogan and Roche 2004a); this was dated to 1700–1430 BC. Single or double cordons, either applied or pinched-out, is a common feature as is rilled decoration that consists of rows of shallow horizontal grooves. Decoration tends to be confined to the area below the rim and the belly. Loose lattice patterns, of oblique or vertical and horizontal lines, or oblique lines and heavy twisted cord impressions are common.

Rim Forms	*Structure*	*Vessel Nos Fine Fabric (c. 6.0–10.0mm thick).*	*Vessel Nos Medium Fabric (c. 10.0–14.0mm thick).*	*Vessel Nos Coarse Fabric (c. 14.0–18.6mm thick).*	*Total vessels*
Round rims, many in-turned	1, 2, 3, 4, 5, 6, 7, 9, 10, 12, 13, 14, 15, 17, 19, 23, 26, 27, 28, 29, 31, 33, 37, 38, 41, 42, 43, 47, 48, 51, 52, 53, 54, 56, 58, 59, 64, 65, 69, 71 , enclosure	3, 12, 13, 18, 24, 32, 37, 41, 45, 51, 52, 57, 59, 61, 66, 67, 69, 73, 103, 107, 110, 114, 126, 129, 143, 187, 190, 195, 229, 240, 255, 280, 289, 295, 300, 302, 305, 319, 326, 330, 338, 391, 405, 407, 410, 436, 437, 441, 476, 480, 486, 492	46, 47, 55, 56, 85, 88, 97, 109, 125, 141, 161, 162, 166, 167, 169, 172, 174, 177, 205, 219, 20, 230, 235, 239, 269, 270, 272, 278, 279, 283, 288, 299, 308, 310, 323, 340, 343, 344, 345, 349, 375, 376, 388, 395, 398, 403, 430, 434, 449, 463, 464, 484, 485, 488, 489	19, 23, 158, 274, 277, 354	112
Round out-turned	12, 45	128, 312			2
Round with inward expansion	13, 37, 38, 40, 54, 56, 65, 69	346, 379, 438	262, 281, 431, 487	297	8
Round with outward expansion	54, 69	362, 439			2
Round with ext. & int. expansions	38		276		1
Round with internal lip	1, 8, 29	14	117, 217		3

Rim Forms	Structure	Vessel Nos Fine Fabric (c. 6.0–10.0mm thick).	Vessel Nos Medium Fabric (c. 10.0–14.0mm thick).	Vessel Nos Coarse Fabric (c. 14.0–18.6mm thick).	Total vessels
Flat rims	1, 2, 3, 4, 5, 6, 7, 8, 9, 12, 13, 14, 16, 17, 19, 20, 21, 27, 28, 31, 33, 35, 37, 38, 40, 41, 42, 43, 45, 46, 48, 52, 53, 54, 55, 56, 58, 59, 60, 65, 69, 70, 71, 72, 73, enclosure	2, 5, 9, 16, 21, 22, 28, 39, 40, 44, 48, 53, 64, 70, 74, 82, 86, 90, 91, 101, 113, 116, 123, 135, 142, 173, 199, 201, 202, 204, 215, 222, 236, 238, 251, 252, 254, 258, 298, 301, 304, 316, 322, 339, 353, 356, 366, 380, 387, 389, 393, 397, 399, 409, 415, 419, 422, 423, 433, 447, 465, 468, 470, 471, 473	17, 36, 43, 49, 77, 79, 87, 89, 102, 118, 120, 130, 131, 132, 133, 134, 138, 140, 150, 157, 164, 165, 170, 178, 180, 181, 182, 183, 194, 196, 200, 208, 213, 221, 233, 245, 247, 253, 257, 259, 261, 263, 264, 266, 271, 284, 285, 286, 287, 290, 291, 292, 294, 307, 313, 333, 335, 347, 348, 357, 359, 360, 361, 365, 369, 377, 378, 381, 382, 392, 406, 414, 416, 421, 442, 444, 448, 450, 451, 467, 469, 472, 490	139, 160, 163, 311, 315, 401, 402, 443, 453	156
Flat inward sloping	4, 5, 6, 13, 21, 41, 52, 53, 69	62, 100, 140, 303, 332, 460, 477–79	71, 72, 184, 341, 440, 452	94	17
Flat outward sloping	1, 4, 5, 6, 26, 28, 35, 38, 51, 54	1, 4, 11, 60, 63, 68, 84, 99, 191, 325	81, 214, 244, 273, 282, 352		16
Flat outward sloping with int lip	1	15	8		2
Flat int lip	1, 2, 4, 5, 8, 35, 57	6, 10, 38, 58, 65, 78, 95, 121	20, 35, 246, 386		12
Flat ext lip	3, 5, 6	83, 111	27, 29, 30		5
Flat with inward expansion	5, 12, 13, 14, 15, 16, 17, 19, 23, 26, 27, 28, 29, 37, 38, 42, 52, 54, 56, 59, 70, ringfort	80, 93, 144, 145, 188, 192, 198, 231, 256, 267, 331, 413	137, 147, 148, 152, 156, 168, 171, 175, 176, 179, 203, 206, 207, 218, 260, 275, 309, 334, 355, 412, 445, 461	154, 155, 197, 336, 374, 411	40

RIM FORMS	STRUCTURE	VESSEL NOS FINE FABRIC (c. 6.0–10.0MM THICK).	VESSEL NOS MEDIUM FABRIC (c. 10.0–14.0MM THICK).	VESSEL NOS COARSE FABRIC (c. 14.0–18.6MM THICK).	TOTAL VESSELS
FLAT WITH OUTWARD EXPANSION	38, 54, 69		268, 351, 358, 435		4
FLAT WITH EXT. & INT. EXPANSIONS	8, 37	265	119		2
BEVELLED RIMS	4, 5, 6, 65	50, 92, 108, 432	75		5
VESSEL WITHOUT ASSIGNED RIM	1, 2, 3, 4, 5, 6, 7, 8, 9, 11, 12, 15, 16, 17, 22, 24, 26, 28, 31, 33, 35, 37, 38, 40, 42, 45, 46, 47, 48, 51, 53, 54, 55, 56, 57, 58, 59, 60, 62, 64, 70, 73, 74, 75, enclosure	7, 31, 33, 42, 104, 105, 106, 115, 124, 151, 153, 186, 189, 209, 212, 224, 248, 293, 296, 314, 328, 329, 350, 364, 367, 368, 370, 371, 372, 396, 400, 418, 420	25, 26, 54, 76, 98, 112, 146, 149, 159, 193, 210, 211, 223, 225, 227, 228, 232, 243, 249, 250, 306, 318, 320, 321, 327, 342, 363, 373, 383, 384, 385, 394, 404, 408, 417, 424, 425, 426, 427, 428, 446, 454, 455, 457, 458	122, 127, 136, 226, 237, 241, 242, 317, 390, 429	88
TOTAL		205	238	33	476

Table 3.4: Middle Bronze Age Rim Types

3.2.2.1 Methodology

To accommodate the classification of this large quantity of sherds, descriptions are categorised with regard to (1) fabric consistency, (2) rim type and (3) decorative motifs. Where possible individual vessels were identified and numbered on the basis of this examination using the additional information provided by feature sherds, principally rims and basesherds, as well as, where present, decorative or additional surface treatment. The fabric has been divided into three main types (a) fine fabric (205 vessels), measuring between *c.* 6.0mm and 10.0mm thick (b), medium fabric (238 vessels) measuring between *c.* 10.0mm and 14.0mm thick, and (c) coarse fabric (33 vessels) measuring between *c.* 14.0mm and 18.6mm thick. A certain degree of latitude has been taken concerning these measurements, in that with some examples the measurements sometimes overlap, as a medium-graded fabric may thicken considerably from rim to base, therefore the measurements should be used as a guide rather than a strict parameter. Three main forms of rim are present: round, flat and bevelled but variation occurred (see Table 3.4). No correlation between rim type and fabric type was noted. Regarding the surface treatment of the vessels three main distinctions can be made: (1) decorated vessels; (2) vessels with a shallow horizontal

Incised Decoration	Impressed linear Decoration	Grooved Decoration	Rilled Decoration	Comb Impressed Decoration	Horizontal Indentation below rim	Cordons	Perforations	Burnished
S1: V7	S3: V32, 33	S2: V25	S3: V31	S38: V293	S2: V21	S6: V105	S3:V30	S1: V6, 7
S2: V25	S9: V124	S6: V102	S5: V85		S3: V28	S55: V370	S4: V48	S3: V33
S3: V28		S8: V119	S13: V490		S4: V43, 44, 49, 62, 68		S19: 171, 177	S4: V43, 49, 58, 62
S4: V42, 62		S19: V164, 165	S38: V278, 294		S5: V94		S42: V308	S5: V76, 85
S5: V76		S20: V182			S6: V109		S54: V359	S6: V105,
S6: V98, 104, 106, 112		S21: V183			S8: V117, 121		S57: V386	S8: V121
S7: V115		Enclosure: V228, 229			S12: V134			S17: V154, 157
S8: V122		S38: V283, 287, 289			S13: V467–70, 472			S19: V178
Enclosure: V227		S42: V305			S16: V152			S21: V183
S42: V305		S54: V351			S19: V167			S27: V196, 197
S43: V343					S28: V202, 205, 208			S28: V203, 207
S44: V350					S33: V238, 239			S29: V218
S48: V400					S35: V243, 246			S33: V239
S73: V452					S37: V247, 259, 260, 263			S35: V243
					S38: V269, 273, 275, 277			S37: V248, 255, 259, 262
					S41: V304			S38: V273, 289, 291, 294
					S42: V307			S40: V298

Incised Decoration	Impressed linear Decoration	Grooved Decoration	Rilled Decoration	Comb Impressed Decoration	Horizontal indentation below rim	Cordons	Perforations	Burnished
					S48: V322			S42: V309
					S53: V339			S43: V310
					S54: V344, 348			S45: V313
					S56: V381			S46: V315, 316
					S57: V386			S47: V318
					S58: V393, 395, 397			S52: V331
					S59: V414			S55: V367, 371
					S69: V438, 442			S56: V372
					S70: V443, 445			S59: V407, 414
					S72: V451			S60: V421, 422
					S73: V452, 453			S62: V426
					S75: V457			S65: V434
								S69: V438, 439, 44
								S70: V445, 447, 44
								S71: V450
								S72: V451
18 Vessels	3 Vessels	14 Vessels	5 Vessels	1 Vessel	54 Vessels	2 Vessels	7 Vessels	55 Vessel

Table 3.5: Middle Bronze Age Vessels – Decorative motifs and other surface treatments (S. =Structure; V. =Vessel)

Residue Exterior	Residue Interior	Residue Both Surfaces	Fire Blackening Exterior	Fire Blackening Interior	Fire Blackening Both Surfaces	Weathered
1: V3, 8, 10, 15, 16, 19, 20, 21	S1: V7	S1: V1, 2, 4, 5, 9	S1: V6, 12	S2: V23	S1: V14	S1: V5, 6, 8, 10, 13, 15
S2: V23	S2: V18, 25	S2: V22, 24	S14: V143		S17: V156	S2: V18, 19, 20, 22, 23, 24, 25
S3: V29, 30, 32	S3: V33	S3: V26, 27, 28, 31	S28: V202, 203		S21: V183	S3: V26, 27, 29, 32
4: V36, 39, 43, 47, 8, 50, 55, 56, 57, 58,), 61, 63, 64, 68,), 71	S4: V41, 42, 59	S4: V37, 38, 40, 46, 49, 51, 52, 53, 65, 70	S33: V236		S41: V303	S4: V35, 37, 40, 41, 42, 45, 46, 47, 48, 50, 51, 52, 53, 54, 56, 57, 62, 65, 67
5: V72, 73, 75, 77, 80, 81, 82, 85, 87, 88, 89, 93, 94	S6: V98, 104, 106, 112	S5: V74, 76, 78, 79, 83, 84, 90, 91, 92	S37: V257, 263			S5: V74, 80, 81, 86, 89, 95
56: V99, 101, 102, 109	S9: V124	S6: V97, 100, 103, 107, 108, 110, 111	S41: V299			S6: V97, 101, 103, 104, 105, 107, 111, 112
12: V133, 134, 138	S13: V139, 462, 473, 474, 481, 483, 489	S7: V113, 114, 115				S7: V113, 114
13: V140, 460, 461, 63, 469, 470, 475–77, 479, 482, 487	S14: V143	S8: V116, 117, 118, 119, 120, 121				S8: V121, 122
S14: V142	S16: V151	S9: V123, 125				S9: V124, 125
S16: V 150	S17: V159, 161	S10: V126				S12: V130, 133, 134
S17: V158, 160	S19: V164	S11: V127				S13: V140
19: V165, 167, 168, 71, 172, 174, 175, 177, 178	S22: V186	S12: V129, 130, 131, 132, 135, 137				S14: V141, 142
S27: V195, 196	S24: V189	S14: V144				S15: V145, 146
28: V200, 204, 206, 213	S26: V193	S15: V145, 146				S16: V 150, 153
Enclosure: V228, 229, 230, 231	S28: V202, 203, 209, 212, 215	S16: V152				S17: V154, 156, 158, 161
S33: V235, 239	S29: V219	S17: V154, 155, 157				S19: V163, 164, 167, 170, 174, 175, 176, 177
S35: V245	S31: V220	S19: V162, 169, 170, 173, 179, 180, 181				S21: V184
37: V253, 258, 260, 261	Enclosure: V226, 227, 232	S20: V182				S23: V187, 188
38: V268, 269, 272, 75, 277, 279, 285, 287, 288, 290, 292	S33: V237, 238, 241	S21: V184				S26: V190, 191, 192, 193
41: V300, 302, 304	S35: V243, 244	S23: V187, 188				S27: V194
S42: V308, 309	S37: V248, 249	S26: V190, 191, 192				S28: V200, 202, 205, 209, 214

Residue Exterior	Residue Interior	Residue Both Surfaces	Fire Blackening Exterior	Fire Blackening Interior	Fire Blackening Both Surfaces	Weathered
S43: V311	S38: V267, 270	S27: V194, 197, 198, 199				S29: V217
S45: V312, 313	S40: V298	S28: V201, 205, 207, 208				S31: V223, 224, 225
S46: V315	S48: V320	S29: V217, 218				Enclosure: V226, 23
S47: V318	S51: V327	S31: V221				S33: V235, 237, 238 241
S48: V322	S52: V330	Enclosure: V233				S35: V246
S52: V: 331, 332, 334, 335	S53: V342	S33: V242				S37: V252
S53: V340	S54: V353, 357, 362	S35: V247				S38: V286, 287
S54: V346, 347, 348, 358	S55: V363, 364, 368, 369	S37: V250, 251, 254, 255, 256, 259, 264, 265, 266				S42: V305, 307, 308
S55: V365	S56: V372, 375, 383	S38: V271, 273, 274, 276, 278, 280, 281, 282, 284, 289, 291, 295				S46: V317
S56: V384	S57: V385	S40: V296, 297				S52: V335, 336
S58: V395, 398, 401, 403, 404	S58: V390, 391, 394, 396, 399	S42: V305				S54: V346, 351, 358 361, 362
S59: V409	S59: V410, 417	S43: V310				S55: V363, 364, 366
S64: V428, 429	S60: V420	S45: V314				S56: V372, 373, 374 375, 377, 378, 379, 380, 381, 384
S65: V433	S62: V425	S46: V316, 317				S57: V385
S69: V435, 442	S64: V427	S47: V319				S58: V387, 388, 389 390, 391, 399, 400, 4
S70: V443, 445	S65: V432	S48: V321, 323				S59: V406, 408, 409 410, 411
S73: V453, 454	S70: V444	S51: V325, 328				S60: V423
Early medieval structure: V455	S75: V458	S52: V333				S62: V424, 425
		S53: V338, 339, 343				S64: V427, 428, 429 430
		S54: V344, 345, 349, 350, 351, 352, 354, 355, 356, 359, 360, 361				S65: V431, 433, 434
		S55: V366, 367, 370, 371				S69: V435, 436, 437 438
		S56: V376, 377, 378, 379, 380, 381, 382				S70: V444, 446
		S57: V386				S71: V449, 450

RESIDUE EXTERIOR	RESIDUE INTERIOR	RESIDUE BOTH SURFACES	FIRE BLACKENING EXTERIOR	FIRE BLACKENING INTERIOR	FIRE BLACKENING BOTH SURFACES	WEATHERED
		S58: V 387, 388, 389, 392, 397, 400, 402, 405				S72: V451
		S59: V406, 407, 408, 412, 413, 414, 415, 416, 418, 419				S73: V453, 454
		S60: V422, 423				Early medieval structure: V455
		S62: V 524, 426				S75: V457
		S64: V430				
		S65: V431, 434				
		S69: V436, 437, 438, 439, 440, 441				
		S70: V446, 447, 448				
		S71: V449, 450				
		S72: V451				
		S73: V452				
140 Vessels	75 Vessels	190 Vessels	9 Vessels	1 Vessel	4 Vessels	166 Vessels

Table 3.6: Evidence for carbonised residue and weathering on Middle Bronze Age Vessels (S. =Structure; V. =Vessel)

indentation on the exterior surface immediately below the rim; and (3) undecorated vessels (Table 3.5). All of this analysis is presented in Tables 3.4–3.6; however, there were a large number of small indistinct or featureless sherds that could not be assigned to individual vessels.

3.2.2.2 Fabric details and vessel construction
The Corrstown vessels were coil-built, tub-shaped with flat, mainly simple angled bases although occasionally pedestal-footed bases occur (Vessels 151 and 165). The fabric is generally medium- to thick-walled, well-executed but loose textured and gritty, ranging in thickness between a very fine 6.0mm to thick-walled coarse fabric measuring 18.6mm thick (Table 3.7) and with inclusions ranging between 1.1mm and 13.1mm in length. The exterior and interior surfaces are mainly orange/brown/black in colour with grey, black and orange cores. The fabric throughout is of exceptionally high standard, relatively uniform in quality, well fired and with good surface preparation. There was little difference noted between the quality and treatment of the undecorated and decorated vessels or in relation to different rim forms; the main visible difference

was the variation in fabric thickness. Five main fabric types were identified: (1) hard, compact, sometimes slightly chalky textured fabric, represented by 199 vessels; (2) chalky textured with a loose-textured matrix, represented by 159 vessels; (3) thin-walled brittle fabric, represented by 65 vessels; (4) poor quality uneven surfaced fabric, represented by 39 vessels, and (5) thick-walled crumbly fabric, represented by 19 vessels (Table 3.7). Although a degree of weathering was observed on 166 vessels, the fabric was mainly fresh, as were the break edges, suggesting that the bulk of the sherds were not exposed to open weather conditions or prolonged surface disturbance. From the examination of the larger rimsherds, base sherds and bodysherds it was clear that the vessels represent wide-mouthed barrel or sometimes straight-sided flat-based vessels in a range of sizes extending from unusually small bowls, with a few measuring as little as 9cm in diameter at the mouth, to examples of larger vessels measuring up to 26.5cm in diameter. The majority of the vessels, however, measure from 16cm up to 20cm in diameter at the mouth (see Table 3.8 for range of rim and base diameters).

With the exception of three possible slab-built pots (Vessels 449, 450 and 452), the vessels were coil-built as is evident from horizontal coil breaks present on sherds from Vessels 33, 110, 138, 180, 187, and 277. Overlaps are not well defined, even on the larger sherds: this is probably a result of 'puddening' the clay during production, a process involving the patting or beating of the clay to ensure consistency as well as to achieve smooth, even surfaces. The added crushed inclusions are well sorted with a broad range of lithics included: crushed flint was visible in Vessels 17, 35 and 57. Evidence for burnishing (Table 3.5) is evident on sherds from 55 vessels, but generally the exterior surfaces of the sherds have been smoothed, probably just with the hand using a type of slurry wash. Occasionally, as with Vessels 247, 333, 414 and 438, striations are visible on the exterior surface as if fibrous or textured matter had been rubbed across the pots.

Single perforations occurred on the upper portion of six vessels (Nos 30, 48, 171, 177, 308, and 386) and appeared to have been fashioned after firing and possibly after they had been used for some time as the perforations were drilled through carbonised residue. A partly bored perforation was present on the exterior surface of Vessel 359 (Table 3.5).

The assemblage from S4 was distinctive in being fired to a bright orange colour and was generally thin walled with brittle fabric, rather than having a broader range of fabric types. However, carbonised residue on many of the interior surfaces of the vessels demonstrates that, as with the assemblages from the other structures, they were used for cooking purposes. In contrast to other material from Corrstown the sherds from S26 (unlikely to have been a complete dwelling) showed evidence for a greater degree of weathering, which probably indicates that these sherds were exposed to the elements for a greater length of time. Sherds from S41 were noticeably different in being thin walled with a distinctive orange-buff exterior surface and a grey core, which indicates a difference in firing and a possible difference in function. However, broadly speaking, the assemblages from the different houses were quite uniform with few obvious distinctions in form and function emerging and those that were identified were largely superficial.

3.2.2.3 Decorative motifs and surface treatment
Although largely fragmented, 97 vessels were decorated in a variety of forms and motifs (see Table 3.5). Eighteen vessels showed evidence for incised decoration but in no case

THIN-WALLED BRITTLE FABRIC	CHALKY FABRIC LOOSE TEXTURED MATRIX	HARD COMPACT FABRIC	THICK-WALLED CRUMBLY FABRIC	POOR QUALITY UNEVEN FABRIC
S1: V1, 6, 7	S1: V2, 3, 10, 14, 16	S1: V4, 5, 8, 9, 11–13, 15	S2: V19	S4: V47, 50, 65
S2: V17, 18	S2: V20, 23–25	S2: V21, 22	S3: V27, 29, 30	S5: V93
3: V28, 32, 33	S3: V26	S3: V31	S4: V35, 45, 56	S6: V101
4: V41, 43, 49, , 53, 62, 67, 70	S4: V36, 42, 46, 52, 54, 69, 71	S4: V37–40, 44, 48, 55, 57–61, 63, 64, 66, 68	S5: V85	S16: V149
5: V74, 91, 95	S5: V76, 92, 94	S5: V72, 73, 75, 77–84, 86–90	S6: V106, 112	S17: V161
6: V100, 103, 105	S6: V107, 109, 110	S6: V97–99, 102, 104, 108, 111	S8: V122	S19: V173, 177
S7: V113	S12: V131, 138	S7: V114, 115	S12: V134, 136	S26: V190, 192, 193
S8: V121	S13: V459, 461, 466, 173–79, 481–85, 489, 490	S8: V116–120	S13: V140	S28: V210
S9: V125	S14: V141	S9: V123, 124	S17: V160	Enclosure: V226
S12: V135	S15: V146, 490–92	S10: V126, 127	S48: V320	S35: V246
3: V465, 468, 486	S16: V147, 150	S12: V129, 130, 132, 133, 137	S55: V363	S37: V252
4: V142, 143, 144	S16: V147, 150	S13: V139, 140, 462, 463, 467, 469–72, 480, 487	S56: V378	S37: V252
9: V165, 171, 175	S17: V154, 156, 158, 159	S15: V145	S70: V443	S37: V256
S23: V187	S19: V 162–164, 166–170, 172, 174, 176, 178, 179, 181	S16: V 148, 151–153		S38: V295
S27: V199	S21: V183, 184	S17: V155, 157		S40: V298
28: V202, 212	S23: V188	S19: V180		S42: V305
S31: V224	S24: V189	S20: V182		S42: V307
closure: V229	S26: V191	S22: V186		S47: V319
S33: V236	S27: V194, 197, 198	S27: V195, 196		S48: V322
37: V255, 265	S28: V 200–205, 207, 208	S28: V206, 209, 211, 213–215		S52: V336
38: V280, 289	S29: V217, 218	S29: V219		S53: V339–341
S41: V301	S31: V221, 223, 225	S31: V220, 222		S54: V358, 362
S43: V310	S33: V237–239	Enclosure: V227, 228, 230–233		S56: V379, 381, 383
S45: V314	S35: V243–245	S33: V235, 240–242		S58: V387, 403
51: V325, 328, 329	S37: V247–250, 253, 259, 260, 262, 263, 266	S37: V251, 254, 257, 258, 261, 264		S59: V406, 410

THIN-WALLED BRITTLE FABRIC	CHALKY FABRIC LOOSE TEXTURED MATRIX	HARD COMPACT FABRIC	THICK-WALLED CRUMBLY FABRIC	POOR QUALITY UNEVEN FABRIC
S54: V344, 350	S38: V268, 269, 271–276, 278, 279, 284, 285, 287, 292, 294	S38: V267, 270, 277, 281–283, 286, 288, 290, 291, 293		S64: V429, 430
S55: V366, 367	S40: V297	S 40: V296		S69: V437
S56: V380	S41: V300	S41: V299, 302, 303		
S58: V393, 397, 400, 405	S42: V306	S42: V308, 309		
S59: V409, 415	S43: V311	S45: V312		
S69: V439	S45: V313	S46: V315–317		
S71: V449	S47: V318	S48: V321		
	S48: V323	S51: V326, 327		
	S52: V335	S52: V330–334		
	S54: V345, 347, 349, 351–353, 355	S53: V338, 342, 343		
	S55 V365, 368, 370	S54: V346, 348, 354, 356, 357, 359, 360, 361		
	S56: V372, 384	S55: V364, 369, 371		
	S57: V385, 386	S56: V373–377, 382		
	S58: V398, 402	S58: V388–392, 394–396, 399, 401, 404		
	S59: V407, 408, 411–414, 416, 418, 419	S59: V417		
	S62: V425	S60: V420–423		
	S64: V428	S62: V424, 426		
	S65: V431	S64: V427		
	S69: V438	S65: V432–434		
	S70: V445, 448	S69: V435, 436, 440–442		
	S73: V453	S70: V444, 446, 447		
	S75: V457	S71: V450		
		S72: V451		
		S73: V452, 454		
		Early medieval structure: V455		
		S75: V458		
65 Vessels	159 Vessels	199 Vessels	19 Vessels	39 Vessels

Table 3.7: Middle Bronze Age fabric types (S. =Structure; V. =Vessel)

STRUCTURE	VESSEL	RIM DIAMETER	BASE DIAMETER
1	15	21cm	
2	17	16cm	
3	26	-	12.6cm
4	36	18cm	
4	37	14cm	
4	50	16cm	
4	52	21cm	
4	60	14cm	
6	100	–	8.2cm
7	113	15cm	13cm
12	137	–	11.3cm
17	159	–	8.5cm
21	184	15cm	9.4cm
22	186	–	8.3cm
27	195	18.5cm	
28	205	–	16.8cm
37	247	23cm	
37	253	20.5cm	
38	276	21cm	
38	277	20cm	
38	280	11cm	
38	294	22.4cm	
41	303	9cm	
54	347	18cm	
54	352	16cm	
57	386	21cm	
58	394	15.5	
58	395	21cm	
58	398	17cm	
59	414	23cm	
65	431	26.5cm	
71	449	22cm	
71	450	21cm	
72	451	19.5cm	
73	452	10.7cm	
73	453	22cm	

Table 3.8: Rim and base diameters from Middle Bronze Age Vessels

was it possible to reconstruct the overall decorative motif. The most complete were portions of carelessly executed chevrons and triangles present on Vessels 350, 400 and 452, but most just consisted of portions of horizontal, oblique, curved, and overlapping incised lines. Impressed linear motifs were present on Vessels 32, 33 and 124. Portions of both shallow and oblique horizontal and oblique grooves were present on sherds representing 13 vessels. In two examples both incised and grooved decoration was present (Vessels 25 and 305), but it was not possible to interpret the complete motif. Only one example of comb-impressed decoration was identified (Vessel 293) where comb-impressed oblique and horizontal lines possibly formed triangles. Only two examples of cordons were identified. Two low cordons were present on the exterior surface of Vessel 105 and a single cordon was present on Vessel 370. The nature of this limited evidence for decorative motifs is reminiscent of funerary cordoned urns from Altanagh, Co. Tyrone (Williams 1986, fig. 30), Killinchy, Co. Down (Mallory and McNeill 1991, figs 3–9), and Claragh, Co. Londonderry (Kavanagh 1976, fig. 27:12). Similar domestic Bronze Age pottery has also been found on settlement sites in Northumberland in northern Britain (Burgess 1995, 145–158). A range of dates has been obtained from these sites, mainly ranging from 1400–1010 BC. At Standrop Rigg, which produced a date of 1390–1130 BC, there are rimsherds decorated with incised horizontal lines and triangles below the rim similar to the Corrstown examples (*ibid.*, fig. 13.4, nos 2–9). Comparable vessels were also found at Bracken Rigg where a reconstructed vessel shows that decoration was limited to the area below the rim (*ibid.*, fig. 13.4, nos 1–2), similar to the decorative arrangement on funerary cordoned urns.

Five vessels (Nos 31, 85, 139, 278, 294 and 490) were ornamented with 'rilled' decoration, a motif consisting of two or more horizontal rows of shallow grooves extending from just below the rim and continuing down the belly of the pot. Similar pottery has been found at Site C, Lough Gur, Co. Limerick, Knowth, Co. Meath, and Rathgall, Co. Wicklow (Ó Ríordáin 1954, fig. 17:1; Eogan 1984, pl. 75, no. 1418; Roche forthcoming b).

A group of 54 vessels has an interesting and rather unusual feature consisting of a single or occasionally two shallow horizontal indentations immediately below the rim. Though not strictly a decorative motif it appears to be ornamental rather than representing a functional element. With the exception of three examples all vessels bearing this feature appear to have no further decorative motifs. However, Vessels 28, 62 and 452 have slight evidence for incised decoration in the form of portions of incised triangle, horizontal and oblique incised lines. The most elaborate example is a large vessel (No. 247) with a rim diameter of about 23cm. Only part of the upper portion survives and the decoration present consists of two shallow horizontal indentations on the exterior surface just below the rim. Below this are vertical raised ribs extending down the belly of the pot. Vertical and oblique striations are present on the exterior surface but they appear to be accidental and are somewhat similar to wipe marks on the interior surface.

The distribution of funerary cordoned urns is mainly concentrated in Ulster, decreasing in numbers through north Leinster with scattered examples extending into the Midlands, in areas of Connaught, south Leinster and south Munster (Waddell 1998, fig. 59). Domestic urns similar to the Corrstown assemblage have been identified from an increasing number of settlement sites and have a dispersed distribution throughout the country. Close parallels are found at Downpatrick, Co. Down (Pollock and Waterman 1964), where vessels of the cordoned urn tradition were associated with a roundhouse. In north Leinster examples have been found in settlement contexts at Moynagh Lough, Baltrasna and Barronstown, Co. Meath, and Kilshane, Co. Dublin (Bradley 2004; Roche and Grogan 2005b; 2005c; Grogan and Roche 2006b). The largest collection of domestic cordoned urns is found in the south western part of the country at Lough Gur, Co. Limerick, including Sites C and D (Ó Ríordáin 1954, 333–40 and 392–4, figs 18.7–9, 19.1–6, 34.26, pl. 34), Circle L and Site 10 (Grogan and Eogan 1987, 405 and 449–51, figs 45.891, 68.893–11). Further southern examples have been found at Ballinaspig More 5, Scartbarry 2 and Ballybrowney Lower 1, all in Co. Cork (Danaher 2004; Grogan and Roche 2004a; Roche and Grogan 2005a).

3.2.2.4 *Undecorated vessels*

As already stated, the bulk of the Middle Bronze Age vessels from Corrstown are undecorated and at first glance, and without the addition of a suite of solid Middle Bronze Age dates, they could be mistaken for Late Bronze Age flat-based, barrel-shaped coarseware. However, under closer examination and especially in comparing the decorated and undecorated examples, certain fabric differences can be noted from what is accepted as typical Late Bronze Age pottery. In examining the decorated and undecorated vessels no obvious difference was noted in the fabric matrix and examples of all five fabric types (discussed above) were identified in both decorated and undecorated vessels. Two fabric details that were particularly significant were the chalky textured surfaces and the loose textured matrix that were consistent within the Middle Bronze Age assemblage from Corrstown. These features are not consistent with Irish Late Bronze Age pottery which generally has a harder gritty matrix. The identification of a large body of plain Middle Bronze Age domestic pottery, together with some other recent discoveries and the re-examination of some older assemblages, has dramatically altered our understanding of ceramic developments in the latter part of the Bronze Age (see below).

It should be noted that S9 and S13 did produce dates which ranged from the Middle Bronze Age into the Late Bronze Age (1260–930 BC and 1028–896 BC), although pottery from these houses was not compatible with Late Bronze Age material, and certainly the Late Bronze Age features in S13 are believed to post-date the occupation of the building. However, it is probable that the undecorated vessels represent the immediate precursors to developed Late Bronze Age pottery and they are an important addition in the study of the Middle Bronze Age/Late Bronze ceramic transition.

3.2.2.5 *General discussion*

Recent excavations have revealed several domestic sites with pottery of Middle Bronze Age that represents a domestic variant of the cordoned urn tradition. This pottery appears to have been for contemporary use with more formally decorated cordoned urns that appear to have been made specifically for funerary use (Kavanagh 1976; Waddell 1995; Grogan 2004b; Cooney and Grogan 1999, 126–29). However, Corrstown represents by far the largest assemblage from Ireland. These vessels feature various combinations of applied cordons and rilling, as well as open lattice or in-filled panels of elongated opposed triangles beneath the rim (see Grogan and Eogan 1987, figs 44, 45, 51, 68; Ó Ríordáin 1954, figs 17–19, 34: 25, 26, pls 34, 35). Decorative application occurs in the form of incision (both fine lines and channels) and cordons. There is a range of rim forms including simple round and flat tops, as well as rims with a straight or slightly curved internal bevel; more sharply curved or stepped bevels also occur (Grogan and Eogan 1987, fig. 68:893, 895, 896). Other assemblages include Ballinaspig More 5 and Ballybrowney, Co. Cork (Danaher 2004; Grogan and Roche 2004a; Cotter 2005; Roche and Grogan 2005a). Reasonably extensive dating indicates a range of *c.* 1750–1450 BC for cordoned urn burials (Brindley 2007) but a slighter longer currency, perhaps down to the beginning of the Late Bronze Age, for the domestic variant.

The most important impact of the Corrstown material is the very considerable proportion of plain coarse, very well-made and fired – by Middle to Late Bronze Age standards – fine fabric. The dating of this material to the latter part of the Middle Bronze Age has re-defined the period of development which up to now had been considered a feature of the Late Bronze Age (see Raftery 1995; Grogan 2005a). Together with the evidence from sites with domestic cordoned urns and plain pottery in Middle Bronze Age contexts this has shifted the origin of plain domestic pottery back to the period *c.* 1500–1400 BC. This has important wider implications but in a purely ceramic context it indicates the need to re-evaluate many other assemblages previously assigned to the end of the Bronze Age through the presence of coarse undecorated vessels.

Domestic pottery of a specific Middle Bronze Age date has not been widely recorded in this region. However, an important early identification of domestic cordoned urns occurred at Downpatrick (Pollock and Waterman 1964). Although no comprehensive study of this material is available it is possible that this tradition forms the background for the emergence of the plain coarse domestic vessels that dominate the Late Bronze Age. At a general level it had appeared that this gradual transformation occurred in the period after 1200 BC towards the end of the Middle Bronze Age. However, generally unpublished dates from a number of mainly funerary sites in east Limerick (Gowen 1988) suggested that plain wares may have developed at an early stage, possibly as early as *c.* 1500 BC (see Grogan 2004b). More recently similar Middle Bronze Age dates have come from cremations in both inverted and upright plain coarse vessels at Priestsnewtown, Co. Wicklow, and Darcytown, Co. Dublin, suggesting the necessity of a thorough review of the chronology of pottery development in this period (Tobin *et al.* 2004; Grogan and Roche 2004b; 2007b).

The date ranges for the occupation of Corrstown provided by the radiocarbon dates, and supported by the non-ceramic artefactual assemblages (this chapter) suggest that the core period of occupation is within the span from *c.* 1500 BC to *c.* 1200 BC. These dates, and those from east Limerick, Ballybrowney, Ballydrehid, Priestsnewtown, and Darcytown, provide a very significant advance in our understanding of the chronological, social and economic contexts for the transition to plain domestic wares.

3.3 Stone artefacts: Eoin Grogan

The geological identifications were made by Stephen Mandal.

This small assemblage, consisting of stone axe fragments, a stone macehead and stone moulds, significantly adds to the understanding of the use and context of ground stone objects in later prehistory. Moulds 1 and 2 can be ascribed to the Middle Bronze Age; however, the remaining moulds were for the casting of small implements that are not readily paralleled and therefore their position within Bronze Age metallurgical chronology is unfortunately currently inconclusive.

3.3.1 Axes

The collection consists of a complete miniature axe (No. 2), five large axe fragments (Nos 1, 3–5) and a small flake (Illustrations 3.11–3.14). The miniature axe was associated with S37 and the five fragments were not stratified and derived from topsoil. The Corrstown

Illustration 3.11: Miniature stone axe (No. 2) (left), axe No. 4 (right) (Jon Sunderland)

Illustration 3.12: Axe No. 3 (left), axe No. 1 (right) (Jon Sunderland)

3cm

2cm

Illustration 3.13: Axe No. 6 (Jon Sunderland)   *Illustration 3.14: Stone axe flake (Jon Sunderland)*

axes, although generally broken and fragmentary, are readily paralleled in shape and production treatment within the overall Irish series (Cooney and Mandal 1998). The axes are well ground and, with the possible exception of No. 5, have generally smooth, highly polished surfaces largely free from the flake scars of primary treatment. While the axes are all broken, the edge breaks and surface flake scars are generally very fresh and the axes show little evidence for edge blunting or surface wear. This suggests that, whatever their origin, these objects saw little functional use at Corrstown.

Although only the miniature axe is complete (Illustration 3.11), conjectural reconstruction indicates that, apart from the miniature axe No. 2, they are small to medium sized, 120–180mm long with length to width ratios of *c.* 2.5–3:1. The axes have generally asymmetric face shapes with one straight side and the other gently curved, with medium symmetrical or asymmetrical profiles and curved or gently curved edge shapes (Cooney and Mandal 1998, 10–24). Despite the fragmentary nature of these artefacts it is clear that they are all recognisably forms that can be widely paralleled on Neolithic sites (Sheridan *et al.* 1992, figs 3–4). The identification of Nos 1–3 and 6 as porcellanite (No. 4 is made from shale and No. 5 from dolerite) tends to further identify the Corrstown axes as of Neolithic origin. Miniature axes, like No. 2 from Corrstown, are also a feature of the Neolithic: a number of axe pendants, miniature axes perforated near the butt for suspension, also occur in both Neolithic and Bronze Age contexts (*ibid.*, 398). Among the latter are examples from Harristown, Co. Waterford, and Site F, Lough Gur, Co. Limerick (Hawkes 1941; Ó Ríordáin 1954, 423, fig. 47.3). Although the specific production period of polished stone axes is not well dated the Lambay axe factory, at least, appears to be entirely Neolithic (Cooney 2003; 2002; 2000) and the dated contexts for porcellanite axes are also principally of this date (Sheridan 1986, table 1). Of course, ground and polished stone implements continued to be produced well into the Bronze Age and these include maceheads, exemplified by the Corrstown example, battle axes and axe hammers (Simpson 1990a; 1990b; 1989; 1988). However, the specific manufacture of stone axes in this period is not supported by any direct evidence and most of the implements found in Bronze Age contexts appear to have been produced in the Neolithic.

Stone axes have come from several sites with Bronze Age occupation activity. The majority of these have derived from insecure contexts on settlements with significant earlier Neolithic activity, such as at Lough Gur, Co. Limerick, and at Dalkey Island, Co. Dublin (Ó Ríordáin 1954; Grogan and Eogan 1987; Liversage 1968). More satisfactorily stratified axes or fragments came from an enclosure (Cleary 2003, 126–29, fig. 16) and the metal production Sites F and Hut 1, Site D, at Lough Gur (Ó Ríordáin 1954, 403–05, 423, figs 39 and 47) (see below). At Knockuregare the settlement, with separate Middle and Late Bronze Age phases, produced Middle Bronze Age pottery and a broken polished stone axe (Taylor 2004; Brindley 2003). A roundhouse at Clonard, Co. Meath, dated to 1449–1319 BC (UB-6162, 3120±31 BP), produced a small, polished porcellanite axehead, five flint waste flakes and angular fragments, and three sherds of unidentifiable prehistoric pottery (Byrnes 2004).

The very occasional use of stone axes as grave goods in Early Bronze Age burials includes Rathbarron, Co. Sligo, and Killycarney, Co. Cavan, as well as a porcellanite chisel from Monasterboice, Co. Louth (Ó Ríordáin and Waddell 1993, nos 328 and 275; Kavanagh 1976, no. 36). In the later period there are a number of examples associated with cremation pits including Ballyconneely, Co. Clare (Read 2000). Other Bronze Age stone axe contexts include *fulachta fiadh* such as Hermitage and Gorteen, Co. Limerick, Sheephouse, Co. Meath, Carrowcor and Clare, Co. Mayo (Collins 2003; Deevy 2000; Campbell 1995; Guinan 2003; Nolan 2003). The continuing special, if perhaps occasional, status of these artefacts is perhaps indicated by the hoard of 12 axes deposited into the Early Bronze Age copper mine at Ballyrisode, Co. Cork (O'Brien 2000).

Several of the axes from Bronze Age contexts appear to have been in good or even pristine condition, including the examples from Monasterboice, Hermitage and Carrowcor, while the Corrstown examples exhibit little post-breakage wear. It is probable that the majority of the axes from later contexts were actually derived from earlier Neolithic deposits or debris; occasionally these deposits were still *in situ* within the Bronze Age occupation, as at sites like Lough Gur and Dalkey Island. Others may constitute stray artefacts or perhaps finished objects, or items broken during manufacture, discarded at production sites like Tievebulliagh.

3.3.2 Macehead

This large implement, made from gabbro, came from a posthole [608;105] in the northern half of S1 (Illustrations 3.15–3.18). It is sub-rectangular in shape with a thick sub-rectangular cross-section and a central cylindrical perforation bored through from both sides. This is a Largs-type macehead, as defined by Roe (1979; 1968) and Simpson (1988, 35–6), with a central perforation and flattened ends, although its face shape can as readily be paralleled by the sub-rectangular forms of several examples of Irish Bush Barrow type (e.g. *ibid.*, nos 27 and 33). The chronology of these maceheads is very poorly defined although a Bush Barrow type example may have been associated with a collared urn in a burial from Tullymurry, Co. Down (Kavanagh 1976, 348; Simpson 1989, 116), and there are also possible collared urn associations for the Largs type from Britain (Simpson 1988, 36–7). A date in the developed part of the Early, extending perhaps into the Middle, Bronze Age is generally accepted. This would clearly overlap with the slightly more reliably contexted battle axes such as the Bann types (Simpson 1990a) associated with a collared urn at Castleboy, Tara, Co. Meath, dated to 1813–1637 BC (O'Sullivan 2005, burial 38, 191–95, fig. 164) and a cordoned urn from Laheen, Co. Donegal (Ó Ríordáin 1967). A boat-shaped battle axe, possibly of Roe's (1966, 212) late Loose Howe Series, came from a cordoned urn burial at Ballintubbrid, Co. Wexford (Ryan 1975; Simpson 1990a, 15).

3.3.3 Moulds

Four stone moulds for the casting of bronze artefacts came from the site (Illustrations 3.19–3.20). Mould 1, one half of a palstave mould, is from the upper fill of a posthole [161] on the northern side of S1, and Mould 2 occurred in the fill of the northern foundation trench of S8. Mould 3 is from the pathway cobbling to the south of S4 and S52, and Mould 4 is from S38. All of the moulds are of dolerite and display a very high quality of production with sharply defined matrices. In the case of Mould 1 (a shield pattern unlooped palstave) and face 1 of Mould 2 (a parallel-sided chisel) the objects can be paralleled in the Middle Bronze Age (see below). Face 1 of Mould 3 may be for the casting of a chisel similar to Mould 2, but face 2 has rounded bevelled ridges on the longitudinal side of the apparent matrix that preclude this side of the mould from fitting with another mould valve. This mould, and that of the palstave, has cylindrical perforations that pierce the item through the matrix: although unusual these appear to have been part of the original mould production rather than later additions. There are no exact parallels for these features. However, the use of dowels, perhaps of non-combustible material, is indicated on a steatite mould for a socket-looped spearhead possibly from the Omagh hoard, Co. Tyrone, as well as on the steatite example probably from Ballydaw, Co. Kilkenny (Coghlan and Raftery 1961, nos 15 and 27, 231, 236, tavola VIII, fig. 15 and XII fig. 27). On Mould 3, which is from the mid-section of a mould, the broken ends have been re-ground and the object appears to have been re-used as a plaque or pendant, taking advantage of the perforations which are centrally positioned within the modified artefact.

On Mould 2 face 2 there are three parallel, slightly tapering matrices: while these might represent mid-ribs on a bladed implement no parallel exists for this specific form and, furthermore, the configuration of this valve leaves no space for a blade. It is probable, therefore, that the mould was for casting separate lozenge-sectioned rods. These may have been pins although no comparable items have been identified within the Middle Bronze Age metal repertoire: disc pins of this period have rounded cross-sections (Eogan 1964, fig. 6.10–11). It is also possible that these rods are the first stage of bracelet production: lozenge-sectioned bracelets with unexpanded or very slightly expanded terminals are a feature of this period (*ibid.*, 277–9, fig. 6.2).

There is a large number of stone moulds in the Irish archaeological record (Coghlan and Raftery 1961; Eogan 1983). Many of these are two-piece moulds of

Illustration 3.15: Macehead (Jon Sunderland)

Illustration 3.16: Macehead (Jon Sunderland)

Illustration 3.17: Macehead (Jon Sunderland)

Illustration 3.18: Macehead (Jon Sunderland)

Illustration 3.19: From left to right: Mould 2, Mould 1, Mould 4 (above), Mould 3 (below) (Jon Sunderland)

Illustration 3.20: From left to right: Mould 3, Mould 1, Mould 4, Mould 2 (Jon Sunderland)

Middle Bronze Age date and include several for the casting of palstave or related axes. The Corrstown axe mould is for an unlooped shield pattern palstave: the shield consists of an elongated raised pendant triangle that extends from the septum onto the middle section of the axe face: while in part decorative, these would have provided additional cushioning for the haft. As is the case with most Irish palstaves the Corrstown axe would have been small (90mm × 32mm × 23mm in maximum dimensions). The mould was open at both ends and the opening at the blade end appears, if the valves were of equal dimensions, to have been at least 4mm wide. Despite this it is probable that, as with similar moulds from Ballyliffin, Co. Donegal, and those provenanced only to 'Ireland', casting was from the butt end (Coghlan and Raftery 1961, 228, 230, tavola IV, fig. 8a–b, VI, fig. 13): the purpose of the blade end slot is not apparent but it is possible that this end was set or encased in clay during the pouring process. The possible use of clay with the Corrstown mould is particularly interesting. The septum (the portion of the axe haft between the hafting flanges) is extremely rough in contrast with the fine smooth finish of the rest of the mould. While this may have been broken during or after use, the damage is confined to the septum itself and given its protected position this could only have been achieved through the deliberate de-commissioning of the mould: there is no evidence that this occurred accidentally during manufacture, for example through the boring of the perforations. Furthermore, the flanges are too low to have gripped the haft and were the mould complete in its present form, the septum would be far thicker than is usual for palstaves. It is possible, therefore, that the Corrstown mould was a composite example that incorporated the use of clay.

In this respect it is very similar to a composite mould from Site D, Lough Gur, where the deliberately rough area of the septum of a looped palstave, with a similar elongated V-shaped shield pattern, was built-up with clay (Ó Ríordáin 1954, 401–03, fig. 40). At Site D clay mould fragments from the production of socket-looped spearheads were associated with the palstave mould (*ibid.*, 400–03, fig. 40). Other composite moulds occur at, for example, those provenanced only to 'Ireland', and Killymaddy, Co. Antrim, although in these cases the clay consisted of cores to form the sockets of spearheads (Coghlan and Raftery 1961, 231–32, tavola VI, fig. 15, 232, VII, fig. 17). Nevertheless, the use of composite moulds presages the move to the exclusive use of clay moulds in the Late Bronze Age.

While palstave axes are a feature of the Middle Bronze Age in Ireland their precise chronology is poorly understood (Ramsay 1995, 57; Eogan 1964, 270, fig. 2). They are certainly contemporary in their early stages with a range of other flanged axe types; however, they also continue into the final stages of the period as indicated by their presence in the Annesborough, Co. Armagh, and Bishopsland, Co. Kildare, hoards (Eogan 1983, nos 7 and 16, 278, 36–38, figs 6A.1 and 10.1). Bishopsland also contained a rectangular-sectioned chisel possibly similar to the object from face 1 of Mould 2 at Corrstown (see above). While it may be that the small Corrstown palstave belongs to an earlier phase the possible composite nature of this mould may indicate a later date, as the so-called *Hadermarschen* type socketed axe and the socketed hammers from Bishopsland, with rope moulding around the socket, must have been cast in clay moulds (Herity and Eogan 1977, 173).

There are very few palstave moulds from secure contexts. At Raheen, Co. Limerick, part of a mould came from a settlement enclosure in association with plain coarse domestic pottery (Gowen 1988, 86–7, 92–3, fig. 45). The Site D, Lough Gur, example came from a production site centred on House 1 that also produced socket-looped spearheads: other artefacts of relevance to Corrstown include stone axes, plain coarse domestic pottery, as well as vessels with lightly incised ornament and rilled decoration, and a bronze bracelet with an oval cross-section (Ó Ríordáin 1954, 392–4, 400–03, 412, figs 34, 40 and 43.10). The Site F workshop produced clay moulds for the casting of socket-looped spearheads as well as Group IV rapiers and is also of developed Middle Bronze Age date (Herity and Eogan 1977, 170; Ó Ríordáin 1954, 415–25). Plain domestic coarse pottery also came from the site as did an axe pendant identical in shape and size to the Corrstown miniature axe (Ó Ríordáin 1954, 423, fig. 47.3).

None of the Corrstown moulds display direct evidence, in the form of scorching or wear, for use although this does not mean that they had not been utilised. Furthermore, there was no evidence from the site for metal production, in the form of crucibles or metal/casting waste. In the absence of any copper-alloy artefacts from the site and, indeed, the absence of any personal items, it may be that the occupants were not of sufficient social or economic standing to have access to high status artefacts. This interpretation is highlighted by the extensive lithic assemblage and the predominance of a basic and expedient production technology and also by the large but mainly plain domestic pottery assemblage.

3.3.4 A note on the stone types: Stephen Mandal

Porcellanite is known from only two sources in Ireland, namely Tievebulliagh, Co. Antrim, and Rathlin Island, off the north coast of Northern Ireland. It is an extremely unusual rock type, resulting from the metamorphosis of a lens of lateritic soil incorporated into a dolerite plug which developed in the last phase of volcanism at Tievebulliagh and at Brockley on Rathlin Island. Both of the source sites show clear evidence of large scale exploitation of the porcellanite outcrops in the production of stone axeheads (e.g. see Mallory 1990). It is likely that the porcellanite stone axeheads in this assemblage came from one or other of these sources. While it is not possible to differentiate between these sources by macroscopic (hand specimen) examination, or indeed in thin section, x-ray fluorescence geochemical analysis of samples taken from the sources has identified a difference in the trace element concentrations, particularly of strontium (see Mandal *et al*. 1997). This method has been used to match porcellanite axeheads to the sources (*ibid*.).

Dolerite occurs in several locations close to the site, most notably in outcrop on the coastal sections to the north along the Londonderry–Antrim coast. It is possible that the dolerite objects in this assemblage were sourced from one of these outcrops. They could also have been sourced from secondary sources such as the glacial tills in the vicinity of the site.

The closest outcrop sources of gabbro in the area occur to the south towards Tyrone (the Tyrone Basic Igneous Complex). However, the gabbro macehead has been manufactured from a water-rolled cobble. Thus, it is likely that this was sourced locally from a secondary source such as a beach cobble.

Shale is a very common rock type in Ireland, in particular making up discrete horizons with the carboniferous limestones that make up much of the midlands of Ireland. The closest outcrops of shale to the site occur to the west towards Limavady, Co. Londonderry. However, shale is very common in the glacial tills of the country, and it is likely that the shale axeheads in this assemblage were made from such secondary sources.

3.4 Seed Analysis: Örni Akeret (Palaeocology Research Services (PRS))

Only large plant remains were present in the material investigated; in most cases, only cereal grains were recovered and no chaff was present (Table 3.9). The only weed represented was black-bindweed, a species with relatively large fruits. As the samples had already been sorted before being sent to PRS, there remains some uncertainty as to whether the absence of chaff and small seeds is a genuine characteristic of the assemblage or whether inconspicuous plant remains were present but not detected during sorting. Chaff remains are not only of value for the identification of cereals, but also for the reconstruction of crop processing stages, while weed seeds can provide useful ecological information.

Overall, the range of the cereals identified is similar to finds from contemporaneous sites in Ireland (e.g. Hjelmqvist 1980; Greig 1991). The dominance of barley, and notably naked barley, is characteristic of this period, while the other crops known from Bronze Age sites elsewhere in the British Isles are absent or rare.

Among the barley grains (approximately 150) from stakehole [5466] (S58), there was a single grain of rye (these may have actually come from an adjacent pit). This closely resembles the assemblage recovered from a site at Carrowmore, Co. Sligo, where 'some few rye grains were intermingled among barley' (Hjelmqvist 1980). Single rye grains have been found in many assemblages from Neolithic to Iron Age sites in various parts of Europe, but their rarity suggests that the species only occurred as a weed. It is only from the pre-Roman Iron Age that there is evidence for the deliberate cultivation of rye (Behre 1992).

A small number of wheat grains, some of them being emmer wheat (*Triticum dicoccum* Schübl.), and others which could not be assigned to either emmer or spelt wheat (*Triticum dicoccum/spelta*), were recovered. No wheat chaff was found in any of the samples. On current evidence, the presence of wheat on prehistoric Irish sites seems to be a somewhat rare occurrence.

Structure No.	Context	Sample	Latin name
4	Posthole in inner postring	Barley (3 charred grains), 5 unidentifiable grains	*Hordeum distichon* L. *H. vulgare* L.
8	Fill of internal feature, possible hearth	25 charred cereal grains (barley, where identifiable) and emmer or spelt wheat	*Triticum dicoccum* Schubl.*T. spelta* L.
8	Internal spread	6 charred seed fragments, unidentifiable	
13	Fill of posthole associated with outer ditch	*c.* 90 charred cereal grains, those identifiable all barley (naked and hulled)	*Hordeum distichon/ vulgare*
14	Internal burnt spread	*c.* 80 charred barley grains (naked and hulled)	*Hordeum distichon/ vulgare*
14	Fill of outer postring posthole	4 whole cereal grains (2 hulled barley)	*Hordeum distichon/ vulgare*
25	Fill of internal stakehole	*c.* 450 charred barley grains (naked and hulled)	*Hordeum distichon/ vulgare*
30	Fill of outer ditch	16 charred cereal grains (barley where identifiable, naked where recognizable)	*Hordeum distichon/ vulgare*
37	Fill of internal pit	30 whole charred cereal grains (barley and emmer wheat in similar proportions)	*Hordeum distichon/ vulgare Triticum dicoccum*
58	Fill of outer postring posthole	*c.* 80 charred cereal grains and some cereal grain fragments, majority naked barley	*Hordeum distichon/ vulgare*
58	Fill of outer ditch	*c.* 100 charred cereal grains, barley (naked and hulled) and emmer or spelt wheat identified	*Hordeum distichon/ vulgare Triticum dicoccum*
58	Fill of internal stakehole	*c.* 150 charred cereal grains, barley (naked prevalent, also hulled) and a single grain of rye	*Hordeum distichon/ vulgare Secale cereale* L.
69	Entrance pathway	*c.* 300 cereal grains, barley (naked prevalent, also hulled) and one fruit of black-bindweed	*Hordeum distichon/ vulgare Fallopia convolvulus* (L.) A. Love
69	Fill of external ditches	4 complete charred cereal grains and fragments (3 barley)	*Hordeum distichon/ vulgare*
69	Fill of outer ditch	*c.* 450 charred cereal grains, barley (naked) and two fruits of black-bindweed	*Hordeum distichon/ vulgare Fallopia convolvulus*
70	Fill of outer ditch	15 whole charred cereal grains and fragments, majority barley (naked), and one grain of emmer wheat	*Hordeum distichon/ vulgare Triticum dicoccum*

Table 3.9: Seed analysis

Chapter 4

Analysis of the Corrstown Site

4.1 Summary

In Chapters 2 and 3 the constituent components of Bronze Age Corrstown were outlined, from the individual descriptions of the structures to the analysis of the artefacts. An assessment of how these components functioned and operated together is presented in this chapter. The detailed archaeological footprint of the 76 structures was somewhat varied and often complicated, not only due to the effect of medieval occupation (Appendix II) and post-medieval ploughing, but also due to the complex design of the original structures and the succeeding phases of modification, repair and rebuilding. Therefore, the reconstruction of these structures proved somewhat problematic and various interpretations arose during excavation and post excavation; this chapter attempts to portray all of these interpretations.

The Type 1 Corrstown structures represent a rather heterogeneous group, although they share enough common elements to be best regarded as a single diverse group rather than as a multitude of different structural types. The dimensions of the structures varied, from the smallest (S28: 6.2m diameter, S74: 6.6m × 6m and S30: 6.8m × 6m) to the largest (S76: 12m diameter, S44: 12m to 12m terminus to terminus and S13: 11.2m × 11m); however, overall they are considerably smaller than their Type 2 counterparts (see Illustration 1.7). It will be suggested below that the smaller structures, which were often built against the side of or adjacent to a larger structure, represented annexes. However, despite a possible functional variation and a range of structure sizes, the ground plans between the smaller and the larger structures were frequently similar in many regards.

The Type 1 structures were surrounded, or partially surrounded, by wide and shallow ditches, which had a distinctly segmented nature. In some cases the ditch circuit consisted of numerous small oval segments separated by narrow gaps. In other instances the ditches consisted of longer sections which repeatedly constricted to give a segmented appearance without actual separation. In numerous cases the perimeter of a structure was defined by a mixture of small separated ditches and the longer repeatedly constricted ditches. These outer ditches often had extensive cobbling on their bases and in many instances this cobbling had been covered over by layers of large flat stones (Illustration 4.1). In other cases the layer of flat stones lay directly on the base of the ditch and no cobbling was present.

Illustration 4.1: S31 (mid excavation, from the north) showing the cobble fill in the segmented outer ditch

Within the area defined by the outer segmented ditches a ring of outer postholes was located and was set concentrically to the outer ditch. The number of postholes recorded within this postring varied considerably, but it is thought that in most cases a single structural phase would have contained between eight and 13 posts. Occasionally, additional postholes formed notable clusters or groups and these represent repair and modification to the original building. These posts would have supported a ring beam that was one of the key structural elements of the building. By converting the expansive downward force exerted by the roof into a contained radial force, the ring beam allowed the outer ring of posts to support the roof's weight.

In some examples a second inner ditch was present within the interior of the structure. This inner ditch was similar in form to the segmented outer ditch. In only a very few instances were complete circuits of inner ditch recorded. Most often only a single segment of inner ditch was present. These inner ditch segments also commonly contained either cobbled bases or layers of large flat stones covering cobbled bases.

Within the interior of the structures numerous features were present. In most cases the central area was devoid of features but in several instances a bowl-shaped pit was recorded in relative isolation close to the very centre of the interior. These pits may have been hearths but their fills were generally lacking in the charcoal-rich deposits and fire-reddened sides and bases normally associated with such use. The most important of the internal features, structurally speaking, were postholes that could sometimes be identified as forming inner postrings which were concentric with the outer postring. This second postring was present in numerous examples and could therefore have supported a second ring beam and therefore be interpreted as being integral to the structure's design. However, more frequently there were not enough internal posts to form complete postrings, and it seems these internal posts connected directly onto the rafters, and may have been used simply to reinforce a failing structure. Shallow pits were also recorded in great number within the interior of the structure, often concentrated around the entrance and around the line of the outer postring. Stakeholes were recorded within many of the structures in a variety of arrangements, some of which indicate the former presence of wattle panels dividing the internal space. In other cases small circles of stakeholes were suggestive of the positioning of household items, such as furniture and cooking apparatus. In a small number of structures there were stakeholes in such profusion that no particular pattern could be identified.

Entrances were generally southeast facing and again demonstrated considerable variation around a common theme. In some examples there was a simple gap marked by pairs of postholes lining up with a break in the circuit of ditches. In other instances several pairs of postholes extended beyond the building on either side of the entrance, demonstrating the presence of a porch. In many houses the entrance was marked by a long shallow cut feature, often with a cobbled base, that extended several metres beyond the structure's perimeter (Illustration 4.2). In some cases this 'sunken' entrance feature was accompanied by pairs of postholes located on either side; these also are interpreted as representing porches. Finally, in some cases, single lines of postholes extended along one side of the entrance only, and these are interpreted as having held simple wind breaks or fences rather than complete porches. These single lines of postholes were recorded at structures with simple flat entrances and also at structures

Illustration 4.2: S47 (mid excavation, from the north) showing paved feature leading up to S38

Illustration 4.3: S4 (mid excavation, from the northeast), showing the western side of the structure with walling evident; external drain runs from the outer ditch in the top right of the photograph

Illustration 4.4: Large external pit located to the west of S4 (from the north)

with sunken entrances. Further elaboration of the sunken entrances was represented by layers of large flat stones that often covered the base and frequently overlay the basal layer of cobbling. The similarity between this layer of stones found within the sunken entrance features and the layers of large flat stones found in many of the segmented ditches is discussed below.

External drains in the form of linear channels running away from the outer ditch were recorded at a small number of the structures (Illustration 4.3). In addition, a small number of postholes and pits was recorded in the vicinity of many of the structures, frequently occurring on either side of the entrance (Illustration 4.4).

The Type 2 structures at Corrstown occurred in small numbers and were of a different design, although there were some structures which shared features common to both types, suggestive of an evolutionary design process. The Type 2 structures had

Illustration 4.5: S18, taken from the east

much simpler archaeological footprints (Illustration 4.5). They were defined by an almost continuous circular slot-trench, which was narrow in width, had vertical sides and a flat base. Entrances, where identified, consisted of simple gaps in the slot-trench at the south or southeast, although some minor elaboration was present. Within the interior was a single postring consisting of a set of regularly spaced postholes located a consistent distance away from the slot-trench. It is thought that a continuous timber wall stood in the slot-trench and that this would have been topped by a wall plate. The inner posts supported a ring beam. Both elements were likely to have had a role in supporting the weight of the roof. Type 2 structures were considerably larger than the Type 1 structures (see Illustration 1.7).

Four anomalous structures were also recorded within the Corrstown settlement. These may have been structures of either type that were too badly damaged to properly recognise, or structures of a different types altogether that are not easily interpreted by their archaeological remains.

Doody (2000)	Classification
Single ring of posts	1
Double ring of posts	2
Single wall slot	3
Double wall slot	4
External wall, internal posts for roof supports	5

Table 4.1: Classification of Bronze Age structures

4.2 Structure types

From Doody's studies (Doody 2000) of Bronze Age houses excavated in Ireland an image of the typical Middle Bronze Age house emerges: circular in shape, the conical roof supported by a postring consisting of evenly spaced postholes and possibly an outer slot-trench to facilitate a wall created of wattle and daub. Doody classified the structures into one of five different groups according to the number of rings present in the perimeter wall, the presence of a footing trench and the use of internal roof supports (2000, 137, Table 4.1); these groups conformed to the types of Bronze Age houses recognised in Britain.

The two types of structure present at the Corrstown settlement cannot be adequately identified with Doody's classifications, although both of the Corrstown types contain elements from Doody's scheme, such as the evenly spaced postholes.

4.2.1 Type 1 structures

This type of structure was the predominant form on site accounting for 66 of the 76 structures. This group is represented by a range of buildings that followed a similar set of design decisions – an architectural style – rather than an exactly repeated ground plan. Type 1 structures varied considerably in size and complexity and certain examples were almost certainly never free-standing buildings in their own right but were lean-to additions on already standing buildings. Other examples, while free standing, appeared to be too small to have been independent domestic buildings and should be considered as annexes. The variety of ground plans demonstrated by the Type 1 structures necessitated their sub-division into six categories (see below, 4.2.2), to facilitate better clarity in the discussion. These six sub-divisions are rather arbitrary and a certain number of structures could have been located in multiple sub-categories.

4.2.1.1 Shared features of the Type 1 structures: ditches
The Type 1 structures are characterized by the segmented ditches that define their perimeters and which are present within the building's interior in some of the more complicated examples (Illustration 4.6). The segmented nature of these ditches and the manner in which they often fail to encompass the entire building is problematic when ascribing them a structural function. In addition, many of the ditch segments contained a significant amount of stone (present in S1, S2, S4, S5, S7, S8, S13, S14, S15, S27, S37, S43, S51, S55, S57, S60, and S61).

Why the ditch should have been segmented, rather than continuous, is not discernable from the extant evidence at Corrstown; perhaps the creation of a continuous ditch was simply unnecessary. Similar segmented ditches were observed at the Bronze Age settlement sites of Cappagh Beg, Co. Londonderry (Appendix IIII), and also at Ballyhenry, Co. Antrim (McManus 1997), although no internal postholes were discovered at Ballyhenry. It was thought (e.g. MacDonald *et al.* 2005) that this segmentation may have been a regional, northern architectural development until the subsequent discovery of Bronze Age houses at Caltragh, Co. Sligo, in 2005 (McCabe 2005) (although this example was dated to the Early Bronze Age), at Knockdomny, Co. Westmeath, in 2002

Illustration 4.6: Example of a Type 1 structure: mid excavation of S43 (from the northeast)

in advance of the construction of a gas pipeline (Hull 2007), and at Grange 3, Co. Meath, in 2007 as part of the M3 Clonee–North of Kells Motorway Scheme (Kelly 2008). The site at Knockdomny consisted of a single slightly oval-shaped building defined by a mixture of long curvilinear ditch segments and shorter pit-like ditch segments, with a simple southeastern entrance, which was surrounded by a scatter of non-structural pits (Hull 2007). A single linear feature inside the northeastern part of the interior is noticeably similar to the single sections of internal ditch found in some of the structures at Corrstown, and overall the building is highly similar to the smaller examples of the Type 1 structures at Corrstown. Two secure radiocarbon dates were acquired from this structure, 1429–1303 BC and 1527–1415 BC, both at two sigma, while a third of AD 1409–1454 was disregarded as medieval contamination (*ibid*. 8). The excavator interpreted the segmented outer ditch as having held 'horizontal earth fast beams' which held timber uprights, although neither the reason for the segmentation nor an explanation of how such a segmented foundation could function in combination with timber sill beams were not offered (*ibid*. 8). At Grange 3, two Bronze Age structures were formed by what the director, Amanda Kelly, defined as 'interrupted pits'. These pits are not dissimilar, on ground plan at least, to the segmented ditches at Corrstown and may be interpreted as the same phenomenon (Kelly 2008). At Grange 3, some of the pits contained artefacts, including a large stone adze which had been re-used as a hammer and a large saddle quern and a rubbing stone. The presence of these artefacts indicates that the 'interrupted pits' were unlikely to have been structural.

At Ballyprior Beg, Co. Antrim (Suddaby 2003), and Ballyutoag, Co. Antrim (MacDonald *et al*. 2005), Bronze Age roundhouses also exhibited evidence for a double ditch, although the outer ditch was not segmented in these two sites. As at Grange

3, this outer ditch was not ascribed a structural function; indeed, the outer ditches at Ballyutoag, Co. Antrim, were interpreted as 'quarries for material used in the construction of the roundhouses' (MacDonald *et al.* 2005, 58), with the same explanation being offered as a possibility by the authors for those at Corrstown.

At Corrstown, many of the outer ditch segments contained stones (Illustration 4.7). Often these stones seemed to be set in courses and it was initially thought that these external ditches may have formed the foundations for an outer, non-load bearing wall; however, their segmented and discontinuous nature makes this interpretation unlikely. Instead, it seems that some of the stone within the outer ditch segments may have directly related to their role as part of a drainage system (this was explicitly observed with S4, see below), and further drains were observed running from several structures (see below). By examining the sections through the ditch segments it could be noted that in some cases there was a concentration of stone at the base of the ditch and then further stones were mixed through the infilling material at various heights. This suggested that the basal layer of stone was *in situ* while the higher more dispersed stones had derived from the collapse of a stone-built feature, such as a wall, which may have been positioned adjacent to the ditch.

In the absence of any structural function or regional idiosyncratic trait it seems most likely that the external segmented ditches had a triple function. Initially, they functioned as quarry pits for the extraction of material used in the construction of the buildings before being cobbled or paved in order to facilitate drainage. Finally, they would also have served as convenient receptacles for domestic waste, as shown by the inclusion of pottery sherds and residue lithic material in their fills and by the recutting of several segments (e.g. S41). That some of these deposits may have been ritually charged is a possibility (see below).

Illustration 4.7: Stones in the outer ditch segment of S40

The nature of the internal segmented ditches is also problematic. Those at Caltragh, Co. Sligo, were interpreted by the excavator as storage pits which were possibly covered with a lid. They were also present at Ballyprior Beg, Co. Antrim (Suddaby 2003, 54–7, figs 3, 4, 7), possibly at Whitepark Bay, Co. Antrim (Knowles 1886, 107, pl. 1), and at Ballyutoag, Co. Antrim (MacDonald *et al.* 2005), where a subsequent floor surface covered over the ditch segments / pits, thus indicating that the segments / pits pre-dated the actual occupation of the house. At Corrstown it is likely that the internal segmented ditches functioned in a manner similar to those at Caltragh, and that their cobbling and lining may have facilitated storage or that they were left open (Conway *et al.* 2004, 122), although it is also suggested that they may have functioned as internal divisions and that, in some cases, they could feasibly also represent evidence for earlier structures (see below).

4.2.1.2 Shared features of the Type 1 structures: walls
As the above discussion indicates, there was insufficient evidence to conclude that either the inner or the outer ditches supported walls or wall foundations. Instead, it seemed that there was, in some structures, a low non-load bearing wall set beside the outer ditch.

In S4 a well-laid stone foundation was identified around the northwest and north of the structure, the only definite recorded example of extant *in situ* walling identified on the site. It was located on the outer half of the bank between the outer and inner segmented ditch circuits. The foundation was up to 0.8m wide and consisted of a single course of flat stones pushed firmly into the clay subsoil. There was a significant gap between the inner edge of the wall foundation and the line of the outer postring which was located close to the outer edge of the inner ditch which itself had a cobbled base. At the northeast, the inner edge of the wall foundation had a semi-circular indentation in which two stakeholes were located. Those outer ditch segments adjacent to the wall foundation contained loose stone which derived from the collapse of the rest of the wall. When this was removed it was found that the sides of the ditch segments had originally been revetted with large flat stones and that the bases of some segments had been covered in fine cobble. This arrangement seemed to suggest that the outer ditch segments had been used for drainage, an idea that was reinforced when it was discovered that an earlier phase of this structure had a shallower outer ditch that was connected to a long linear drain running off from the northwest (Illustration 4.3). When the outer ditch was subsequently deepened this drain had been blocked off by the stones used to revet the deepened ditch's sides.

None of the other structures on the site produced definite evidence of *in situ* wall foundations although many other examples contained a large quantity of jumbled and un-sorted stones within the fills of the ditch segments. There are two, non-mutually exclusive, functions for this stone. In some cases this stone represents drainage (see below) but it is also possible that in some examples the loose stone represents wall collapse. In light of the evidence from S4 it is suggested that it is possible that a small non-load-bearing wall on the Type 1 structures was located between the outer ditch and the outer postring; it was only archaeologically visible in S4. It is possible that when the structures were abandoned, the walls collapsed and filled the ditch segments with a jumble of loose stone, while the foundation of the wall was, in the majority of cases, eventually removed by ploughing or other agricultural activity.

4.2.1.3 Shared features of the Type 1 structures: entrances

The majority of the Type 1 houses had long sunken entrances between 2m and 5m long, 1.5m and 2m wide and around 0.3m lower than the surrounding subsoil. Many of the sunken entrance passages were flanked by pairs of postholes, which in some cases extended to the end of the entrance, but in others stopped halfway along the length. These pairs of postholes were interpreted as indicating the presence of a porch which covered part or all of the length of the sunken entrance. In a few cases postholes were present along only one side of the sunken passage, suggesting that a wind-break was used, rather than a covered porch. The bases of these entrances were often covered in fine cobble, and in some cases this extended beyond the end of the entrance and joined onto adjacent pathways or the surface of the roadway. It is suggested that this cobbling was used to stop the entrance from eroding. In one example, S45, the probable position of the door was marked by a low mound of hard-packed clay running across the entrance between a pair of postholes (Illustration 4.8). Almost all of the entrances were orientated to the southeast or SSE, and where this was not the case it is suspected that the entrance had been diverted around a building that was already in place, as with S45 and S6. The entrances of 20 of the structures contained an area of large flat stones. In some cases these filled the entire entrance feature, as with S4, while in others it was found only in one area, as with S13, most often at the end of the entrance furthest away from the structure. The similarity between the stones laid in the entrance features and the stone layers found in the bases of the ditch segments was noticeable, supporting the idea that the stone layers in the outer ditches were not foundations for walls.

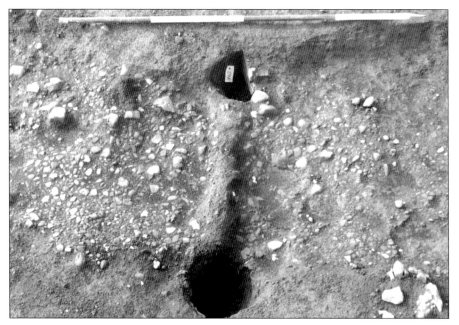

Illustration 4.8: The clay threshold in the entrance feature of S45

Evidence for a pair of large opposing pits located close to the door jambs was frequently identified. In some instances additional pairs of opposing pits were found further along the line of the entrance. These pits were invariably placed on the same line as the walls of the covered porches and so it is possible that they could not have been used once the porch had been constructed. Alternatively, the porch may have simply been a set of timbers supporting a roof with no wall connecting the bottom of the roof to the ground. If this was the case these pits, which often contained considerable quantities of domestic waste, would have been accessible from within the entrance.

The structures which did not have the extended sunken entrances either had simple entrances marked by pairs of door jambs or had lines of postholes extending from the entrance, which in some cases represented covered porches and in others represented only a single-sided wind-break or fence. Where there was no sunken entrance an elongated pit was often found just to one side of the entrance and this may have had an original drainage function before being used as refuse pits.

4.2.1.4 Shared features of the Type 1 structures: postrings
In the Type 1 structures the superstructure of the building was supported by one or two rings of internal posts. In the simpler examples of the Type 1 structure the outer ring of posts was typically set between 0.5m and 0.8m inside the line of the outer ditch and would have supported a ring beam. In approximately 20% of cases an inner ring was set concentrically inside the outer postring, between 1m and 2m closer to the building's centre. In most instances this inner postring contained fewer and smaller posts than the outer postring. In the examples of the Type 1 structure with double ditches the outer ring of posts was located on the bank between the double ditches. The exact position of this postring varies, in S4 it is close to the inner ditch, in S13 it is in the middle of the bank, and in S5 it is closer to the outer ditch.

It appears that there were two types of inner postring, one type consisting of around eight or nine posts which would have supported a second ring beam, and a second type which consisted of only a few posts. The latter is seen most clearly in S45, where three postholes may have held posts that may have been tied directly into the roof's apex or onto particular rafters, rather than supporting a second ring beam.

4.2.1.5 Shared features of the Type 1 structures: drains
As stated above, the outer ditch segments functioned as drains, facilitating run-off from the roof. Many of these drains were filled with loose stone which either derived from collapsed material from a possible wall set on the bank of the ditch or which represents the draining material. A small number of the buildings (six out of 74 roundhouses) had linear drains running away from the northern side of the double ditch; these were all Type 1 structures. All of these examples were located towards the northern half of the settlement which was the down slope end and may have been more prone to inundation from surface water than the southern buildings positioned further upslope. Apart from the drain attached to S4, the drains were small, 3–6m in length and up to 0.4m in width. The drain of S4 is particularly interesting as it ran for approximately 11m to the northwest, encroaching upon the area of the first-phase roadway, prior to the construction of the road's cobbled surface in its second phase (see below; Illustration

4.3). It was subsequently blocked off, backfilled and covered over by the second-phase road surface. The drain was blocked by placing a large stone into the point where it joined the structure's outer ditch, after the ditch had been deepened and revetted. These details suggest that the function of the outer ditch of S4 was definitely drainage, that in essence it was an elaborate eaves-drip gully.

A possible drainage channel ran from the west side of S1 for several metres before running into the eastern ditch of S8. During the excavation it was noted that water naturally accumulated in the area around S1 and indeed the excavation of S1 had to be halted frequently because of flooding. It therefore seems likely that water was being drawn away from S1 into the perimeter ditch of S8, and that may explain the exceptional width and depth of the ditch around the north of S8. Further drains were noted elsewhere across the site, including at the entrances to S13, S25 and S55. Similar drains have been noted in Britain where particular structures, as at Shaugh Moore, Devon (Wainwright and Smith 1980), sometimes had drains which ran from the inner postring to outside their drystone walls, although the examples in Devon were later than those at Corrstown, dating to around 1000 BC.

4.2.1.6 Shared features of the Type 1 structures: internal features
The majority of Type 1 structures contained significant numbers of internal features in addition to the postrings which were identified primarily as stakeholes and pits. These features tended not to be located at the very centre of the structure but to cluster around the sides. In the structures with double ditches the majority of internal features were located inside the inner ditch, in and around the inner postring. The position and density of the internal stakeholes suggested that they had resulted from the placing of screens in order to divide off the central area from the peripheral areas. Other stakehole groups may have related to the setting of pieces of equipment. It was clear from the quantity of stakeholes recorded that such features were more temporary than the main superstructure elements and were moved or replaced reasonably often.

The distribution of pits was also concentrated around the periphery of the interior space with the central area largely devoid of such features. A small number of centrally placed possible hearths was located, as in S6, S9 or S33, but as with other roundhouses of this date, their discovery was not common. In a number of other structures centrally located pits may have been used as hearths but if this was the case they had been thoroughly cleaned out before they had become filled in with sterile material. In total, nine other buildings (S7, S8, S14, S15, S21, S27, S35, S37, and S70) contained possible hearths, but the evidence in each instance was rather inconclusive. Even if all of these examples did represent hearths, a total of 60 of the roundhouses would still not contain an identifiable hearth.

Small patches of cobbling were recorded in the interior of three buildings: S10, S62 and S65. These may represent intact fragments of floor surfaces, although it is not possible to prove that they were contemporary with the occupation, and in the case of S65, it seems more likely that an earlier cobbled patch was cut through by the structure. Some of the larger buildings had slightly sunken interiors that should have allowed better preservation of any cobbled surfaces, but as these were not found it is suspected that these were not a standard feature in most of the structures. Four of the buildings, S7, S8, S9, and S43, also had large sunken areas within their interiors that were filled with layers of flat stone. Again, these may have represented floor surfaces but as they are either extensions of the sunken entrance, or the segmented ditch, it is hard to classify them as they may have been created for more complicated purposes, such as repairing eroded areas of the interior. All of these buildings are concentrated in the northern third of the settlement and these features may reflect the overall chronology of the settlement described below.

4.2.1.7 Shared features of the Type 1 structures: internal space
The stakeholes and postholes found in many of the structures indicate internal divisions and possible screens used to sub-divide the internal space. The inner ditches and second, inner postrings, may have formed part of an earlier, smaller structure although conclusive stratigraphic evidence for which was not forthcoming. It is therefore also possible that they were also used to demarcate spatial zones. If all these features were contemporary then two concentric zones may be defined: the outer zone around the perimeter of the structures and an inner zone in the centre of the building. This division is very clearly demarcated in the more elaborate structures with both inner ditches and inner postrings. In those structures the outer zone lay between the outside wall and the line of the inner postring, and contained the inner ditch segments and numerous small pits and stakeholes, and the central zone was the area inside the inner postring which was largely devoid of features. This concentric division of space was present in numerous roundhouse reconstructions at other sites, but rarely has it been found to be as clearly demarcated as at Corrstown. While initial impressions of the outer zone were of a low space under the eaves of the roof, reconstructions which place the angle of the roof at 45 degrees or more give a roof height between 2m and 2.5m over the area of the segmented inner ditch. This 'ceiling' height, the fine cobbling laid into each ditch segment, and the wattle screens dividing off the outer zone from the inner zone rather give an impression of comfort and privacy. This division of space may have included sleeping areas.

Internal spatial divisions were also seen at Troopersland, Co. Antrim (McConway 2000), where a central division (2.6m wide) was formed by two linear slots (2 and 1.4m long). North–south internal divisions formed by stakeholes were noted at Structure 1, Caltragh, Co. Sligo (McCabe 2005, 47) and at Kerlogue, Co. Wexford (McLoughlin 2002), and these most likely separated the front of the house from the back. East–west divisions were noted at Structure B, Ballybrowney (Cotter 2005) and at Cloghlucas, Co. Cork (Gowen 1988, 17).

4.2.2 Sub-division of the Type 1 structures

A further sub-division of the Type 1 structures can be advocated in order to facilitate comprehension of the site's complexity. The following structures all remain part of the Type 1 form and as such, despite some differences, share certain common features: the segmented ditch, the presence of stone in the ditches, the occurrence of internal features, the use of linear drains in some examples, and the creation of elaborate entrances. The sub-divisions are based primarily on the extant archaeological footprint.

4.2.2.1 Type 1A: single segmented ditch roundhouse
Structures: S3, S6, S7, S8, S9, S10, S14, S17, S20, S21, S22, S23, S25, S38, S40, S41, S43, S51, S52, S55, S56, S58, S59, S66, S68, S69, S70, S73, and S76 (Illustration 4.9).

This type of structure was the most predominant form on the site, and 29 examples were recorded. The outer ditch comprised between two and nine individual segments, with an average of 4.5 segments; these segments may have been entirely separated from each other, joined together at their narrow ends, or a mixture of both. In many instances there was one main segment that defined most of the perimeter and was flanked by a number of smaller segments. The ditch segments were typically around 0.8m wide and 0.3m in depth, but there was variation in this. The perimeter ditch generally defined an oval-shaped structure, with the long axis extending along the line of the entrance. The long axis was typically 10% longer than the short axis and the length of the long axis varied between 7m and 11m.

Inside the structure was a postring, which was typically set 0.5m beyond the inner edge of the segmented ditch. The number of postholes in this postring varied considerably, from five to 28, and it is thought that in any singular building phase a ring of between five and 13 posts was used with between eight and 11 being the most common. The evidence did not suggest differential truncation and therefore it could be concluded that some of these postrings intentionally only included a small number of posts.

Illustration 4.9: Examples of Type 1A structures: S25 (from the south), S38 (from the north), S59 (from the south)

Occasionally postholes were recorded in the interior of the structure inside the area defined by the outer postring, but in no instances were enough discovered to suggest the presence of a second, inner postring (as were seen in Types 1B and 1C), and it is thought these postholes represent posts designed to stabilise a sagging roof or that they related to internal features.

Although these structures did not have complete inner ditches as seen in Type 1B and 1C structures, five examples of single ditch segments, or perhaps more correctly shallow pits that resembled the ditch segment form, were recorded in five of the structures. These were normally located opposite the entrance and while these did not form complete circuits it seems likely that they were used in the same way as the inner ditch segments seen in the Type 1B and 1C structures.

A variety of entrance features was associated with these structures, the majority of which faced to the southeast or SSE. The most elaborate were long sunken features that extended for several metres, had cobbled bases and were flanked by pairs of postholes. Other examples were simpler, defined either by a short run of paired postholes or by a single pair of postholes just beyond the line of the segmented ditch.

4.2.2.2 Type 1B: concentric segmented ditch roundhouse
Structures: S1, S2, S15, S16, S19, S42, and S45 (Illustration 4.10).

These seven structures were very similar in size and complexity to those of Type 1A but with the addition of a second segmented ditch set concentrically within the first and located inside the line of the first postring, and outside the line of the second, inner postring, where it was present. In the case of the Type 1B structures, the addition of the second concentric segmented ditch did not fulfil a structural function and instead had some use in the organization of activities within the building. There were no instances of Type 1B structures where the inner ditch formed a complete circuit, and no examples where it could be concluded that the inner ditch was replaced by, or post-dated the outer ditches, and no examples where postholes from one phase pre-dated or post-dated the inner ditch. It therefore seems most likely that the inner ditch segments were contemporary with the main occupation of the structures. In most of these examples the inner postring was fully developed and comprised between three and 15 posts, but it is thought that only between three and eight of these postholes

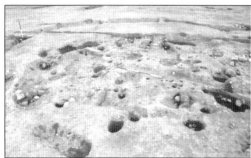

Illustration 4.10: Examples of Type 1B structures: S19 (interior, from the west) and S42 (from the southwest)

were used during a single building phase. S45 was a particularly important structure because it was evidently a single-phase structure and the clarity of its plan was of great use when attempting to interpret other more complicated structures. S45 was sub-circular (9.1m × 8.4m, externally) and no postholes or stakeholes cut the five outer ditch segments, while the outer postring consisted of nine postholes with no evidence for repair or replacement. Three inner ditch segments and an additional two areas of cobbling represented the inner ditch which was concentric with the outer ditch. The area enclosed by the inner ditch measured *c*. 4m and contained three postholes which would have been insufficient to support a second ringbeam. Two adjacent postholes positioned along the cobbled entrance suggest the presence of a projecting doorway, or a small porch.

4.2.2.3 Type 1C: conjoined concentric segmented ditch roundhouse
Structures: S4, S5 and S13 (Illustration 4.11).

These three structures were undoubtedly the most complicated examples recorded on the site. Similar in most respects to the first two types, the major difference was the scale and complexity of the ditches defining the perimeter. In these structures the concentric ditches were conjoined and the outer ditch was on average twice the depth of the inner ditch. A low bank that was lower than the surface of the surrounding subsoil separated the ditches. In effect, the ditches formed a distorted or unbalanced W-shape in profile. All of these structures demonstrated clear evidence of being multi-phase structures. In all of the examples the first postring was located on the bank between the outer and inner segmented ditch. In two of the examples, S4 and S13, there was a more developed second, inner postring, but in S5 there were only three inner postholes, which were located around the southern side in association with a line of stakeholes. Stakeholes were also located in profusion among the postholes of the western side of the inner ring of S4.

The Type 1C structures were the largest and most elaborate buildings on the site, and as such a particular status and importance could be assigned to them. Indeed, the artefact evidence goes someway to support this (see below). They are arranged roughly equidistant from each other in the centre of the settlement, and may have been the residences of important people or may have had particular functions, such as

Illustration 4.11: Examples of Type 1C structures: S4 (from the south) and S13 (mid excavation, from the northeast)

the location of a specific activity or the focus of some ritualised behaviour. However, it could also be hypothesised that the double ditch foundation was a result of the rebuilding of a previous structure on the spot that had left the subsoil badly disturbed. It can be argued that the conjoined ditch was constructed in order to remove the foundation of an earlier building and allow for a new structure. The multi-phased nature of these structures, in particular S4 which had truncated postholes sealed under stone footings and a sealed-up drainage channel, could certainly be seen to fit with this explanation. Even in light of this more pragmatic explanation, the Type 1C structures were undeniably large and complicated and produced large assemblages of artefacts, which surely indicate some difference in status. S5 may have an even more specific explanation for its particular form. It is possible that the inner ditch of this structure is actually the remains of a Type 1D that pre-dated or post-dated the outer ditch of a Type 1A building. This interpretation reflects the way in which the inner ditch is not concentric with the outer ditch, and the absence of postholes within the area enclosed by the inner ditch.

4.2.2.4 Type 1D: freestanding structure
Structures: S12, S28, S29, S46, S47, S48, S57, S60, S61, S62, S67, S71, and S74 (Illustration 4.12).

These structures were reasonably common across the site with 13 examples being recorded. They were very similar in nature to the Type 1A structure with three important differences. These structures, although of a significant size (maximum lengths of typically 7–8m), had noticeably smaller dimensions than the Type 1A structures. These structures were noticeably more circular in plan than the Type 1A structures, although the majority were still marginally oval shaped. Thirdly, these structures did not stand in isolation. They were situated adjacent to another, normally larger, structure (e.g. S12 and S2, S46 and S5), with the exception of S61 and S62 which were adjacent to each other. For these reasons it is considered that the Type 1D structures were not independent houses, but were instead ancillary structures used by the neighbouring buildings, either for some particular function or activity, or simply to create additional enclosed space. In determining whether or not to classify a structure as Type 1A or Type 1C when the dimensions permitted either

Illustration 4.12: Examples of Type 1D structures: S46 (from the south) and S61 (from the north)

choice, the presence of a larger adjacent structure was often a deciding factor, and the rather arbitrary nature of this determination should be recognised. For instance S12 and S14 were similar in most respects but as S12 was located immediately west of the much larger S2 it was classed as a Type 1C structure, whereas S14 stood in isolation and was therefore categorised as being Type 1A. There were no examples of this structure type that had fully developed inner ditches or inner postrings, although several had isolated ditch segments and postholes, in a similar manner to Type 1A structures.

4.2.2.5 Type 1E: small abutting structure
Structures: S11, S30, S31, S34, S53, S54, and S65 (Illustration 4.13).

This type of structure, of which seven examples were identified, was very similar to the Type 1Ds, but these roundhouses were more directly connected to the adjacent larger structures and indeed shared structural elements. In this way the Type 1E building can be seen to have never been a freestanding independent structure and the ancillary function is confirmed. The Type 1E structures had small dimensions and a fairly varied shape ranging from small circular and oval, to a very small crescent. The Type 1E structures invariably consisted of only a single segmented ditch, and only one example, S31, contained a second, inner postring. The most interesting arrangement of these structures involved the Type 2 S33, which potentially had the small Type 1E S31 built up against its eastern side, and which in turn had the even smaller Type 1E S30 built up against its eastern side. Both of these structures had external entrances

Illustration 4.13: Example of a Type 1E structure: S30 (from the northeast)

independent of the larger adjacent building, but there may also have been access to the structures from within the adjacent larger building.

4.2.2.6 *Type 1F: undetermined segmented ditch roundhouse*
Structures: S27, S32, S35, S36, S37, S44, and S75.

Seven of the structures on the site were too badly damaged by later features, such as the early medieval ditch, the early modern field boundaries or by ploughing and other agricultural processes, to be sub-classified. Although these structures were incomplete, enough survived to allow for the recognition of the segmented ditch, which is the common link between the Type 1 structures. It is for this reason that these seven structures have been identified as Type 1F rather than being placed into the Anomalous Class described below.

4.2.3 *Type 2: narrow slot roundhouses*
There were six structures (S18, S33, S39, S49, S63, and S64) which differed substantially from the others on site and therefore warranted a different classification (Illustration 4.14). One of these, S63, had certain similarities with the Type 1 structures and may be considered as a hybrid form. The typical ground plan of these Type 2 structures comprised a narrow circular slot-trench defining the perimeter and an internal ring of postholes. The slot-trench was narrow with vertical sides and a depth between

Illustration 4.14: Example of a Type 2 structure: S18 (from the east)

0.2m and 0.4m. The internal ring of postholes was located between 1m and 2m from the slot-trench in the interior and contained between eight and 15 evenly spaced postholes. The structures were between 10m and 15m in diameter and had entrances to the south or SSE.

These structures are similar to Doody's Type 1 structure and examples are known from throughout Ireland including at Kilmurray, Co. Wicklow (Ó Néill 2001), Lisheen Site A, Co. Tipperary (Ó Néill 2005), Ballybrowney, Structures B–E, Co. Cork (Cotter 2005), Ballyhenry, Site 2, Co. Antrim (McManus 2002), Ballyrenan, Site 3, Co. Antrim (McQuillan 1999), and Townparks, House B, Co. Antrim (Ballin Smith 2003). All of these examples were dated to the Middle Bronze Age, either by virtue of radiocarbon analysis, or through associated chronologically diagnostic artefacts. There is no known regional, functional or chronological difference between this type of structure, and those structures without a slot-trench or with multiple internal postrings. Certainly, at Corrstown, the broadly contemporary nature of the two types was suggested by S33. This Type 2 structure may have had two Type 1 structures, S31 and S30, built up against its eastern side in a lean-to manner. A radiocarbon date from S33 demonstrated a date range identical to that provided by numerous Type 1 structures, strongly indicating that this structure, at least, was in use contemporaneously with the Type 1 buildings.

Structurally, the Type 2 examples functioned in a similar manner to the Type 1 examples: the internal ring of posts would have held a ring beam that would have supported the rafters of the roof. The precise function of the slot-trench remains open to discussion: it may have formed an eaves-drip gully (Ladle and Woodward 2003, 275), it may have contained a palisade of upright wooden planks (Cotter 2005), or it may have provided a foundation for an external light wooden wall formed of wattle and daub (Ballin Smith 2003, 42). Certainly, the latter two hypotheses seem more probable explanations of the Type 2 structures at Corrstown. The profile of the slot-trench was narrow and deep with vertical sides and a flat base and was perfectly shaped to have held a timber wall. The slot-trench of S49 was substantially truncated but the extant remains did contain evidence for three postholes, set into the slot-trench. Stones were located in the fills of S18, S33, S63, and S64 and the excavators of S18 and S64 argued that these medium-sized and large stones represented disturbed packing material and, as such, evidence for a continuous wooden palisade.

The number of internal postholes varied within the Type 2 structures (Table 4.2). It appears that, at least for those structures with a low occurrence of internal postholes, most of the weight of the roof must have been borne by an outer wall, as it could not have been fully supported by an incomplete internal postring. It is not clear from the archaeological evidence whether any of the Type 2 structures ever had a full internal postring, as the replacement of four or five internal posts in successive phases could create a similar pattern, and so S49 and S69 could be viewed as a two-phased structure and S18 as a three-phased structure. However, the regular spacing of the posts in S49 and S63 does seem to suggest a complete postring, while the clustering of posts in S18 seems to indicate at least one phase of replacement.

Entrances to the Type 2 structures, where they were intact, appeared to be simple gaps in the slot-trench. Part of a more complicated entrance arrangement survived

Structure	No of postholes in postring
S18	15
S33	4
S39	1
S49	10
S63	9
S64	5

Table 4.2: Type 2 Structures

at the south of S18, but most of this had been removed by a modern field boundary and reconstruction is not possible. Similarly, the entire southern end of S49 had been removed by a modern field boundary and no entrance was apparent around the rest of the structure. S64 had two large pits outside the southern side, similar to some of the pits found outside the entrances to the Type 1 examples but it is not clear whether these should be associated with S64 or the adjacent Type 1 structure, the largely destroyed S77.

Apart from the internal postring very few features were recorded inside the Type 2 structures with the exception of S33. In addition not all of the Type 2 buildings contained associated artefacts and only S33 produced a dateable quantity of charcoal.

As mentioned above S63 may have been a hybrid form featuring a segmented slot-trench akin to those seen in the Type 1 structures. It was included as a Type 2 structure because of the lack of postholes and internal features. Likewise S25 had elements of both types but was included as a Type 1 because of the quantity of postholes and internal features that were recorded. S38 may also have been a hybrid form. Its entrance led onto the largest and deepest section of cobbled pathway F101, which also served a number of Type 1 structures, again suggesting that both building types were contemporaneous.

The largest of the Type 2 structures was S33, located at the southwest edge of the settlement. In terms of its basic construction this building clearly fits into the Type 2 category as it was defined by a narrow, circular slot-trench. Apart from this most basic of criteria this building diverged from the rest of the Type 2 group in a number of important ways. There was an abundance of internal features within this structure, including a probable hearth, and many of these features contained pottery and charcoal. A small Type 1E structure, S30, appeared to have been constructed against the eastern side of S33, and an even smaller Type 1E structure, S31, had been built against the eastern side of this. Unlike the other structures in this group, S33 therefore appears to have been used in a similar way to the Type 1 structures.

4.2.4 Anomalous structures

Four of the structures on site (S24, S26, S50, and S52) could not be classified as either Type 1 or Type 2. Instead, they are described here. Two of these structures, S26 and S24, were similar and consisted of shallow slot-trenches forming two adjacent semi-circles, making the overall ground plan look like a squashed 'W'. S26 was open to the north while S24 was open to the south, and overlay the Type 1 structure S23. It is possible that these represented the partial remains of four Type 2 structures; however, there was a general lack of associated postholes which makes it almost impossible to perceive how the weight of a roof could have been borne. It is also hard to determine a way in which the ground level could have been reduced to leave this pattern of sub-surface remains as the only surviving remnants from complete houses. It is therefore suggested that these two structures are best interpreted as drainage gullies located outside curving wattle fence lines representing wind-breaks where the associated stakeholes have not survived. Such wind-breaks could have been required for various reasons and the areas north of S26 and south of S24 were probably areas where some form of activity took place that has left no other recoverable trace. The weathered and abraded nature of the pottery recovered from S26 is consistent with an open-roofed interpretation.

S50 is perhaps the most difficult structure to explain. It consisted of a semi-circular ditch open to the west, overlaying an earlier posthole of considerable depth. It appears to be too substantial to be a simple drainage gully in the manner used to explain S24 and S26, but if it was part of a building then that building was either never completed or left no other recoverable traces.

S53 was defined by a very narrow sub-oval slot-trench and presumably represented a small shed or animal pen. This is the only such structure on the site but several circles of stakeholes to the west of S4 probably represent simple structures or fences which were comparable in size. There are numerous explanations for what such small open buildings or pens could be used for and they may have been roofed or un-roofed, for animals or storage.

4.3 Roundhouse reconstructions

Reconstruction drawings of the two types of structures were drawn by Ella Hassett after detailed consultation with the authors. Illustration 4.15 shows an external view of one of the Type 1 buildings. It does not represent any one particular structure and instead is based on the type as a whole. Therefore, it represents a kind of informative composite and illustrates what one of the buildings may have looked like during a particular construction phase. Illustration 4.15 shows a thatched roof with a pitch of 45 degrees, although of course this could have been considerably steeper and the roof may have been covered in sods rather than thatch. The low stone wall is shown within a circuit of discontinuous ditches, and the turf or sod wall which would have connected the top of the stone wall with the thatch is not shown as it is hidden by the extent of the roof. The sunken entrance porch is covered with a long thatched roof and flanked with pits. There was no evidence to suggest that the wall which defined the perimeter of the house also demarcated the extent of the porch (certainly, there was insufficient space between the postholes and the external, flanking pits). The porch in Illustration 4.15 is shown as open; however, it is likely that some form of wattle, perhaps made from hazel, would have been interwoven between the postholes. It is also possible that the porch was left open, and that therefore the external pits could have been accessed from the sunken entrance.

The second reconstruction is of a Type 2 building (Illustration 4.16). Again this is not based on a single specific example but represents the building type as a whole. The roof is shown as thatched with a pitch of 45 degrees, but as with Illustration 4.15 this may have been steeper or constructed with a different material (although the evidence from S33 which burnt down seems to indicate thatch was used on that particular structure at least). The continuous outer wall is shown with the timbers emerging from the backfilled slot-trench leaving no above-ground trace of this feature other than some disturbed ground. The timbers are spilt into halves, with the rounded sides facing outwards. The gaps between these timbers would have been sealed, perhaps with clay or some other organic material. A single post from the internal ring of posts is visible through the entrance. Illustration 4.16 depicts a simple, open entrance, without a door which could have been derived from animal skins. The internal postring would have been connected to a ring beam. It is beyond the remit (and knowledge) of the authors to give a detailed structural reconstruction of the roundhouses and others with more expertise have published on the matter (see as exemplar Reynolds 1982).

Illustration 4.15: Reconstruction of a Type 1 structure (Ella Hassett)

Illustration 4.16: Reconstruction of a Type 2 structure (Ella Hassett)

4.4 Rebuilding cycles

It has been already mentioned that certain structures were rebuilt numerous times on the same place, leaving archaeological remains that are best considered as 'house footprints' rather than as singular buildings. Doody (2000, 147) discovered that this successive re-use of a particular area was common in Bronze Age settlements and, as there was no spatial reason for such rebuilding, he interpreted this as the sequential replacement of a single homestead. In just under half of the excavated structures at Corrstown it is thought that the remains represent multiple building phases, either being major overhauls or complete rebuilds. The structural elements are almost totally lacking horizontal stratigraphic relationships and it was all but impossible to separate out individual phases through excavation; therefore, only rough approximations were given in Table 2.1.

   In many prehistoric sites if the inhabitants wished to completely rebuild their structure they generally did so either adjacent to or near the original, soon to be defunct, structure. This was also the case at Caltragh, Co. Sligo, where one structure had been built over the location of a previous one (McCabe 2005, 47) as well as at Lisheen, Co. Tipperary (Houses A and B) (Ó Néill 2005), and at Ballypriorbeg (Suddaby 2003). In some instances the new structures were partially built over the old ones, re-using as much of the same constructional material as possible. In these cases, overlapping and settlement shift was evident, as observed at Reading Area 5 (Brossler *et al.* 2004) and Navan Fort (Lynn 2003), although in the Late Bronze Age/Iron Age at Navan the same building area was used repeatedly, up to seven or eight times. It is this pattern of overlapping circles which is often used in the identification of individual buildings among a mass of postholes, and ultimately enables the excavator to total up the number constructed over time (Moore 1992, 15–29). Such patterns were not commonly observed at the Corrstown settlement and it was difficult to interpret how many buildings were built on each house footprint. Using the lowest estimates for each building, it is suggested that a minimum of 100 structures were constructed on the 74 house footprints (not including the two W-shaped structures classified above as Anomalous), although the actual total could conceivably be rather higher (Table 2.1).

Why then did the inhabitants of the Corrstown settlement decide to rebuild their structures on the same spot? The likely answer would relate to some constructional component which necessitated the retention of the same area. Once the outer ditches of the Type 1 structures were of considerable depth the house platform was unlikely to change. Yet this depth may only have been reached during the final years of the structure's use-life. It seems more likely that there was some kind of social, rather than architectural, mechanism which involved the maintenance of the same house site. Unlike at most other known Bronze Age settlements in Ireland and Britain, at Corrstown the sheer size of the settlement introduces limitations of space. It is likely that at some point there was simply nowhere else to move to within the bounds of the settlement that was not already occupied or claimed in some way. Thus, when a house needed to be rebuilt, it could only be built in approximately the same location. This may also be relevant at sites where the location, while not overcrowded, was considered special in some way, and therefore required rebuilding on the same spot, as this may have been the case at Navan Fort.

The duration of the lifespan of a roundhouse has been subject to much debate. In a recent review Pope dismisses the notion that the lifespan of a roundhouse may be equated with the lifespan of a medieval timber building; in the absence of a sill beam the vertical timbers are subject to water uptake and decay rapidly (Pope 2008, 18). The charring of the outsides of vertical timbers is widely regarded as an attempt to delay this process of decay, and appears to explain the quantities of charcoal so often found in the infills of postholes. Experimental reconstructions of roundhouses have demonstrated not only the occurrence of the below-ground surface decay of vertical timbers, but also that this may not have had catastrophic results for the structure. At Butser Ancient Farm it was found that when the Pimperne House was dismantled in 1990 the building was simply standing on the ground surface and that all sub-surface timbers had rotted away. Similar occurrences are recorded at the Peat Moors visitor centre (Townsend 2007, 103). Cunliffe takes the idea a step further in suggesting that once sub-surface posts had decayed a building could be de-thatched and then moved intact to a new location, and explains some of the structural remains at Danebury as having resulted from just such a process (Cunliffe 2003, 88–9). Pope argues that a well-maintained and continually occupied roundhouse may have had the potential to last for 60 years or more, depending on the construction material.

Continual occupation is considered an essential requirement for such a long-standing lifespan because the warming and drying effect of an internal fire is vital to halt decay, and a seasonally abandoned building could be left in a damaged state for many months before the occupants' return, with potentially devastating results. Pope suggests that despite the potential for roundhouses to last for longer periods, the archaeological evidence seems to reflect a pattern whereby most roundhouses were abandoned after less than 30 years (Pope 2008, 18). At the Corrstown site numerous buildings appear to have been completely rebuilt on at least two occasions. Given the range of dates from the site, as described below, this probably occurred over a period of not less than 100 years and not more than 250 years, providing an estimated lifespan for each building of between 30 and 80 years.

The process by which buildings are seen to be replaced before the time when they became unmaintainable may be indicative of a process vital to the transmission of ideas in a pre-literate society: learning through doing. The construction of a roundhouse would be a complicated process involving an array of raw materials that were used in a variety of ways to form quite a complex architecture. In addition to the variety of complicated building procedures that would be used, a complicated series of symbolic procedures may also have been undertaken during the construction, as has been highlighted by Townsend (Townsend 2007, 104–6). In order for the preceding generations to transmit this knowledge to the succeeding generation they would need to repeat these procedures on a regular basis. Thus, when evidence is found that demonstrates the successive replacement of structures at intervals considerably shorter than the estimated maximum lifespan of a structure, we may be seeing evidence of just such communal educational procedures. Indeed, homes needed to be replaced often enough to ensure a transfer of skills. It can be envisaged that from a young age people were involved in house construction, gradually acquiring the full set of skills needed to construct a house. Children may have been involved in simple tasks such as weaving wattle panels or bunching thatch, while they watched their parents and older siblings perform more complicated tasks. As they aged they may have begun helping with carpentry and other tasks which required more strength, dexterity and stamina. Passing into late adolescence and early adulthood they may have been involved in those tasks considered most difficult or which required the greatest physical strength. If such a learning process was not being continually cycled through, then each generation would be tasked with re-inventing the process from scratch, and the archaeological record would be far less consistent over time. The difficulties encountered in certain examples of experimental archaeology illustrate rather well what occurs when this procedural chain has not been transmitted, and the techniques to obtain a particular outcome, whether it is a well-fired pot, properly dried grain, or a stable and weather-proof building, have to be invented freshly. The role of rebuilding as an educational process, rather than as a result of structural failure, has yet to be fully explored in relation to Bronze Age structures in Ireland and Britain.

4.5 Population estimates

A number of researchers have suggested quite high values for the number of people that could occupy a roundhouse. Minimum floor space (MFS) per individual varies greatly depending on the researcher. Byrd (2000, 82) calculated a MFS of *c.* 8.59 m² for his work in the southern Levant, whereas Kuijit (2000) estimated a higher MFS of 9–10 m² for his work, also in the Levant. In addition, Kuijit was able to demonstrate that the population size of the settlement fluctuated over time and that these alterations were reflected in architectural changes.

In suggesting a population level for the Corrstown structures it is worth re-iterating Alcock's insightful illustration which compares the floor plan of a typical Iron Age roundhouse (which would have a slightly larger internal area to those at Corrstown) with the floor plan of a modern two bedroomed bungalow; it finds the floor area of the two to be broadly similar, at around 90m² (Alcock 1972). Alcock emphasises that there is little available data regarding the size of prehistoric family groups, but suggests that each of the roundhouses at South Cadbury may have been occupied by 20 people (*ibid.*, 34, fig. 1). No doubt a modern European would find living in a two bedroomed bungalow with 20 other people unbearably cramped, and there is no evidence to suggest that Bronze Age people would be comfortable with such a high occupational density. A number of occupants between five and 10 is perhaps more plausible for the houses at the Corrstown settlement, and the majority of these inhabitants would most likely have been children. Certainly, if a high value for the number of people occupying each structure at Corrstown was suggested, the value for the total population would be somewhat intimidating. For instance, a value of 10 people per structure could give a population figure between 500 and 700, while a value of 20 people per structure would give a population figure between 1000 and 1400. A lower figure in line with the example of the small family group (30 households of between seven and 10 members occupying two or three structures) would give a population figure between 210 and 300 people.

An alternative method was employed by Cunliffe who used two formulas to estimate the population (P) at Danebury (Cunliffe 2003, 92–3);

$P = 146\sqrt{A}$
Where A is the total estimated area of internal floor surfaces of the settlement in metres squared.

$P = A/10m^2$
Where A is the total area of the settlement in hectares.

There are a lot of variables involved in estimating the two values for A; in particular the lack of a clearly defined perimeter of the settlement makes using these formulae more difficult than with an enclosed site as at Danebury. If for the first equation it is estimated that the settlement had an area of 2.34 hectares (195m × 120m) the figure for P (i.e. the population) is 223. If for the second equation we estimate that at any one time the settlement consisted of 60 buildings with an average of internal space of 50m² (8m × 8m), the figure for P (i.e. the population) is 300. These formulas are based on ethnographic data and it is not intended that they provide anything but very rough estimates. It does seem that all three estimates are in general terms similar and this does support the notion that a population of between 200 and 300 people may be of the correct order.

Certainly any of these estimates, varying between 200 and 1400 people, occupying the site at Corrstown during the zenith of the settlement's duration far exceeds that of any other Bronze Age community in Ireland or Britain.

4.6 Domestic unit

Some of the structures were associated with smaller, perhaps ancillary buildings (Types 1D and 1E) and this relationship may have necessitated retention of the same plot. Indeed, within the general spread of buildings at Corrstown it can be discerned that most of the structures stood as pairs or in groups of three (see Illustration 1.7). It is suggested that only S14 and S19 definitely stood in isolation and that the pair, or small group, of buildings seems to have formed a standard domestic unit within the site. Such pairs or small groups of buildings have often been noted from Bronze Age sites (e.g. Bradley 2007, 190 and notably at Reading Business Park (Brossler *et al*. 2004, 122)) and the most obvious explanation is that they represent the dwellings of a household or small extended family group. Such grouping within the larger settlement may also suggest that while property boundaries and individual plots were not physically outlined by an archaeologically identifiable means (and probably were never actually present at all), concepts of individual property and ownership were. Close examination of the plan of the settlement also reveals a difference in the pattern of grouping between the northern and southern parts of the site. The structures in the north of the site occurred mostly as pairs or small slightly irregular groups. The structures in the south of the settlement occurred mostly in linear arrangements of four structures aligned from east to west (see Illustration 1.7). It was not clear if these alignments comprised two adjacent pairs equating to two separate households, or if all of the buildings in a row formed a single larger household. The implications of this division in the groupings of the buildings between the north and the south of the site are discussed more fully below.

This pairing and grouping of structures can be seen primarily as a function of the limitations of circular architecture. Unlike a longhouse, which can in theory be lengthened indefinitely, as exemplified by the massive longhouses found at La Hersonnais, Brittany, a roundhouse has a maximum diameter determined by the mechanics of the roof design (Tinevez 2002). As the diameter of the outer wall increases, the height of the roof has to increase to maintain a pitch of 45° or greater. Eventually timbers of sufficient length are simply not available or are impractical for using as rafters. Stone roofed structures are even more sensitive to increase of diameter, because there is a very definite limit to how large a span can be covered by un-mortared rough stone corbelling. Therefore, if a family or household expands beyond a certain size, it cannot simply build a bigger roundhouse but either has to construct additional buildings or add circular modules, individually roofed, onto an existing structure. The large modular form of the Hebridean sheiling at Gearraidh

Na H'Aidre Moire recorded by Capt Thomas in the mid-19th century is an extreme example of this principle (Curwen 1938, fig. 18).

4.7 Roads and pathways

The settlement was serviced by a two-tier network of roads and pathways which consisted of one large cobbled roadway (F100), a second probable roadway that was left un-surfaced or from which the surface had been removed, and a multitude of smaller paths leading from the entrances of the houses onto the roadways (Illustrations 1.7 and 4.17–4.18). In some cases the pathways survived as cobbled tracks and in other cases their position is inferred from the location and alignment of entrances and the existence of blank spaces within the overall settlement plan.

The first roadway, F100, was the large cobbled road that ran on a sinuous southeast–northwest course through the northeastern part of the settlement. The evidence for the road terminated at S43. It ran for a total distance of *c.* 95m and was generally around 10m in width. It consisted of a layer of small stones around 0.1m deep and careful recording of the surface revealed numerous areas where it had been repaired with larger stones. S7, S43, S45, S1, and S2 had entrances connected directly onto the surface and S10, S11, S8, S4 S51, and S52 had entrances which would have been connected to it by short pathways, some parts of which had survived (Illustration 4.19). It was clear that the surface of the road was a secondary feature as it covered up and sealed a linear drain coming from S4, a number of other cut features to the west of S4, and

Illustration 4.17: S7 (from the north)

part of the entrance to S43 and had also been laid up against the western side of S7 while it was still standing. However, the secondary cobbled surface must have been laid in the area of an un-surfaced roadway on a very similar alignment because no structures had previously been built in this area and at least 12 structures had been designed so that their entrances led into this area either directly or via pathways. The small cobbled pathway that led to the road surface from S51 and S52 survived in part and its western end had actually been covered over by the road surface.

While the road terminated in the area around S43, at the north of the site, at the eastern end it extended beyond the area of the settlement, maintaining its width and the dense cobbling. Ultimately, the road was traced as far as the large spoil heaps at the eastern boundary of the excavation area, beyond which it would have been destroyed by mid-20th-century housing. The sections of the road which were located within the Corrstown settlement would have had little purpose once the settlement was abandoned. As the road went out of use, it was not subject to the downward erosion pressures which would have ultimately worn away the surface and probably left the road as an extremely difficult to date feature.

The second possible roadway lay towards the west of the settlement running from the south of S6 between S38 and S8, past S53 and S54, between S13 and S14, and then S30 and S23. It was of roughly similar width to the cobbled road surface F100, and again seems integral to the layout and design of the settlement. It was not surfaced in cobble at the same time as F100 was laid, or perhaps the cobbled surface simply did not survive to be excavated. S6, S48, S38, and S54 had large cobbled areas which

Illustration 4.18: Cobbled surface to the south of S38 (mid excavation, from the northwest)

Illustration 4.19: S10 and S11 with the road running along the top of the photograph (mid excavation, from the west)

would have led onto the second roadway, and S53, S14, S30, S31, and S33 were all in locations that suggest they had pathways that also connected to the second road. If the full length of the second roadway is accepted then the implication is clear: both the northern and southern halves of the settlement were occupied simultaneously.

The network of pathways is another aspect of the settlement that indicates that many of the buildings were simultaneously occupied. From the ends of the entrances the paths ran directly east–west, obviously avoiding the rears of the structures located to the south. A particularly interesting example of this is the un-surfaced pathway that must have been used to leave S41, past the entrances of S40, S11 and S10 and onto the roadway F100. Here, although the second road is physically closer, access is blocked by the rears of S48, S6, S5, and S45. Certain pathways existed that could be used to access both roadways, such as the path to the south of S1 and S8, or the path to the south of S2 and S12.

In the southern half of the site, the alignment of the entrances of the structures belonging to the east–west groups clearly implies the presence of east–west pathways. Indeed, a long portion of one such path survived as a narrow cobbled surface running from the south of S19 past the entrance of S20 and S56/57 and then connected onto the second roadway. A particularly interesting, if presently unanswered, question is whether the small pathways leading up to groups of buildings led into private spaces for the use of the occupiers, or whether access was freely granted across the site.

4.8 The roads in context

The survival of the roads and trackways at the Corrstown settlement is of particular importance. Prehistoric roads are not very common in the archaeological record, especially in low-land and non-wetland areas. The most famous ancient Irish road, the Esker Riada, runs from Dublin to Galway and follows glacial ridges that would have facilitated travel across the deep bogs of the Irish midlands, and is in essence very similar to the English ridgeways. It is not clear when this routeway was first used but certainly it was well established by the late prehistoric period. The Irish Annals give details of five ancient highways leading from Tara and again prehistoric origins for these have to be suspected. Certainly Jordan and O'Conor have provided a compelling case for the prehistoric origin of the Slí Dala in the vicinity of Turoe, Co. Galway, as well as several lesser roads in that area (Jordan and O' Conor 2003, 112–14). Various pilgrim paths, which run between places of importance to early medieval churches, have also been suspected as having prehistoric foundations. For example, the Tochar Phadraig that runs from Ballintubber Abbey for 22 miles to Croagh Patrick passes numerous (often Christianized) standing stones and the important rock art site, the Boheh Stone (Corlett 1998, 17–18; Morahan 2001, 81), which suggests a prehistoric origin.

More direct evidence of Bronze Age routeways is represented by the large numbers of roads located in the Irish bogs (Raferty 1999, 170). The earliest of these roads date from the Neolithic but their use and construction extends into the medieval period and beyond, and there is a clear concentration of them which date to the Bronze Age. Their construction is often assumed to reflect increasingly wet conditions which resulted in an expansion of the amount of bogland in Ireland. Constructed in a variety of ways these trackways were used to cross wet areas, or to access their interiors. The trackways demonstrate the ability of people to undertake large civil engineering schemes and imply varying degrees of social organization and resource management (Coles *et al.* 1978, 19). The frequency at with which they have been located suggests that they were built in great number, as typified by the multitude of tracks found in proximity at Derryoghil, Co. Longford. However, for various reasons it has not yet been possible to directly translate this frequency of wetland routeways to dryland sites (Raferty 1999). The majority of the dryland tracks which have been identified are quite ephemeral routes, seemingly suitable only for pedestrian traffic. However, the well-known Iron Age timber road found in Corlea, Co. Longford, and the recently discovered example in Annaholty, Co. Tipperary, are of a far larger scale, and compare well with the width of the road at Corrstown (Rafterry 1995; Taylor 2008). The Corlea road had little sign of wear and has been interpreted as having a symbolic function, possibly leading out into the deep bog to a sacred location of some sort; the excavator of the more recently discovered site at Annaholty offers a more pragmatic explanation and suggests that this road is simply part of a large network running across the bog and linking areas of higher ground.

The physical remains of prehistoric roads have been much harder to identify on drier land. The authors have only been able to identify a single excavated Irish site that has unequivocal evidence of a formally surfaced prehistoric road: Tullyallen, Co. Louth, where two shallow linear features with cobbled bases ran across the site

(Linnane 2002). The tracks were around 2m in width and although incomplete, their courses could be traced right across the site, a distance of around 200m. The base of the track contained two parallel groves which the excavator interpreted as being created by carts with an axle width of 1.5m. The tracks were not internal features of the settlement area, although they presumably were accessed from the settlement. The trackways appeared to be medium distance route-ways running from the River Boyne to the Hill of Rath, a distance of approximately 1.5km. The dating of this site is unclear but it was thought by the excavator to belong to the Bronze Age. Examples of later prehistoric roads seem to be a regular component of ritual complexes later associated with the inauguration ceremonies of the high kings, such as the numerous examples recorded with the Rathcroghan complex in Co. Roscommon, and possibly the Riverstown earthwork close to the Hill of Tara (Condit 1993; Waddell 1983). These possible roadways have not been subject to any particularly intensive study and at present little is unknown about their date or function. Indeed, when they are described they are often called ceremonial ways, and their relevance to the purely functional roads and paths found at Corrstown may be limited.

Perhaps the most intriguing aspect of the road at Corrstown was that it was last recorded disappearing beyond the eastern boundary of the site, where it had retained its size for a considerable distance beyond the core settlement area. It is simply not possible to determine where the road originated, but two possibilities can be suggested. The road may have been the terminal of a long track leading to the settlement from somewhere to the east. Alternatively, the road may have branched off a long distance routeway leading from the coast, much like the track found at Tullyallen that ran from the Boyne to the Hill of Rath (Linnane 2002).

4.9 Enclosure

Although unenclosed Middle Bronze Age settlements exist (e.g. Kerlogue, Co. Wexford, Kilmurray, Co. Wicklow, and Lisheen, Co. Tipperary (McLoughlin 2002; Ó Néill 2005; Ó Néill 2001)) it was relatively common on Middle Bronze Age settlement sites to be located in an enclosing ditch. Brück (1997) found that 65% of Middle Bronze Age sites in Britain were enclosed and as the buildings at the Corrstown site formed a dense, oval-shaped cluster, such an enclosure might have been expected. However, no evidence for an enclosing element was discovered, despite a large area of empty ground being exposed along the east and south of the site. A small but steeply sided valley, containing a small stream, marked the western side of the site, and this may have acted as a natural barrier on this side of the settlement. At Reading Business Park it was noted that the houses formed an almost circular cluster despite there being no evidence for an enclosing ditch. There it was suggested that a hedge might have performed this function (Brossler *et al.* 2004, 121).

The road surface, F100, continued uninterrupted out beyond the eastern boundary of the site, and this rather implies that the settlement could be freely accessed; there was no evidence for a barrier or gate.

4.10 Chronology

At some stage during the Middle Bronze Age, *c.* 1550 BC, the settlement at Corrstown became occupied. A Neolithic presence on the site was attested to by the presence of some of the stone artefacts and the pottery but no direct settlement evidence prior to these Bronze Age roundhouses was forthcoming during the excavations. A total of 37 radiocarbon dates was obtained for the site, of which 29 were associated with the original excavation (28 samples (unidentified charcoal) were processed at CHRONO and one sample (alder) was processed at Beta Analytic Inc, Florida) and a further eight samples (identified to species) were funded by and processed at CHRONO. Four early medieval dates were returned, along with one Iron Age and one Mesolithic date (the prehistoric dates are given in Table 4.3; Illustration 4.20).

An unfortunate side-effect of the unidentified charcoal samples was the possibility that they may have all derived from oak. The returned radiocarbon dates then could have unknowingly suffered from the 'old wood' effect, and date the older wood, rather than the occupation of the settlement. As oak can grow for hundreds of years the 'old wood' effect can have a considerable impact upon interpreting chronologies. Lorna O'Donnell identified predominantly hazel and alder in the additional eight samples (a ninth sample was identified as oak and therefore not submitted for dating). In some instances (e.g. S4, S33 and S47) the new dates did help to reduce the range associated with the structure by 30–40 years. In other instances (e.g. S17, S23, S37, and S40) the ranges increased by 10–50 years; however, as these dates have associated identified charcoal they reflect a more accurate depiction.

Overall, the majority of these dates returned a remarkable degree of consistency and had a reasonably low error range, averaging ±33 years. The sample taken from the ditch of S1 (2016–1772 BC, UBA-6230) pre-dates the others by a considerable period. As it is considerably earlier than the remaining dates it is likely that the charcoal derived from residual material. The latest date in the sequence was obtained from a pit located in the entrance of S13 (1022–844 BC; UB-6245). This pit contained burnt stones in a charcoal-rich matrix and represented the only example of possible burnt mound activity on the site. It was positioned in the entrance of S13 and therefore post-dated the occupation of this structure. The later date suggests that it may also post-date occupation of the settlement as a whole.

Two diseparate sets of dates were obtained from S33: the latest (1261–1022 BC; UB-6233 and 1260–1055 BC; UBA-16609) from a spread overlying the house and the earliest (1490–1305 BC; UB-6235) from a stakehole beneath the spread. The later dates may relate to the destruction of the house or to an activity which took place thereafter. The earlier date is more closely associated with the occuapation of the structure and accords with the date obtained from S31 (1497–1318 BC; UB-6236), a house abutting the east of S33. The dates may also represent the lifespan of the occupation of the house: although the range, at 45–468 years, is considerable.

The remaining radiocarbon dates span the period from *c.* 1600–1000 BC, with a concentration between *c.* 1500 and 1300 BC. When the earliest and latest dates are removed, Illustration 4.20 suggests three broad phases of activity, with the majority of the houses being broadly contemporary. McSparron (Appendix I) modelled the

Structure	Lab	Lab Code	Date Type	Calibrated Date	Conventional Date	13C/12C	Charcoal
S1	UB	6230	AMS	2016–1772 BC	3556±34	N/A	Unidentified
S4	UB	6231	AMS	1431–1270 BC	3090±32	N/A	Unidentified
S4	*UBA*	*16615*	*AMS*	*1424–1302 BC*	*3089±24*	*-21.8*	*Hazel*
S8	UB	6240	AMS	1601–1415 BC	3210±33	N/A	Unidentified
S9	Beta	190132	AMS	1261–935 BC	2900±50	N/A	Alder
S13	UB	6245	AMS	1022–844 BC	2796±32	N/A	Unidentified
S15	UB	6378	AMS	1410–1211 BC	3041±34	-26.9	Unidentified
S15	UB	6242	AMS	359–95 BC	2157±31	N/A	Unidentified
S17	UB	6381	AMS	1429–1268 BC	3086±34	-26.1	Unidentified
S17	*UBA*	*16611*	*AMS*	*1413–1213 BC*	*3050±35*	*-23.7*	*Hazel*
S19	UB	6247	AMS	1665–1497 BC	3293±32	N/A	Unidentified
S19	UB	6246	AMS	1614–1452 BC	3256±32	N/A	Unidentified
S21	UB	6379	AMS	1531–1409 BC	3199±35	-27.7	Unidentified
S23	UB	6249	AMS	1408–1213 BC	3041±32	N/A	Unidentified
S23	*UBA*	*16610*	*AMS*	*1260–1055 BC*	*2946±25*	*-34.9*	*Hazel*
S30	UB	6234	AMS	1416–1265 BC	3072±32	N/A	Unidentified
S31	UB	6236	AMS	1497–1318 BC	3141±33	N/A	Unidentified
S33	UB	6235	AMS	1490–1305 BC	3117±33	N/A	Unidentified
S33	UB	6233	AMS	1261–1022 BC	2932±33	N/A	Unidentified
S33	*UBA*	*16609*	*AMS*	*1260–1055 BC*	*2946±27*	*-29.5*	*Alder*
S37	UB	6238	AMS	1440–1293 BC	3101±32	N/A	Unidentified
S37	*UBA*	*16612*	*AMS*	*1384–1212 BC*	*3024±22*	*-26.1*	*Alder*
S40	UB	6241	AMS	1410–1215 BC	3048±32	N/A	Unidentified
S40	*UBA*	*16614*	*AMS*	*1374–1130 BC*	*3003±24*	*-29.6*	*Alder*
S43	UB	6239	AMS	1497–1320 BC	3143±33	N/A	Unidentified
S45	UB	6248	AMS	1416–1264 BC	3068±31	N/A	Unidentified
S47	UB	6382	AMS	1502–1322 BC	3156±35	N/A	Unidentified
S47	*UBA*	*16608*	*AMS*	*1432–1312 BC*	*3103±26*	*-32.8*	*Hazel*
S58	UB	6243	AMS	1511–1406 BC	3178±32	N/A	Unidentified
S65	UB	6244	AMS	1499–1324 BC	3153±32	N/A	Unidentified
S68	UB	6380	AMS	1421–1265 BC	3076±34	-25.1	Unidentified
S70	UB	6250	AMS	6461–6255 BC	7522±44	N/A	Unidentified
S76	UB	6251	AMS	1493–1312 BC	3129±31	N/A	Unidentified

IntCal 09

Reimer, P. J., Baillie, M. G. L., Bard, E., Bayliss, A., Bayliss, A., Beck, J. W., Blackwell, P. G., Bronk Ramsey, C., Buck, C. E. Burr, G. S., Edwards, R. L., Friedrich, M., Grootes, P. M., Guilderson, T. P., Hajdas, I., Heaton, T. J., Hogg, A. G., Hughen, K. A., Kaiser, K. F., Kromer, B., McCormac, F. G., Manning, S. W., Reimer, R. W., Richards, D. A., Southon, J. R., Talamo, S., Turney, C. S. M., van der Plicht, J., Weyhenmeyer, C. E. (2009) IntCal09 and Marine09 Radiocaron Calibration Curves, 0–50,000 Years cal BP. *Radiocarbon* 51, 1111–50.

Dates in italics were funded by Chrono as part of Ginn's PhD research and kindly identified by Lorna O'Donnell

Table 4.3: Prehistoric radiocarbon dates from Corrstown (those in italics are those obtained from Chrono, QUB, as part of Ginn's PhD research)

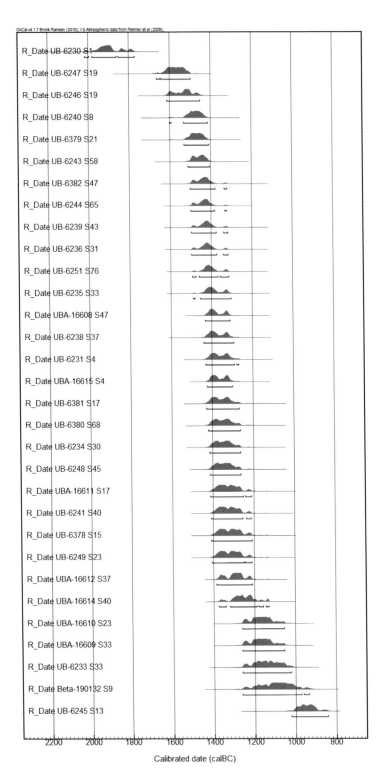

OxCal v4.1.7 Bronk Ramsey (2010); r:5 Atmospheric data from Reimer et al (2009);

R_Date UB-6230 S1
R_Date UB-6247 S19
R_Date UB-6246 S19
R_Date UB-6240 S8
R_Date UB-6379 S21
R_Date UB-6243 S58
R_Date UB-6382 S47
R_Date UB-6244 S65
R_Date UB-6239 S43
R_Date UB-6236 S31
R_Date UB-6251 S76
R_Date UB-6235 S33
R_Date UBA-16608 S47
R_Date UB-6238 S37
R_Date UB-6231 S4
R_Date UBA-16615 S4
R_Date UB-6381 S17
R_Date UB-6380 S68
R_Date UB-6234 S30
R_Date UB-6248 S45
R_Date UBA-16611 S17
R_Date UB-6241 S40
R_Date UB-6378 S15
R_Date UB-6249 S23
R_Date UBA-16612 S37
R_Date UBA-16614 S40
R_Date UBA-16610 S23
R_Date UBA-16609 S33
R_Date UB-6233 S33
R_Date Beta-190132 S9
R_Date UB-6245 S13

2200   2000   1800   1600   1400   1200   1000   800

Calibrated date (calBC)

Illustration 4.20: Chart displaying the Bronze Age radiocarbon dates

radiocarbon dates and tightened the chronological resolution of the three phases, describing them as the Growth Phase (commencing after 1550 BC, most likely after 1460 BC and lasting between 0 and 260 years), the Village Phase (commencing 1360–1270 BC and lasting between 35 and 155 years), and the Decline Phase (commencing after 1150 BC and lasting between 80 and 300 years).

That much of the activity was concentrated to one phase was also borne out in the spatial organization of the site and the retention of individual house sites even during periods of modification and rebuild. As the houses respect each other and modifications and rebuilds generally occurred on the same spot, it was difficult to ascertain a sequence of development. Spatial and typological analyses did indicate that some of the more centrally located structures, such as S4 and S19, could have been among the earliest constructed roundhouses (see below). Certainly, two of the earliest dates come from S19, which is the only structure to be enclosed with an additional ditch and it is likely that this house represents the origin of the Corrstown settlement. Modelling the radiocarbon dates suggested that activity on site neither began nor ended abruptly and instead most likely grew from an initial nucleus of structures (McSparron, Appendix I). When McSparron colour-coded the structures according to their radiocarbon phase the likelihood that S19 represents the focal point of the settlement was visually demonstrated (Illustration AI.6).

The combination of the radiocarbon dates, the structural analysis and the spatial analysis suggest that the overall duration of the occupation at the Corrstown settlement was relatively succinct, *c.* 250 years. The artefact assemblage is also remarkably consistent, and with the noticeable exception of a small quantity of residual Neolithic pottery and the polished stone axe fragments, there is no indication of a wide chronology within either the pottery or lithic assemblages. It should be noted, however, that due to the plain nature of the pottery and the crude nature of the flint work, this material is not particularly conclusive to precise or sequential dating. Modelling of the radiocarbon dates (McSparron: Appendix I) suggested that the occupation was slightly shorter: *c.* 200 years long. Certainly, the main occuapational phase of the settlement must have endured for at least several generations, given the numbers of repairs and rebuilds evident on the majority of the structures. It is therefore likely that the Village Phase lasted between 100 and 200 years.

The overall layout of the structures within the settlement emphasises a well-organized aspect, strongly indicative of some form of planning process occurring prior to or at the very beginning of construction. With the possible exception of S19, no single point of nucleation was apparent and no evidence of settlement drift has been identified. While the radiocarbon dates demonstrate that many of the buildings were broadly contemporary, they do not provide enough resolution to determine a precise chronology of development within the settlement. Fortunately, analysis of spatial patterning among the building and artefact distribution across the site has permitted a slightly more developed understanding of the settlement's internal chronology.

4.11 Spatial analysis

Three westsouthwest–eastnortheast rows of structures are present at the centre of the site: S13, S15, S55, S27, and S60 form the first and approximately 20m south of this row lies S22, S21, S56, and S20. Approximately 20m south again from this row is S70/S76/S69, S58, S59, S68, and S73; all forming a grid pattern (Illustration 4.21). Two long double northwest–southeast alignments are also apparent and formed by S43, S10, S45, S1, S2, S74, S27, S44, S20, S68, S71, and S64 along the most easterly and S40, S11, S5, S8, S12, S16, S55, S29, S28, S56, S72, S59, S67, and S65 along the more westerly, with the structures on either side forming west–east 'side streets' (e.g. S13, S15 and S60 as well as S23, S22, S21, and S19) (Illustration 4.21). The majority of the structures associated with these alignments are located in the north of the settlement. They are characterised by pairs and small groups of buildings set adjacent to each other in a way that the entrances opened onto east–west-aligned paths that led to the roads. These two approaches are not necessarily chronologically mutually exclusive as the three rows of structures exist to the south of the site and the two alignments are more discernable in the north.

The above-mentioned patterns indicate that the northern and southern halves of the site may have been organized differently or may have developed at different times. Indeed, the north of the site is characterised by small pairs or groups of structures aligned to either side of the two roadways, while the south of the site is primarily formed by the three rows. The distribution of the artefacts suggested that the northern part of the site may be older than the southern and eastern parts (see below). McSparron's modelling of the radiocarbon dates indicated that three of the houses in the southern half of the site were among the initial Growth Phase of the settlement's development (Illustration AI.6). However, houses belonging to the Village Phase were present in both the northern and southern halves. The available radiocarbon dating evidence does then seem to suggest that the southern half of the site developed earlier than the northern and that S19 did provide a focus for growth. This two-fold division is common in villages and there is a tendency for such settlements to divide in two on a social level: such as upper and lower, north and south (Chris Lynn, pers. comm.).

4.11.1 Typological analysis

The categorisation and sub-division of the structure types, albeit slightly arbitrary, can perhaps shed light on the sequence of development on the site. When plotted on the site plan (Illustration 4.22) four patterns are immediately apparent: the Type 2 structures were located around the periphery of the site, noticeably to the south and, apart from S33, they were not associated with any other structures; Type 1E structures, the abutting structures that shared elements with their neighbours, were predominantly located along the west of the site; five of the Type 1B (concentric, segmented ditch), structures ran in a north–south alignment while the other two are located close by, one on the other side of road F100; and the Type 1A (single segmented ditch) structures lay beyond the Type 1C (conjoined segmented ditch) and Type 1B structures but, for the most part, did not spread beyond the Type 2 examples.

Illustration 4.21: Spatial analysis of the site, note the three WSW–ENE rows and the two northwest–southeast alignments

Illustration 4.22: Typological analysis of the structure types

Structure Number	No of Pottery Sherds	MNV (Pottery)	Amount of Strat Flint (kg)	Unstrat flint
18	0	0	0	0
25	0	0	0	0
32	0	0	0	0
39	0	0	0	0
49	0	0	1.439	0
61	0	0	7.517	0
63	0	0	0.266	0.195
66	0	0	2.761	0
67	0	0	0.255	0
68	0	0	0.383	0
76	0	0	0.208	0
34	1	0	1.605	0
36	1	0	0	0
50	1	0	0	0
44	2	0	0	0
74	2	0	0	0
10	3	1	5.562	0.36
62	4	3	0.314	0.99
24	5	1	0.23	0
64	5	4	0	0
20	6	1	0.256	0
11	8	1	1.938	0
30	8	0	1.097	0
75	12	2	1.12	0
46	15	3	4.039	0.493
60	15	4	0	0
47	18	2	5.772	0
73	20	3	1.282	0
31	21	6	4.894	0
22	24	1	0.128	0
43	25	2	3.531	0
14	26	4	10.036	0
35	26	4	2.342	0
45	26	3	4.61	0
71	27	2	0.5	0.198
29	28	3	8.755	0
40	29	3	2.394	0
65	29	4	0.863	0
27	31	6	0.25	0

Structure Number	No of Pottery Sherds	MNV (Pottery)	Amount of Strat Flint (kg)	Unstrat flint
57	33	8	2.985	0
48	35	4	10.621	3.83
51	37	5	2.034	0
23	38	2	1.239	0
41	42	6	2.377	4.092
72	51	1	3.356	0
9	53	3	2.286	0
21	55	2	2.859	0
52	57	7	8.878	0.254
42	66	5	10.795	0
7	79	3	10.229	0
17	83	8	2.565	3.017
33	83	8	15.222	0.3
55	86	9	6.54	0
2	90	9	8.242	4.288
53	94	6	2.891	0
16	95	7	13.81	0.02
26	102	4	0.254	0
69	114	7	2.009	0
56	119	13	11.799	0
28	140	16	3.957	3.895
70	146	6	5.08	1.988
59	161	14	10.192	2.32
19	166	20	5.794	0
15	173	2	6.968	3.011
Road	176	-	0.048	0
8	193	7	21.189	0.555
3	195	8	2.05	0
37	196	20	33.266	0
12	198	10	10.89	3.585
38	226	29	50.799	8.46
54	264	19	4.627	0
58	265	19	21.431	4.517
5	268	24	37.572	0
6	291	16	13.682	0
1	294	16	30.354	2.666
13	697	2	30.23	12
4	711	36	41.179	1.954

Table 4.4: Artefact analysis

Illustration 4.23: Artefact analysis based on the quantity of pottery sherds per structure

4.11.2 Artefact analysis

It was felt that the pottery sherds, rather than the flint, would be most appropriate to analyse, as most of the flint represented waste rather than tools. As with the sub-division of the Type 1 structures, the categories for the pottery sherd quantities were somewhat arbitrary. In Illustration 4.23 and Table 4.4 the groups and distinctions can be observed. Those structures with no pottery sherds were present along the eastern edge and southern side of the settlement while those with only very limited quantities (1–49) were represented either by ancillaries and annexes or by somewhat peripheral structures along the north and south of the site. The structures with the greatest concentration of pottery sherds were present in the centre of the site, with the exception of S38 and S58. S4 had over 300 sherds of associated pottery and S38, S54, S58, S5, S6, and S1 had substantial quantities: over 200 sherds.

This pattern was tested using the minimum number of vessels associated with the structures, in case the results differed greatly. The differences were not substantial, and the structures with the highest numbers of pottery sherds also had the highest MNV (see Table 4.4).

Just in case there were any parallels between the flint and the pottery count and this pattern, the flint was added to the table (Table 4.4). For many of the structures there was not a strong correlation; however, the structures with the most flint and pottery were S5, S38 (associated with a mould), S8 (associated with a mould), S1 (associated with a mould and the macehead), S4 (road nearby associated with a mould), S37 (associated with the miniature axe), S13, and S58.

4.11.3 Discussion

When the evidence from these analyses is combined, it would seem most likely that, unless the Type 1B and 1C structures were functionally very different, they were the earliest on site, or more accurately, they were the locations of the longest periods of occupation. The artefact analysis goes some way to supporting this argument as does the morphology of Type 1B structures which seems to represent multiple phases of rebuilding on the same site. These particular structures were sited close to the road, in a rough north–south alignment in the north section of the site, thereby giving weight to elements of the above-mentioned spatial analysis. All three aspects of this analysis, spatial, typological and artefact, suggest that the structures in the southern half of the site, and those along the eastern periphery, were perhaps the latest in the development sequence; they were ordered roughly southwest–northeast (indicating organization, planning and perhaps an element of control), have dissimilar, indeed simpler, extant archaeological footprints, and have few or no associated pottery sherds.

Chapter 5

From Inception to Abandonment

In this chapter a more detailed assessment regarding the lives and activities of the Corrstown inhabitants is given.

5.1 The significance of the Corrstown landscape: with contributions by Maria Lear

The north Irish coastline is very particular in its structure and natural formation process that occurred during the time immediately following the deglaciation of the late Quaternary period (Cooper *et al*. 2002, 369). Portrush (*c*. 1km north of the site at Corrstown), or more specifically, Ramore Headland, was formed on a promontory of bedrock, one of many (e.g. nearby at Portstewart) along the north coast and has remained largely unchanged for millennia. Pocket beaches such as Curran Strand and Portstewart Strand intersperse these promontories. The seafloor of the Malin Sea near Portrush is generally sandy (Lawlor 2000) and sand dunes, up to 25m in height, extend inland for several kilometres (Carter and Bartlett 1990). Before the end of the Mesolithic period, it has been estimated that the sea-level was approximately 30m lower than it currently is (Cooper *et al*. 2002). However, attempts at modelling the levels of sea and land in this area in the post-Mesolithic period have been detrimentally affected by the paucity of data (Lambeck 1996). Cooper *et al*. (2002) and Kelley *et al*. (2006) have demonstrated that peat deposits in this area, now located off-shore on the continental shelf, were once part of the Mesolithic dry landscape: the lowland shoreline position had shifted by a distance of approximately 30m after the Mesolithic period. Dating this shift has been difficult (Cooper *et al*. 2002 and Kelley *et al*. 2006) but it is likely that by the time that Corrstown was inhabited in the Bronze Age it had already occurred and the coastline, with the exception of the more mobile sand dune elements, resembled its present form.

The suitability of this landscape for habitation is evidenced by several large megalithic tombs (SMR ANT 006:016, SMR ANT 006:017 and SMR ANT 006:009) in the vicinity of Corrstown, by the undated prehistoric settlement site at the White Rocks, close to Corrstown (SMR ANT 002:012) (Knowles 1886) and by the presence of the Mesolithic site at Mount Sandel (Woodman 1985) at nearby Coleraine. Excavation in advance of an extension of the car park at Portrush Golf Course uncovered an old land surface peppered with Neolithic flints, debitage and pottery sherds, as well as a small, stone-built cist which contained an adult skeleton but which remains undated (Collins 1971, 3).

With the basalt promontories remaining almost constant and the stabilisation of the sea-level, the inhabitants of Bronze Age Corrstown were ideally positioned (20–30m above the coastline) to exploit a permanent, relatively unchanging landscape. The immediate vicinity of the site would most likely have been dominated by sand dunes and possibly salt marsh and probably extended as far as the coast.

The coast, visible from the site, is a short walk away, and such proximity must have been an enticing factor when deciding to settle in the area as the short distance to the sea would have provided access to salt water food resources and marine life. The Skerries, a chain of islands that were formed by the presence of a dolerite sill, may have been both visible and also accessible from the coast.

Rathlin Island, with its source of porcellanite, is visible from the coastline and is only 29km away by boat and Scotland, located 55km to the east and also visible from Portrush, would have been reachable by boat in less than a day (Armit 1996, 6). While the evidence indicates that there was not a land bridge between Ireland and Scotland during the Holocene and post-Holocene period, it does demonstrate the presence of shallow waters, shoals and small islands between the north coast of Ireland and the west coast of Scotland which could have facilitated sailing between the two countries and may have even provided a semi-dry route. However, considering the seasonal nature of the currents in the Irish Sea it would have been easier to make certain journeys at particular times which may otherwise have been difficult (Brown *et al.* 2003). The coast of Co. Donegal is startlingly visible from the site and could have been accessed more easily by sea than overland. Indeed, the inhabitants of Corrstown could have had good maritime connections, not only around the north coast of Ireland and the Atlantic coast of Scotland, but the longer routes of the Atlantic Seaways would also have been accessible to them (Cunliffe 2001). Although not visible from the site or the immediate coastline, the Rivers Foyle, Bann and Bush were all in proximity to the settlement at Corrstown. The River Bann was the closest and would have provided easy access into the interior of the country. Inland waterways were navigated by boats, of which examples survive in the form of dugout canoes/boats (e.g. Lanting and Brindley 1996). The greatest concentration of the earliest Early Bronze Age swords (Class 1) has come from the River Bann (Waddell 1998). A look at the artefacts' distributions for the Bronze Age repeatedly suggests a link between Co. Antrim, and in particular the River Bann, and the Thames Estuary (*ibid.* figs 82, 94 and 132; Waddell 1991) and perhaps some of the Corrstown inhabitants were aware of or even involved in this trade. With these routeways and waterways, the Corrstown settlement was ideally situated to maximise the opportunities for trade and communication.

The inland landscape was neither less accessible nor less attractive than that of the coastal areas. The land behind the site continues to rise and two standing stones, one, the 'White Wife' (SMR LDY 003:011), located on a low ridge and visible from a wide distance and the other, the 'stone of gold' (SMR ANT 006:011), are still located on two high points behind the site. A further two standing stones were located within the immediate vicinity of the site (SMR ANT 003:050–051) but their precise locations are no longer known. Other possible Bronze Age monuments and sites exist in the vicinity, including an urned cremation at Ballywillan church (SMR ANT 006:015) a mere 0.59km east of the site, although recent attempts to more accurately identify the precise placement of the urn have unfortunately not been successful.

The ground beneath the settlement at Corrstown is a basalt till characterised by brown, relatively dry or moist gley soil indicating well-drained ground conditions. The area was used for pasture throughout the post-medieval period and must have provided attractive agricultural land during the Bronze Age, even if direct evidence for agrarian activity was limited to the small quantities of carbonised grain and seed.

It is likely that the site was surrounded with available resources to be exploited, such as a sustainable supply of timber. Only one wood identification was initially obtained during the excavations: alder from S9. Further species identification was carried out on the remaining eight samples by Lorna O'Donnell and both hazel and alder were discerned. Alder is frequently located in damp areas, such as damp woodland, streams and rivers and survives in poor soils (O'Donnell 2007, 29; Orme and Coles 1985, 7). It burns quickly and does not give out much heat and is therefore uncommon as a fuel; it is more suitable for construction as it is light, soft, and easy to work and durable when immersed in water (O'Donnell 2007, 29; Gale and Cutler 2000). Alder was frequently used to make axe handles and it would have also been used in the construction of buildings (O'Donnell 2007, 31). Hazel grows in dry–wet conditions, is frequently associated with managed oak and has traditionally been recovered in Bronze Age contexts as wattle (*ibid.* 29). Other wood species, notably oak (*Quercus* spp.), were also used in the construction of Bronze Age roundhouses and are most likely to be present at Corrstown. Alder and hazel, oak, and ash (*Faxinus excelsior*) would have been used for cooking, oak for cremations, hazel for construction, and oak for metalworking (O'Donnell 2007, 64–5).

Local deforestation may have taken place as and when required and much wood would have been needed to construct and maintain all the 74 roundhouses at the Corrstown site. It was found that a single reconstructed roundhouse at Castle Henllys, Pembrokeshire, required 26 oak roof rafters, 24 oak wall posts, 3,125 hazel poles, 2,000 bundles of reeds, 600m of hemp rope, 2,000m of tarred hemp twine, and 15 tonnes of clay mixed with cow dung (Mytum 1999; Mytum 1987). Although the reconstructed house at Castle Henllys is a different type of house, it is a useful comparison. Obviously if these figures were scaled up to accommodate the number of buildings present at the Corrstown settlement then the volume of materials would become quite staggering. Such resources would have necessitated the considerable exploitation and maintenance of the surrounding area.

The location of Bronze Age settlements is very diverse (Waddell 1998, 205) and both low-lying and upland areas were used to a greater degree than they had been previously (Cooney and Grogan 1999, 105). The geology of the area, the abundant sources of flint, the unique sources of porcellanite at Rathlin Island and Tievebulliagh in nearby Ballycastle, the proximity to fresh and salt water, the accessibility and suitability of the hinterland for farming would have all combined as important factors as to why the land at Corrstown was chosen for settlement.

5.2 The diet of the Corrstown inhabitants

Unfortunately, the acidity level of the soil in the area was such that little faunal evidence was recovered (a hypothetical portrayal of the animals that would have played a vital role in the daily life of Corrstown is shown in Illustration 1.7). Only a few internal hearths were noted in the roundhouses and there was no evidence of a communal burnt stone mound as has been recorded at some other Bronze Age settlement sites e.g. Reading Business Park (Brossler *et al.* 2004). Conclusive data on patterns of Bronze Age livestock consumption in Ireland are not forthcoming in the published literature and only a small number of sites, such as Ballyveelish, Co. Tipperary, and Lough Gur, Co. Limerick (Doody 1987), have had a significant corpus of faunal material examined by specialists. At Ballyveelish, Co. Tipperary (*ibid.*), which was occupied slightly later than the Corrstown settlement, 1130–810 BC, the faunal remains indicated that cattle were predominant on site (42.9%) followed by pig (35.7%) and then sheep/goat (16.7%) whereas at the lakeside settlement of Lough Gur, Co. Limerick (occupied 1200–800 BC), pig remains represented 50.5% of the remains, followed by cattle (38%) and then sheep/goat (10%). As both of these sites were very different from the settlement at Corrstown the faunal analysis cannot be used to suggest exactly what the inhabitants at Corrstown consumed. The proximity of the Corrstown settlement to the coast would have facilitated access to marine food reserves and seafood would have surely been exploited and consumed on a regular basis by the Corrstown inhabitants.

Cereals would also have formed an important part of the Corrstown diet. Barley was the predominant cereal identified in the Corrstown assemblage (Chapter 3) and it was, especially towards the Late Bronze Age and the Iron Age, the most common cereal of the era (Johnston 2007, 70; Greig 1991; Hjelmqvist 1980). Wheat was also represented at Corrstown, but in lesser quantities. This Middle–Late Bronze Age preference for barley rather than the previously commonly consumed wheat, also seen at Charlesland, Co. Wicklow, which occurred in the Middle Bronze Age / Late Bronze Age transition may represent 'another facet' (Johnston 2007, 73) of the social and cultural Late Bronze Age changes as demonstrated primarily through new settlement patterns and material culture (Waddell 1998; O'Kelly 1989, 151).

It is possible that much of the food the inhabitants required could have been obtained from trading with smaller farming groups in the surrounding area (perhaps, for example, Cappagh Beg (Appendix IIII)). There is evidence that some sites acquired produce that was processed elsewhere, such as at Haughey's Fort, Co. Armagh (Weir 1993). Although it seems likely that this phenomenon was restricted to high status sites, it is also likely that produce was shared, at least within the settlement at Corrstown. With such a large population undoubtedly a substantial amount of food would have been required and cooked on a daily basis. As mentioned above, there were few structures with definite evidence for internal hearths (e.g. S6, S9 and S33) but this is a recognisable trend in the Bronze Age (Doody 2000, 145) and indicates that the hearths were most likely set above the ground level or that communal cooking was practised.

Plunkett's work at Garry Bog, less than 10km from the Corrstown settlement, has demonstrated the existence of two phases of agricultural activity in the Bronze Age which correspond with the occupation of the settlement at Corrstown (Plunkett 1999).

During the first phase, the flora suggests a mixed economy, with multiple crops, that persisted for at least two centuries, up until approximately the beginning of 1100 BC. An expansion was noted in the second phase which corresponded with a hiatus in bog growth (approximately during 1150 and 1140 BC). Wetter conditions then increased and bog growth resumed; there was no evidence for arable agriculture in this phase of activity. This onset of wetter climatic conditions and reduction in arable agriculture in the locality coincides with the lower end of the spread of radiocarbon dates obtained from the site. The abandonment of the settlement may relate directly to this environmental change, although more work would have to be done both in terms of refining the date of both the environmental decline and the abandonment of the settlement before this suggestion could be properly assessed.

Other work in Antrim (Hanna 1993; Francis 1987; Goddard, A. 1971), although not close enough to Corrstown to merit detailed emphasis, notes human influence on vegetation throughout the Middle–Late Bronze Age. This evidence emphasises the results of Plunkett's work and again indicates the predominance of a pastoral economy in the later Bronze Age. Indeed, the Late Bronze Age wall structures forming field systems at Lough na Trosk and Galboly, Co. Antrim (Francis 1987), have been associated with clearance activity perhaps akin to modern slash and burn cattle farming (Plunkett 1999). Doyle and Moore (1997, 41) raised the possibility that the pastoral economy was more significant in the Late Bronze Age economy as the arable land was located at a distance from the settlement, while A. Goddard's 1971 analysis revealed that both clearance and the promotion of grazing were suggested by high charcoal values resulting from burning. Thus, the importance of a pastoral economy can be identified within the archaeological record, and the types of crops grown can be ascertained by extant remains; however, understanding of how crops were grown or of the typical livestock management techniques remains limited at best.

5.3 Building alignment

Of the 65 structures at the Corrstown settlement whose entrance alignment could be positively identified, 29 lay to southeast, 18 lay to SSE, one lay to the ESE, seven lay to the south, nine lay to east, and one lay to the west. S45, which had its entrance aligned to the east, appears to be late in the sequence of the settlement, when space had become congested, and its entrance was diverted to avoid S1 (Illustration 5.1). There was therefore a prominent, but not overwhelming, orientation towards the southeast. This alignment follows a well-attested pattern in Bronze Age and Iron Age houses. It is now commonly proposed that this orientation is not a purely functional concern in response to prevailing wind direction, but relates in some way to cosmological notions of the occupants. Statistical analysis by Oswald has produced very convincing data to support this argument, demonstrating that the orientation of doorways is grouped on important sunrises and sunsets, principally on midwinter sunrise, but sometimes linked to other events throughout the year (Oswald 1997).

A more recent analysis utilising a much larger data set refutes this spiritual connection (Pope 2008, 17–18). Rather than the alignment of entrances being used as evidence of some form of sun worship, Pope re-instates the idea that the east and southeastern predominance relates simply to optimising the amount of light entering a building and minimising exposure to the wind. Entrances aligned beyond this 'light/shelter' optimum are explained not as alignments on the lesser solar events of the calendar, but as indicating buildings that were occupied only during certain parts of the year, or where local topographic factors were of importance. It is likely that the entrance orientation represents a mixture of reasons and what perhaps began as a practicality then developed into a tradition with religious or cosmic associations. Whatever the cause of this phenomenon of orientation, the alignment of doorways at the site at Corrstown is representative of the Bronze Age as a whole.

Several other models exist which describe the routine activities within the houses in terms of the 'sunwise' pattern of movement around the interior of a circular structure as the day progresses (Parker Pearson *et al.* 2004, 196–201; Giles and Parker Pearson 1999, 219–28). This hypothesis cannot be applied to many of the structures at Corrstown: the length of the covered porches and the presence of large buildings to the immediate south and east would have almost entirely obstructed direct sunlight from ever entering the interior of the structures, and so there would have been no 'sunwise' traversing of light through the daytime. If such patterns of activity were followed in these structures the rotation of sunlight could only have been metaphorical. Artefact distribution does not assist in this instance either, pottery and flint were found in large quantities in most

Illustration 5.1: S1 with S45 and the road in the background (mid excavation, from the south)

contexts, and no significant grouping or patterning could be identified. Additionally, the high soil acidity of the area allowed only negligible amounts of bone to survive (the vast majority of which was unidentifiable), and thus another important source of information is not present. There are therefore no differences in the concentrations of bones from certain species, from certain structures, nor any evidence of butchery, feasting or votive deposition. That is not to say they did not occur, but if they did then they have left no presence in the archaeological record.

5.4 Structured deposition?

Examples of foundation deposits or closing offerings in Ireland and in Britain are common in the Bronze Age archaeological record. From the unusual burial of three skeletons 'obviously… handled after death', at Cladh Hallan, Scotland, one of which 'was actually composed of bones from three different individuals – the post-cranial skeleton belonged to one man, the head and cervical vertebrae to another and the mandible came from a third' (Parker Pearson *et al.* 2005, 534) and the fragment of an infant's cranium in an internal pit of a house in Lough Gur, Co. Limerick (Waddell 1998, 209), to the deliberate deposition of more mundane artefacts, such as pottery (e.g. Charlesland, Co. Wicklow (Molloy 2003)), possible loom weights (e.g. Grange Rath, Colp West, Co. Meath (O'Hara 2004)), axes (e.g. broken palstave axe at Ballyprior Beg, Co. Antrim (Suddaby 2003)), cereal grain (Adamstown 3, Co. Waterford (Russell and Ginn 2006)), bronze objects, quern stones (e.g. Adamstown 3 (*ibid.*)), saddle querns (e.g. Ballybrowney, Co. Cork (Cotter, 2005)), hammerstones, cremations (e.g. Knocksaggart, Co. Clare (Hanley 2002)), and quartz fragments (e.g. Adamstown 3 (Russell and Ginn 2006)) found in unusual contexts (Brück 1999, 145–66), examples of structured deposition abound.

It might be expected that with such large-scale and prolonged settlement activity at Corrstown many examples of structured deposition would have been recovered during the excavations. At first glance it appears that only one definite example left an archaeological trace: the base of a pot was found intact at the bottom of a pit in the entrance of S58; presumably it was some sort of foundation deposit or subsequent votive deposit positioned to protect or bless the house's entrance. However, not all structured deposits are as obvious as intact pots among broken sherds or the above-mentioned Cladh Hallan mummies. When the extant evidence at the Corrstown site is examined more fully, several further examples of structured deposits emerge. The large, polished stone macehead from S1 (potentially one of the oldest structures on the site) was used as a packing stone for an internal posthole and perhaps formed a votive or protective offering.

It is possible that structured deposition was represented in the cereal remains from the site. 'Piecemeal recovery of carbonised cereal remains from prehistoric settlement sites is reasonably common' (Johnston 2007, 75); however, cereal grains used for cooking purposes are usually located alongside chaff and weeds. No chaff was recovered at Corrstown and only one grain of a possible weed, rye, from the stakehole in S58, was identified. Cereal grains derived from cooking are also usually found in small numbers (under 10 grains) and therefore the discovery of a substantial amount of grain may be somewhat surprising. Some of the grain deposits shown in Table 3.9 are worth re-iterating here: eight charred grains from a posthole at S4, 31 charred grains from an internal spread/hearth at S8, 16 charred grains from the outer ditch of S30, and four charred grains from a posthole along with 80 charred grains from an internal burnt spread at S14 are likely to represent occupational loss. Possible examples of structured deposition were observed at S13 where 90 charred grains were recovered from a posthole, at S70 where 15 charred grains came from the outer ditch and at S30 where 30 were derived from an inner pit. It is worth acknowledging that not all of the postholes or ditches were sampled and that the possible significance of these results could be overplayed. However, the occurrence of large concentrations of cereal grains certainly does merit some attention.

Johnston (2007, 74) highlights the fact that over 100 cereal grains were counted at two ritual sites, Williamstown IV, Co. Waterford, and Ballingayrour, Co. Limerick, and that the identification of the cereal grains contributed to their interpretation as ritual monuments. Certainly then any context not associated with cooking which was to contain more than 100 cereal grains would be of considerable significance. There were three such contexts at Corrstown, all from Type 1A structures: in S25 *c.* 450 charred barley grains were derived from an internal small posthole; at S58 three deposits were located consisting of *c.* 80 charred cereal grains from the fill of an outer postring posthole as well as *c.* 100 charred cereal grains from a fill in the outer ditch and an additional *c.* 150 charred cereal grains from the fill of an internal stakehole; thirdly in S69 four charred grains came from the fill of the external ditch while *c.* 450 charred grains were found in the fill of the outer ditch and a further *c.* 300 cereal grains from the entrance pathway. It is highly unlikely that these deposits represent casual loss or an expedient and pragmatic way of getting rid of some disastrous cooking. Instead, these deposits of an everyday, ordinary, staple food convey the sense of deliberate, structured deposition and that the postholes and the pits of the houses were crucial, not just in structural terms, but also in symbolic and metaphorical ways that examination of the archaeological record cannot fully determine.

Other possible examples may be represented by the large concentrations of pottery present in the outer ditches of some structures, such as S13 and S3, but these may have been simply domestic waste and there was nothing about their deposition, apart from the large numbers of sherds left, which indicated any special significance had been attached to them. The other high status objects recovered from the site, including two complete polished stone axes, five polished stone axe fragments, and four complete or partial stone moulds, must also be considered (see Chapter 3 for full details of these artefacts). Most of these items appear to pre-date the settlement by a minimum of several hundred years and the axes in particular either related to the Neolithic pottery found across the site or they were heirlooms retained long after their manufacture. This is particularly apparent when considering the half of a palstave axe mould which was found to the south of S1, and had been drilled through in several places which may have made the item redundant as a mould and may have been used to suspend it in some manner. Indeed, it was observed by Grogan (Chapter 3) that the damage confined to the septum was in such a protected position as to suggest possible deliberate decommissioning of the mould. Combined, the evidence suggests some form of curation and possible deliberate breakage; although it's non-secure resting place indicates casual loss (Illustration 5.2).

Brück suggests that the treatment of inanimate objects in this way is connected with the notion that inanimate objects had 'lifestyles similar to their owners' (2001, 152). This idea is often extended to include buildings. It is often considered that houses go through similar, liminal rites of passages to their inhabitants; during construction, buildings are 'born' and when the house is no longer required it 'dies'. It is often these rites of passage that are marked by special and significant deposits. It is also believed that sometimes the lifecycle of a building is interlinked, metaphorically, with that of its inhabitants and when they die, often the house must also 'die'. Not all houses survived until they completely decayed or until repairs became too energy consuming. Thus, there are examples in the archaeological record of the deliberate, symbolic destruction of habitable houses as at Trethellan Farm, Cornwall (Nowakoswki 2001), and Down Farm, Gussage St Michel (Barrett *et al.* 1991). It is possible that S7 and S9 (associated with one of the axe fragments), the two structures which burnt down, suffered such a fate. It is also feasible that perhaps the rebuilding of and the repeated modifications to the structures were in some way related to the liminal rites of the inhabitants, although this cannot be proven.

Alternatively, the evidence could be viewed in a different light. While maintaining that some of the pottery and stone artefacts may represent deliberate deposition it is possible that there is a lack of clear evidence for symbolic practices and meaning among the remains of the settlement at Corrstown, and that this is at least in part representative of a lack of symbolic deposits made by the inhabitants. This may suggest a more defined separation of the ritual and domestic spheres than has become common in much recent archaeological debate and sides with Pendleton's proposal that 'we revise any assertions of a heavily ritualised Bronze Age society' (Pendleton 2001, 177). In particular the stone artefacts that pre-date the period of the settlements

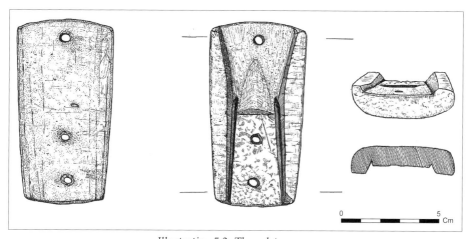

Illustration 5.2: The palstave axe

occupation may, as with the Neolithic pottery found across the site in small quantities, represent residual material from as yet unidentified activity in the area, rather than deliberately curated material. These high quality artefacts were not recovered from particularly significant contexts: the macehead was being used as a packing stone within a posthole while several of the stone moulds, and the miniature stone axe, were recovered from the surfaces of pathways running between structures, and even if they had been curated for several centuries or even longer, ultimately seem to have been discarded unceremoniously. The perforations through the palstave axe mould are, according to the specialist report presented in Chapter 3, original features and were not added to enable the suspension of an heirloom.

Likewise, the environmental evidence should be treated with some caution: the site was not subject to a comprehensive sampling strategy due to the sheer number of contexts discovered, and it is hard to assess the significance of material from a particular context when background levels that would have been provided by more systematic sampling are missing. In addition, it should be noted that the absence of chaff within the samples is a probable result of post-excavation processing; no attempt was made to retrieve micro-fossils from these samples. It is also worth re-iterating Reynolds' observations that while carbonisation of grain will only occur in specific processes, they would subsequently be spread around a settlement through a large number of quite accidental processes. Having directly observed this process, Reynolds was highly dubious of attempts to generate meaningful data from carbonised grains recovered from settlement contexts (Reynolds 1979, 57–8). While the occurrence at ritual sites may require some special explanation (although as Reynolds points out a simple bonfire would produce thousands of carbonised grains if cereal waste was used as kindling or fuel) their occurrence at a large settlement occupied for several generations does not necessitate such interpretations.

5.5 Movement

The major road at Corrstown was last identified exiting the eastern boundary of the site and must have led somewhere. The inhabitants could have travelled along this road, on foot, on horseback, in carts, or in a combination of all three, and they could have travelled relatively far. Horses appear to have been introduced into Ireland in the Late Neolithic period, but remain rare in animal bone assemblages throughout prehistory, although horse riding in one form or another seems to have been an important part of Iron Age society. Sites such as Moynagh Lough, Co. Meath (Bradley 2004, fig. 13.3, No. 62), Ballinderry II, Co. Westmeath (Hencken 1942, e.g. Find 667), and Ballykilleen, Co. Offaly (Wilde 1861, 251), have contained Bronze Age evidence of horse harnesses and related equipment in the form of antler and bone cheek pieces. Unfortunately, no such evidence was recovered from the Corrstown settlement. Early evidence of wheeled transport, whether pulled by horse or oxen, can be cited, as with the pair of wooden block wheels found in a bog at Doogarymore, Co. Roscommon, dated to 760–260 BC and an un-provenanced wooden ox yoke held in the National Museum of Ireland dated to 920–780 BC (Waddell 1998, 118, 274; Coles *et al.* 1978, 17–20). Direct evidence for the early use of a two-wheeled vehicle is demonstrated by the cart tracks found at Tullyallen, Co. Louth, and in Britain at Welland Bank Quarry, Lincolnshire, where parallel wheel ruts that date to the Middle or Late Bronze Age have been recorded (Linanne 2002; Pryor 2001, 221–3).

If wheeled transport was in use, and the network of tracks and routes was reasonably extensive, it may be estimated that the Bronze Age population could have travelled an average of 32km a day. Certainly, in medieval England, once the Roman road system had partially collapsed (Taylor 1979, 85–110), such a distance was feasible for Edward I (January 1300) and distances of 38km a day were recorded in the late 13th and early 14th centuries (Hindle 1982, 9–10).) It would therefore appear reasonable to propose similar distances for travellers with similar technology in the Bronze Age. Such distances would mean it would have been possible for the Corrstown inhabitants to reach the areas around the modern towns of Ballycastle and Ballymean and Londonderry city, as well as the northern end of the Sperrin Mountains and the Glens of Antrim comfortably within a day.

5.6 Burial

'The evidence for how communities buried their dead in Ulster virtually disappears by the Middle Bronze Age' (Mallory and MacNeill 1991, 112). The above-mentioned urned cremation at nearby Ballywillan church (SMR ANT 006:015), a mere 0.59km east of the Corrstown settlement, is the only known Bronze Age burial in the area. This individual burial was typical of the Middle Bronze Age period when the collective burial practices of the Neolithic and the Early Bronze Age died out. While there is no extant evidence for the settlement's deceased, it is known that in the Middle Bronze Age there was a gradual disappearance of the prestigious cinerary urns of the Early Bronze Age and a general abandonment of high status burial offerings. Instead, there was a widespread adoption of more token cremation burials, still with some associated grave goods, interred with coarse pottery such as cordoned urns. Early Bronze Age funerary pottery was found by William Knowles and Edward Watson within the sands and gravels of Co. Antrim, as at Urbalreagh and Bay Farm, Carnlough (Mallory and McNeill 1991), and it is possible that the Middle Bronze Age evidence has been eroded or washed away.

5.7 Organization and property

It is evident that the Corrstown inhabitants were organized. As outlined in Chapter 4 the settlement appears to have developed in an organized fashion and indeed aspects of it, most notably the road – a large engineering scheme – seem planned and convey varying degrees of social organization and resource management (Coles *et al.* 1978, 19). This planning could have materialised in two ways: firstly, it could have been implemented and imposed upon the inhabitants by an authoritative figure, or secondly, it could have resulted from a communal effort derived from many, of not the majority, if the inhabitants.

The pathways leading on to the road at the northern end of the site, and the individual house platforms and plots defined by the deep outer ditches suggest the prevalence of notions of property and imply a sense of ownership of space. The deliberate retention of those house platforms throughout several phases of modification and substantial rebuild could be considered as 'a way of maintaining a sense of continuity with the past and ensuring continued rights of ownership' (Brück 2007; Bailey 1999).

Such a vast number of contemporary Bronze Age structures is currently unparalleled in the British and Irish archaeological record. It is possible that more extensive excavation at some of the sites with Bronze Age structures might have expanded the size of the settlement and the numbers of structures; however, there is a significant number of known single or paired, relatively isolated structures within the settlement record to indicate that large sites such as Corrstown are not representative. Indeed, the commonly occurring trend consists of either scattered homesteads or small conglomerations of 10–20 possible structures, not all occupied simultaneously. There was some overriding social or economic reason as to why so many people clustered and lived together, here on the north coast of Northern Ireland, not transmitted through the extant archaeological record.

5.8 Abandonment

While it has been possible to suggest a number of ways in which the settlement may have developed, it is more difficult to determine the manner in which the settlement was abandoned. The stereotypical model of the development of a settlement describes a trajectory from small beginnings through to a maximum expansion followed by a period of decline and contraction, and McSparron's modelling of the radiocarbon dates demonstrated the presence of these phases at Corrstown (Appendix I). Certainly, Middle Bronze Age settlements in Britain are widely recognised as being short-lived (e.g. Ellison 1975, 391; Cunliffe 1970, 12). However, a well-constructed roundhouse could have the capacity to last for up to a hundred years or more in certain environmental situations. Therefore, a settlement like Corrstown, with possibly 50–70 structures inhabited simultaneously and which displayed evidence for multiple modifications and rebuilds could have endured on a longer-term basis. Even taking into account the relative lack of chronological variations in the Corrstown Middle Bronze Age artefact record, the above-mentioned suggestion that the settlement at Corrstown could have been occupied for 100–250 years still remains valid (and considerably longer than that proposed by Cunliffe and Ellison for the British evidence (*ibid.*)). McSparron's modelling of the dates suggested that the decline of the Corrstown settlement began *c.* 1150 BC and that this phase could have lasted up to 480 years, although in all likelihood it would have been much shorter.

At the Corrstown settlement, there was no conclusive evidence to suggest that any particular area continued in use longer than other areas. The small number of buildings that appeared to have been completely rebuilt twice may have been occupied for longer than the majority of buildings which were only rebuilt once. However, these structures did not form a cluster within the settlement plan as might be expected if the second rebuilding took place as the settlement was contracting. Other explanations can also be offered where the structures which were rebuilt twice may have been originally built earlier in the sequence than the buildings subject to a single rebuild, or the second rebuild could have been necessitated by structural failure or weather damage. Radiocarbon dates from the site do not have the tight resolution which could address this problem.

Three of the buildings had been burnt down: adjacent S7 and S9 located at the north of the site and S33, at the west of the site. S9 seems to have burnt in its entirety, but only the southern and western parts of S7 had been affected. This rather suggests that the burnings were two separate incidents, or at the very least, started with two separate ignitions: if the fire had spread from one building to the other, it would be expected that the adjacent sides would have been burnt. It was argued that the entrance of S9 had been diverted to avoid the linear feature that had been cut through S7, indicating that S7 had been destroyed prior to S9.

S33 had clearly been fully consumed by flames, but the burnt debris had survived as a deep deposit overlying the building's foundations, indicating that the site was never cleaned up. The adjacent lean-to buildings, S30 and S31, showed no evidence of fire and it must be suggested that if these buildings were indeed contemporary, then they had been demolished prior to the burning of S33.

So why then was the settlement at Corrstown abandoned? A settlement as large as Corrstown would have needed vast resources in order to maintain its structures and its population. As mentioned above in relation to the reconstruction at Castle Henllys, a single roundhouse requires a considerable quantity of raw materials for its construction. The amount of material needed to create, maintain and expand the Corrstown settlement would have been staggering and it is possible that the population simply exhausted the locally available supplies and were forced to disperse to possibly re-group elsewhere. Considering the size of the foundations and the amount of stone involved in the construction, it would seem likely that the abandoned settlement would have remained visible for a very long time.

It is also possible that environmental or agricultural factors had a decisive role in the settlement's demise. At Townparks (Ballin Smith 2003) flooding or enlargement of Lough Neagh was considered responsible for the settlement's abandonment during the Late Middle–Late Bronze Age; a date similar to the downfall of the Corrstown site. The environmental record for this period indicates a marked decrease in tree pollen, a rise in grasses and other indicators of forest clearance *c.* 1200–1000 BC (Mallory and MacNeill 1991, 128) as evidenced at Altnahinch and Sluggan, Co. Antrim (Goddard, A. 1971; Goddard, I. 1971), indicating intensified agricultural activity. Plunkett's 2007 analysis demonstrated that the levels of pollen for particular tree species (e.g. hazel, oak and alder) in the later second millennium BC were so low as to be comparable to those in the medieval period (Plunkett 2007). A corresponding rise in open ground species (e.g. heather, grasses, ribwort) was also comparable with levels from AD 1000. However, as mentioned above, in the areas surrounding Corrstown, such as at Garry Bog, the evidence indicated that there was a decrease in arable agriculture from the 1140s onwards, perhaps due to the increase in bog growth. This indicates that the levels of deforestation and exploitation were uneven, and that localised patterns would have been of paramount significance.

The effects environmental and climatic events have on communities, and how they can be traced in the archaeological record, are open to debate. One such event within the chronology of the Bronze Age is represented by Hekla 3, a volcanic eruption which occurred 1300km north of Ulster during this time and to which much of the environmental, and consequently social, change of this period has been attributed. Mallory and MacNeill (1991, 128) describe it as a 'mini version of the dreaded nuclear winter' when rainfall dramatically increased and the temperatures fell. John Barber attributes Hekla 3 as part of the cause of the abandonment in *c*. 1000 BC of Late Bronze Age huts on Caithness (*ibid*. 128). Burgess describes the effects as a 'catastrophe' in the 12th century BC and attributes it to the disappearance of settlements over much of Britain. Hekla 3 is registered by Irish tree rings between 1159 and 1141 BC and seen by Baillie as heralding major alterations in the Irish landscape (Baillie 1989; Baillie and Munro 1988). However, many archaeologists reject these claims on the grounds of a lack of evidence and describe interpretations of catastrophic changes as 'extremely controversial' (Bradley 2007, 184). There is environmental evidence that indicates climatic changes began before the volcanic eruption occurred and archaeological evidence, such as the construction of wooden pathways across damp areas of ground (*ibid*. 184), that demonstrates human response to such change. 'There is no need to postulate a major crisis at this time' (*ibid*. 202).

However, even if the effects of Hekla 3 are ruled out as explaining the site at Corrstown's demise, it is still probable that environmental factors were significant. There were several phases of increased wetness or coldness occurring between the 16th and sixth centuries BC and there is substantial evidence for the depletion of bog oaks in Ireland in the tenth century. Plunkett's work at Garry Bog, 3km north of Ballymoney, 4km south of the Antrim coast, and less than 10km from the Corrstown settlement is currently the closest place where known environmental research has been conducted. Two phases (see above) of activity corresponding to when the site at Corrstown was occupied were noted. During the first phase there was evidence for a mixed economy with varieties of crops; however, following the hiatus in bog growth, there was a wetter period during which there was no longer evidence for arable agriculture. At Gortcorbies, Co. Londonderry, less than 15km from Corrstown, the pollen record demonstrated a gradual decline of woodland from the Early Bronze Age onwards (Smith 1975; Goddard, I. 1971). This evidence also registered an intensification of human activity (*c*. 1250 BC) as the arboreal pollen declined to almost 20%. According to the pollen record in this area it was another 150–200 years before wood regeneration began. Further clearance was not seen again until the Early Iron Age. Evidence for continuous activity throughout the Middle–Late Bronze Age was noted at Lough na Trosk (Francis 1987), Breen Bog 2 and Glens Bridge (Goddard, A. 1971). Periods of expansion are observed at Gruig Top, Loughaveema (*ibid*.) during the Middle Bronze Age and at Galboly Lower (Francis 1987). Combined, this evidence indicates periods of localised growth and contraction which, overall, fit into the broader landscape patterns. The Gortcorbies evidence indicates a period of almost two centuries when there was little human impact upon tree cover which suggests either careful, long-term planning with the maintenance of resources, or that the area was abandoned in the years after 1250 BC; the same period in which the Corrstown settlement was abandoned. This could have been a result of the wet period demonstrated in Plunkett's evidence from Garry Bog.

Plunkett acknowledges that, 'A cultural break is observed at *c*. 1200 BC as settlements appear to contract to certain core areas and evidence for a distinctive material culture dissipates… The break would seem to have arisen largely from internal socio-political changes. These changes appear to begin prior to climate deterioration in the 12th century BC but may have been aggravated by environmental downturn' (Plunkett 1999).

The demise of the Bronze Age settlement in Corrstown in the 12th and 11th centuries BC is not atypical and fits in with wider settlement patterns of contraction and growth within the Middle–Late Bronze Age, in Ireland and in Scotland and Britain. Settlement on the continent also fluctuated and climatic deterioration towards the end of the 12th century BC corresponds with the collapse of civilisations in the Aegean and Mediterranean (Weiss 1982), and a general cooling in Europe (Brice 1981). The interrelationships and associations between the socio-political atmosphere and environmental factors, although not conclusively determinable through the available evidence, cannot be denied.

After the settlement was abandoned there was apparently very little activity on the site until the early medieval period. A bowl-shaped pit was dug through the central area of S13 and then filled with heat-shattered stone, indicating its use as a trough for heating water, but this was not in use long enough for a burnt stone mound to develop. A radiocarbon date from this pit dated the activity to between 1022 and 844 BC (UB-6245), possibly several hundred years after the settlement was abandoned. A possible Iron Age structure or arrangement of posts may have been dug in the area around S15, as discussed above. Details on the early medieval features are located in Appendix II.

Chapter 6

Corrstown in Context

In this chapter the site at Corrstown is set within its immediate context of the Irish north coast, as well as within the wider Irish evidence.

6.1 The North Coast: an economic and social landscape

During the 1990s it was speculated that the north coast of Ireland must have been heavily populated in the Bronze Age. In *The Archaeology of Ulster* (1991, 100) Mallory and MacNeill acknowledged that

> 'County Antrim has produced more bronzes than any other county in Ireland which alerts us to the same problem... encountered in the Mesolithic – do the bronzes indicate the density of prehistoric settlement or the disproportionate effect of the northern collectors on the distribution of prehistoric objects?'

The Late Bronze Age field walls in the Antrim uplands (e.g. Lough na Trosk and Galboly, dating to between the 12th and ninth centuries BC (Francis 1987)), combined with the evidence from the pollen record from nearby Garry Bog (Plunkett 1999), suggested not only considerable agricultural activity, but also settlement occupation. As Plunkett noted in 1999 'extensive settlement in this region is probable'.

However, until the late 1990s the evidence for Bronze Age activity along this section of the north coast was confined to a scatter of SMR entries, with few extensively dated and excavated sites. The settlement site at the White Rocks with multiple roundhouses, excavated by Knowles in the late 19th century, has been considered to be Bronze Age in date (Knowles 1886) and fragments of clay moulds for casting Late Bronze Age swords were collected here (Collins 1970 in Waddell 1998, 269) but other known settlement evidence in this area was scarce. As mentioned in the previous chapter, two standing stones are located on high points in the landscape (SMR LDY 003:001, SMR ANT 006:001) behind Corrstown, along with a further two in the vicinity (SMR ANT 003:050–051). It is feasible that these standing stones were in position when the Corrstown settlement was occupied. The only known Bronze Age burial in the area was discovered nearby, 0.59km to the east, at Ballywillan church (SMR ANT 006:015). No further burials were recorded and no burnt mound sites were known in the vicinity, although post-medieval ploughing may have destroyed any evidence for these.

However, more recent excavations in the area, particularly due to housing developments in Portrush and Portstewart, have dramatically altered previous perceptions of this coastal area. Adjacent to the Corrstown site, in Magheramenagh, NAC Ltd excavated five structures, one of which was a roundhouse of Bronze Age date located close to the townland boundary. Radiocarbon determinations from Magheramenagh have been provided in advance of the publication of the project's findings by Stephen Gilmore (further details regarding the excavation of this adjacent site were not available for consultation) and two of the five dates obtained are from the Bronze Age: one from the roundhouse structure (1450–1260 BC, Beta-186553, 3130±50 BP), dating to the Middle Bronze Age, and the other from a ringditch (1920–1680 BC, Beta-186552, 3490±50 BP), dating to the Early Bronze Age. The roundhouse date is closely comparable to the Middle Bronze Age dates available for Corrstown and should be considered as a possible contemporary structure, and as part of the complex.

In 1994 at Crossreagh West, Co. Londonderry, which is situated *c.* 4.8km to the west of Corrstown, excavations by Declan Hurl investigated a series of northwest–southeast stone alignments set on a platform (Hurl 1994). Early Bronze Age and Neolithic pottery was recovered and several pits, including one containing cremated bone which was sealed by an inverted saddle quern and one with pulverised bone and half a crude mudstone macehead, were also noted (*ibid.*). A ploughed-out burnt mound was also identified by John Ó Néill from Hurl's descriptions of these excavations (MacDonald 2002). In the adjacent townland of Crossreagh East, Co. Londonderry, two large Middle Bronze Age structures were excavated (NGR: 282099 436514). Structure 1 was a sub-rectangular, post and wicker construction formed by pits and gullies and associated with a porch, areas of cobbling, and possible stone footed, turf walls; a radiocarbon date of 1360–920 BC (Beta-157017) was derived (McSparron 2001). Structure 2 was sub-circular, of slot-trench and posthole construction, with a circular annex and an apparent doorway between them. It was not dated but was believed to be contemporary (*ibid.*). McSparron points out that, according to the Book of Leinster, a public assembly and games took place in this area and that an alleged battle of the second century BC occurred on the same site, thus highlighting the potential significance of the locale (*ibid.*). In 2002 the Centre for Archaeological Fieldword undertook further research excavations in the area but no significant archaeology was discovered (MacDonald 2002). In 2004 Early Bronze Age pottery was recovered from a slot-trench in a possible settlement area, also close by at Glebe (Bowen 2004).

Excavations at Cappagh Beg (NGR: 8240 3656; Portstewart, Co. Londonderry) in 2003 for Kennedy Holidays (Coleraine) Ltd revealed the remains of two or three houses, two boundary ditches and a single cremation pit with a possibly associated hearth. The site was situated *c.* 1.6km from the coast and from the north of the River Bann and the features were located in a low-lying area (31m OD) consisting of soft, orange sand which overlay the limestone bedrock. Structure A consisted of pits, postholes and ditch sections which created an oval structure 9m north–south by 7m west–east with at least two phases of construction, evidence for wattle and charcoal (*Alnus/Corylus*) which returned a radiocarbon date of 1491–1058 BC (Beta-188622). Structure B comprised eight outer ditch sections, 11m in diameter, with an internal 11-posthole postring, 8.5m diameter. A radiocarbon date of 1433–1122 BC (Beta-188623) was derived from a sample of various large twig/small roundwood material. Structure C was a D-shaped ditch while Structure D represented another circular house with two phases of construction, both of which consisted of a series of irregular ditch sections, pits and occasional stake- and postholes forming circular enclosures of *c.* 6.5m internal diameter. Full details of the excavation of this site are located in Appendix IIII. As well as the neighbouring Crossreagh sites, various other sites and monuments are recorded in the vicinity of Cappagh Beg, including two unlocated standing stones and one prone stone (1.10m in length) located to the southeast (SMR 003:020; 003:021; 003:074). Two further standing stones are situated to the west (SMR 003:004; 003:005). There was also a prehistoric settlement site on the coast, although its location is unknown (SMR 003:043).

It is therefore apparent that the Corrstown settlement was part of a wider thriving landscape. The upsurge in housing developments along the north coast was paralleled by continued road developments across Ireland which has greatly increased the known Bronze Age direct settlement record. Overviews of this material are now emerging (take Ó Néill forthcoming as exemplar) and some unpublished surveys have helped to establish patterns and trends across the Middle–Late Bronze Age settlement record.

6.2 The Corrstown settlement in an Irish context

As can be observed from the parallels drawn with other Irish sites in Chapters 4–5 the settlement at Corrstown shares similarities with these. At only 28m above sea level it represents a relatively low-lying settlement (the adjacent site at Magheramenagh was recorded as 30m OD) and is on a similar height above sea level as Townparks and Whitepark Bay (17m and 30m OD, respectively). It was evident that as a result of the site's position, towards the base of a long slope which would have resulted in heavy surface run-off, waterlogging proved problematic. The segmented outer ditches that functioned as drains combined with the phases of entrance paving and cobbling indicate that the inhabitants suffered from the threat or realisation of flooding. This issue is further emphasised by the onset of wetter climatic conditions, as evidenced by the pollen record in the nearby areas, especially in Garry Bog. Despite these problems, the site at Corrstown was obviously perceived to be a suitable place for habitation. Certainly, although located in a low-lying landscape most likely dominated by sand dunes, the settlement was well-placed to exploit the variety of other natural landscapes, including varying terrain and soil types, apparent in the surrounding hinterland. Other broadly contemporary settlement sites were located in proximity which could have facilitated the creation of an abstract, social landscape, the importance of which is likely to have been as significant as the economic aspect of the site. Grogan has identified a similar settlement pattern in Munster, where habitation sites were located in close proximity to each other, and suggested the possibility that several families formed larger units or communities (Grogan 2005b, 74). Such clusters of settlement sites are often associated with burial, ritual and communal feasting or cooking sites. This clustering of funerary, ritual and domestic sites is a pattern observed elsewhere in Ireland, which for Munster at least, Grogan has interpreted as a reflection of sub-regional social divisions or kinship groups. Of course, the absence of such monuments and sites in the Corrstown area could be attributed to a lack of excavation, or to a regional trend.

As outlined in Chapters 4–5 the roundhouses at Corrstown share constructional and functional similarities with each other and with other such structures from across Ireland. The segmented ditches, once considered a regional variation, have since also been identified in counties Sligo and Meath. The size, shape, internal organization, and orientation of the Corrstown roundhouses also accord with wider patterns (see Ó Néill forthcoming). There is a great deal of variance in the Corrstown roundhouses, which suggests a functional variety. Some of the smaller roundhouses built against larger examples represent annexes (e.g. S30 and S11), some were likely to have stores, others, e.g. S53, probably functioned as animal pens or sheds, and some had an undeterminable function. This sense of functional variability is matched by the layout of the settlement and the integration of the entrances and the road network, and indicates that the Corrstown settlement was a well-structured and organized community in which to live. Structures and settlements were internally and externally organized alike in the Middle–Late Bronze Age and Cleary (2007) and Ó Néill (forthcoming) have examined the evidence for this organization, in the form of structural ground plans, the deposition of material culture, and the built settlement environment, including ratios of built to unbuilt space. The Corrstown settlement, albeit on a larger scale than the rest of the settlements in Ireland, accords well with the wider patterns they have identified.

In terms of the chronological developments, the Corrstown settlement displays some similar patterns to other sites. The pre-dating Neolithic activity is a common factor on Bronze Age settlement sites, as outlined by Grogan in Chapter 3. The origins of the settlement at Corrstown were in the Middle Bronze Age, and it has been demonstrated by a combination of the radiocarbon dates and artefact analysis that the zenith of its occupation occurred in the Middle Bronze Age, sometime between 1500 and 1250 BC. During this period, other large groups of structures emerge in Ireland, such as Chancellorsland and Curraghatoor, although none on the same scale as that of Corrstown. As Ó Néill (forthcoming) acknowledges, this 250 year period in the Middle Bronze Age produced the largest number of structures throughout the Bronze Age and also the sites with the highest density of structures; Ó Néill goes so far as to suggest that the '*raison d'etre*' for Corrstown may be linked to a higher density of settlement in this period as a whole (Ó Néill forthcoming). However, without a more tightly constructed chronology of the settlement activity and detailed analysis of available associated radiocarbon dates during the Middle–Late Bronze Age, density patterns cannot be interpreted with any degree of certainty.

Of particular interest is the prominence of multiple structures enclosed within hillforts that seems to occur between 1000–750 BC (Ó Néill forthcoming). One such occupied hillfort was located further along the coast from Corrstown, at Knockdhu, Co. Antrim (Phil MacDonald, pers comm.). There a settlement with multiple roundhouse platforms was located within the confines of the triple rampart promontory fort and was partially excavated in 2008. Some of these structures were built on terraces and others on artificial platforms and various construction techniques were observed, including earthen walls, earthen walls built on stone footings, and clay-bonded stone walls. A range of radiocarbon dates were derived from short-lived species (charcoal) associated with some of the structures and indicated occupation between the tenth–eighth centuries BC (including 972–825 BC; UB-10957; 2746±26 BP; 836–784BC; UB-10955; 2635±27 BP;

969–814 BC; UB-10965; 2735±30 BP; 822-768 BC; UB-10964; 2609±28 BP (kindly provided by Phil MacDonald)). This occupation therefore commences after the demise and abandonment of the settlement at Corrstown. The demise of larger settlements, such as Chancellorsland and Corrstown, and the phenomenon of occupied hillforts may therefore be somewhat associated and reflect wider social and cultural changes that seem to have occurred around this time.

6.2.1 *Status*

Traditionally, the above-mentioned social and cultural changes in the Late Bronze Age included the emergence of hillforts as a site type and the archaeologically visible development of a stratified society based around tribal identity and warfare (O'Sullivan 1998, 70). It was also acknowledged that hierarchy, based on the theory that social ranking can be reflected through differences in settlement form and associated assemblages, becomes apparent in the archaeological record in the Late Bronze Age (Grogan 2005c; Eogan 1998; Grogan *et al.* 1996). However, as the origins of hillforts are pushed back even earlier than the Late Bronze Age, to the Middle Bronze Age (e.g. Rathgall: *c.* 1200–900 BC; Dun Aonghasa: 1100–800 BC; Mooghaun: 900–800 BC; Eoin Grogan, pers. comm.) and as evidence for the Middle Bronze Age settlement record continues to emerge, it is now apparent that social and cultural changes were also occurring in the Middle Bronze Age. Social and settlement stratification is, however, much more difficult to ascertain in the Middle Bronze Age as the size of the Middle Bronze Age settlements and their structure types hitherto lacked variance and diversification. It has therefore been difficult to acknowledge the existence of a structural hierarchy based purely on settlement type (Brück 2007), although Waddell (2000) proposed that perhaps hierarchy was embedded in settlement location and that, for example, hilltop sites (prominent, visible, defensive) were a proclamation of status. Generally, a small and uniform set of artefacts is recovered from Middle Bronze Age settlements and there is no evidence for any 'rich' sites based on artefacts either (Brück 1999, 146–50), although the evidence for weapon manufacture, such as moulds, 'may denote specialist importance' (Waddell 2000, 221).

Corrstown is a site unique; it does not fall into any known Middle or Late Bronze Age settlement types. Its size suggests importance, yet its location perhaps does not. It has small houses (?low status) as well as larger houses (?high status). It was unenclosed and apparently undefended which could indicate that it had nothing of worth to enclose or defend (?low-status), or that it was at no risk from attack (?high status). The nature of its pottery (excepting the date range) and lithic assemblages is not of a noticeably high quality (?low status) yet we do not know what artefacts to expect from a high-grade settlement. The presence of moulds could denote high status; however, there were no associated metalworking features, residues or artefacts to indicate that the moulds were used by the Corrstown inhabitants. Certainly, the creation and maintenance of the road network implies significance, especially as it extended beyond the site. Cooney (2000, 24) recommends that a settlement with a significant number of structures, with large structures and with evidence for the possession and deliberate deposition of fine metalwork, combined with a lack of defensive measures be considered as high status. Corrstown, as demonstrated, meets all these criteria, except for the deposition or creation of fine metalwork. It therefore currently sits awkwardly as evidently neither high status nor low status.

6.3 Categorising the Corrstown Settlement

How then should Corrstown be categorised? Even during the early stages of the excavations at Corrstown, it was apparent that the scale of the occupation was exceptional for the Irish Bronze Age, and indeed for the prehistoric period as a whole. The sheer number of the structures and the apparent degree of contemporaneity and nucleation have led to the question of whether or not the Corrstown settlement can be categorized as a village. The question of the existence of villages in prehistoric Ireland and Britain is a complicated one, due to the inconsistent way in which the term has been used by different archaeologists, and this has been addressed more fully elsewhere (Rathbone in prep).

There has been a tendency to classify any settlement consisting of more than a handful of houses as a prehistoric village, when perhaps the term hamlet is far more appropriate. Indeed, some examples may in reality have simply been single farmsteads occupied by an extended family group. The tendency to label small prehistoric settlements is not as common in Ireland as in Britain, where the village is a noticeably less common part of the modern settlement pattern, and is most often seen as a foreign import: 'The 'village' is noticeably scarce across Ireland as a whole, and is best regarded as a predominantly early Anglo-Norman phenomenon' (Barry 1988, 345–6). However, sites such as the Bronze Age settlement at Ballybrowney, Co. Cork, have been termed villages when the designation cannot really be justified (Cotter 2005, 42). The situation in Britain is less satisfactory and any number of sites have been labelled as prehistoric villages. Dubious examples abound, such as the small Bronze Age settlements in southern England at Black Patch, Itford Hill and Thorny Down. The contemporary nature of the buildings at these sites has been questioned, and Brück, in her more recent in-depth analysis of Middle Bronze Age settlements in southern England, concludes that, 'most were occupied by a single household, perhaps comprising a nuclear or small extended family group', although she stresses that the majority of sites in this region and period were single phase settlements (Brück 1999, 145–7). More satisfactory use of the term village can be cited with some of the broch villages and densely occupied hillforts of the Iron Age, and perhaps some of the major Neolithic sites in Orkney, but in the majority of cases the use of the term lacks the necessary rigour.

Only two excavated sites contemporary with the Corrstown settlement even approach the same scale and density of occupation: Ronaldsway Airport on the Isle of Man, and Area 3000/3100 at Reading Business Park. At Ronaldsway a combination of re-interpreted evidence from excavations conducted in the 1930s, modern excavations, and geophysical surveys have resulted in the identification of a settlement consisting of between 10 and 20 households that was apparently continuously occupied from around 1500 BC to 800 BC (www.britarch.ac.uk/ba/ba102/news.shtml). This site may be of particular relevance to Corrstown because of its location in the Irish Sea and partially overlapping date range, and further details are eagerly awaited. The site at Reading Business Park Area 3000/31000 consisted of a dense circular cluster of roundhouses, of which the excavators argued up to 14 may have stood at one time (Brossler *et al.* 2004, 122). It was suggested that a wide linear space running through the settlement was a roadway, and despite the lack of evidence that this was surfaced, this roadway is the only identified direct parallel to the arrangement at Corrstown.

However, caution should be exerted when defining these settlements as villages. Fourteen roundhouses, which appear to represent seven households or even 20 roundhouses, may not form a large enough settlement to justify the designation. At present the scale of the settlement at Corrstown remains unique for this period in Ireland and Britain, probably by an order of magnitude, and it is one of only three sites, perhaps even the only site, from this period where the term village can be used comfortably. Unexcavated sites that may represent villages but are currently classified in other ways are known from outside of Ireland, such as at Legis Tor and Whittenknowles Rocks, both in Devon where around 50 buildings were present at each site (Balaam *et al.* 1982, fig. 17). Until such sites are more fully investigated it remains difficult to assess whether they are truly villages or not.

6.4 Conclusions

The village at Corrstown does much to reinforce contemporary understanding of Irish Bronze Age settlement. Its low-lying, coastal location close to other sites and areas of varying topography and soil quality meant the settlement was well placed to exploit its hinterland and to communicate with its neighbours. The 74 roundhouses, although of varying types, were constructed with similar methods to those already well documented in the archaeological record. The segmented double ditches, observed in significant quantities within the site, although relatively uncommon outside Corrstown, do have parallels in the locale and beyond. The size of the structures, orientation of entrances and internal divisions also all accord with wider settlement patterns identified by Cleary (2007), Carlin (2006) and Ó Néill (forthcoming). The range of artefacts was, as at the majority of Middle Bronze Age settlements, limited and confined predominantly to flint and pottery, only surpassing that of other contemporary sites in terms of quantity, rather than of quality. The emphasis on the retention of the same house plots over successive repairs and rebuilds and on the organization of the settlement space underlines a sense of belonging, both on a personal and on a communal level. The two-phased road network that extended beyond the site indicates a substantial investment of time in terms of creation and maintenance. Such evidence for roads on dryland sites is not frequently forthcoming in the archaeological record and the presence of the Corrstown road, combined with its provision as a focal point for the orientation and layout of the roundhouses, emphasises the organizational capacity of the inhabitants. With estimated population levels of 200–300 during the Village Phase and a likely duration of 100–200 years, investment at the Corrstown settlement was considerable. It is the scale and organization of the Corrstown settlement that sets it apart from other domestic sites; the implications of its scale are wide ranging, from the amount of resources required to create, sustain and modify the settlement and its inhabitants to the social networks required to maintain the Corrstown economy. It is possible that it was the very scale of the Corrstown settlement that proved its demise and it has been suggested (e.g. John Ó Néill) that part of its abandonment could be attributed to over-exploitation of its economic hinterland. However, it is also likely that wider social, cultural, and environmental influences impacted upon the demise of this once densely inhabited settlement.

Bibliography

Alcock, L. (1972) Excavations at Cadbury-Camelot, 1966–70. *Antiquity* 46 (181), 29–38.

ApSimon, A. (1976) Ballynagilly at the beginning and end of the Irish Neolithic. In S. J. de Laet (ed.) *Acculturation and Continuity in Atlantic Europe*, 15–38. Bruges, Dissertationes Archaeologicae Gandenses.

Armit, I. (1996) *The Archaeology of Skye and the Western Isles*. Edinburgh, Edinburgh University Press.

Bailey, D. W. (1999) What is a tell? Settlement in fifth millennium Bulgaria. In J. Brück and M. Goodmand (eds) *Making Places in the Prehistoric World: Themes in Settlement Archaeology*, 94–111. London, University College London Press.

Baillie, M. (1989) Hekla 3: how big was it? *Endeavour* 13, 78–81.

Baillie, M. and Munro M. (1988) Irish tree rings, Santorini and volcanic dust veils. *Nature* 332, 344–6.

Balaam, N. D., Smith, K. and Wainwright, G. J. (1983) The Shaugh Moor Project: Fourth Report – environment, context and conclusion. *Proceedings of the Prehistoric Society* 48, 203–78.

Ballin Smith, B. (2003) The excavation of two Late Bronze Age roundhouses at Ballypriorbeg, Island Magee, Co. Antrim. *Ulster Journal of Archaeology* 62, 16–45.

Barrett, J. C., Bradley, R., and Green, M. (1991) *Landscape, Monuments and Society: The prehistory of Cranborne Chase*. Cambridge, Cambridge University Press.

Barry, T. (1988) 'The people of the country…dwell scattered'. The pattern of rural settlement in Ireland in the Later Middle Ages. In J. Bradley (ed.) *Settlement and Society in Medieval Ireland*, 345–60. Kilkenny, Boethius Press.

Behre, K. E. (1992) The history of rye cultivation in Europe. *Vegetation History and Archaeobotany* 1, 141–56.

Bowen, P. (2004) 'Caslandoo', Glebe. www.excavations.ie.

Bradley R. (2004) Moynagh Lough, Co. Meath, in the Late Bronze Age. In H. Roche, E. Grogan, J. Bradley, J. Coles, and B. Raftery (eds) *From Megaliths to Metals. Essays in Honour of George Eogan*, 91–8. Oxford, Oxbow Books.

Bradley, R. (2007) *The Prehistoric of Britain and Ireland*. Cambridge, Cambridge World Archaeology, Cambridge University Press.

Brice, W. C. (1998) Climatic change and ethnic movements in the Early Iron Age. In C. Delano Smith and M. Parry (eds) *Consequences of Climatic Change*, 124–8. Nottingham, Department of Geography, University of Nottingham.

Brindley, A. (2003) *Report on prehistoric pottery from Knockuregare, Co. Limerick (02E0394)*. Unpublished report prepared for Margaret Gowen and Co. Ltd.

Brindley, A. (2007) *The dating of food vessels and urns in Ireland*. Galway, Bronze Age Studies 7, Department of Archaeology, National University of Ireland.

Brossler, A., Early, R. and Allen, C. (2004) *Green Park (Reading Business Park) Phase 2 excavations 1995 – Neolithic and Bronze Age*. Oxford, Oxford University School of Archaeology.

Brown, J., Carrillo, L., Fernand, L., Horsburgh, K. J., Hill, A. E., Young, E. F., and Medler, K. J. (2003) Observations of the physical structure and seasonal jet-like circulation of the Celtic Sea and St George's Channel of the Irish Sea. *Continental Shelf Research* 23 (6), 533–61.

Brück, J. (1997) *The Early-Middle Bronze Age transition in Wessex, Sussex, and the Thames Valley*. Unpublished PhD thesis, University of Cambridge.

Brück, J. (ed.) (2001) *Bronze Age landscapes: Tradition and Transformation*. Oxford, Oxbow Books.

Brück, J. (1999) Houses, lifestyles and deposition on the Middle Bronze Age settlements in Southern England. *Proceedings of the Prehistoric Society* 65, 145–66.

Brück, J. (2007) The Character of Late Bronze Age settlement in Southern Britain. In C. Haselgrove and R. Pope *The Earlier Iron Age in Britain and the Near Continent* , 24–38. Oxford, Oxbow Books.

Burgess, C. (1995) Bronze Age Settlements and Domestic Pottery in Northern Britain: some suggestions. In I. Kinnes and G. Varndell (eds) *Unbaked Urns of Rudely Shape' Essays on British and Irish Pottery*, 145–158. Oxbow Monograph 55. Oxford, Oxbow Books.

Byrd, B. F. (2000) Households in Transition: Neolithic Social Organization within southeast Asia. In I. Kuijt (ed.) *Life in Neolithic Farming Communities: Social Organization, Identity and Differentiation*, 63–98. New York / London, Kluwer Academic Publishers.

Byrnes, E. (1999) Recent excavations at Richardstown, Co. Louth. *Archaeology Ireland* 13 (4), 33.

Byrnes, E. (2004) Clonard or Folkstown Great, Co. Meath. Bronze Age roundhouse. In I. Bennett (ed.) *Excavations 2002: Summary Accounts of Archaeological Excavations in Ireland*, 135–6. Dublin, Wordwell.

Campbell, K. (1995) *Sheephouse, Co. Meath. Fulachta fiadh*. In I. Bennett (ed.) *Excavations 1994: Summary Accounts of Archaeological Excavations in Ireland*, 73–4. Dublin, Wordwell.

Carlin, N. (2006) *Bronze Age Houses*. Unpublished Research Report prepared for Archaeological Consultancy Services Ltd.

Carter, R. W. G. and Bartlett, D. (1990) Coastal erosion in Northeast Ireland – Part 1L sand beaches, dune sand river mouths. *Irish Geography* 26, 141–6.

Case, H. (1961) Irish Neolithic Pottery: Distribution and Sequence. *Proceedings of the Prehistoric Society* 9, 174–233.

Cleary, R. (2003) Enclosed Late Bronze Age habitation site and boundary wall at Lough Gur, Co. Limerick. *Proceedings of the Royal Irish Academy* 103C, 97–189.

Cleary, K. (2006) Irish Bronze Age settlements: more than meets the eye? *Archaeology Ireland* 20, (76), 18–21.

Cleary, K. (2007) *Irish Bronze Age Settlements: Spatial Organization and the Deposition of Material Culture*. Unpublished PhD thesis, University College Cork.

Coghlan, H. and Raftery, J. (1961) Irish Prehistoric Casting Moulds. *Sibrium* 6, 223–44.

Coles, B. and Coles, J. (1986) *Sweet Track to Glastonbury*. London, Thames & Hudson.

Coles, J. M., Heal, S. V. E. and Orme, B. J. (1978) The use and character of wood in prehistoric Britain and Ireland. *Proceedings of the Prehistoric Society* 44, 1–46.

Collins, A. E. P. (1971) Ballymacrea Neolithic settlement site. *Excavations 1971: Summary Accounts of Archaeological Excavations in Ireland*, 135–6. Dublin, Wordwell.

Collins, T. (2003) Hermitage, Co. Limerick. Prehistoric. In I. Bennett (ed.) *Excavations 2001: Summary Accounts of Archaeological Excavations in Ireland*, 232–33. Dublin, Wordwell.

Condit, T. (1993) Travelling Earthwork Arrives at Tara. *Archaeology Ireland* 7(4), 10–12.

Conway, M. (2003) Corrstown Co. Derry: Assesment. In I. Bennett (ed.) *Excavations 2001: Summary Accounts of Archaeological Excavations in Ireland*, 60–1. Dublin, Wordwell.

Conway, M. (2004) Corrstown Co. Derry: Prehistoric and Early Christian Settlement. In I. Bennett (ed.) *Excavations 2002: Summary Accounts of Archaeological Excavations in Ireland*, 100–102. Dublin, Wordwell.

Conway, M. (2005) Hopefield Road, Corrstown, Co. Derry. *Archaeology Ireland*, Vol. 19 (71), 4.

Conway, M. (2010) A Bronze Age Village at Corrstown, Co. Londonderry. In E. Murray and P. Logue (ed.), *Battles, Boats and Bones. Archaeological Discoveries in Northern Ireland 1987–2008*. Northern Ireland Environment Agency. Belfast, TSO.

Conway, M., Gahan, A, and Rathbone, S. (2004) Corrstown: a large Middle Bronze Age village. *Current Archaeology* 195, 120–3.

Conway, M., Gahan, A., Rathbone, S., Lear, M. and Ginn, V. (2008) *Corrstown Final Excavation Report*. Unpublished report prepared for Archaeological Consultancy Services Ltd.

Cooney, G. (2000) Lambay Island, Co. Dublin. Neolithic axe production with associated activity. In I. Bennett (ed.), *Excavations 1999: Summary Accounts of Archaeological Excavations in Ireland*, 88. Dublin, Wordwell.

Cooney, G. (2002) Lambay Island, Co. Dublin. Neolithic axe production with associated activity. In I. Bennett (ed.), *Excavations 2000: Summary Accounts of Archaeological Excavations in Ireland*, 109–11. Dublin, Wordwell.

Cooney, G. (2003) Lambay Island, Co. Dublin. Neolithic axe production with associated activity. In I. Bennett (ed.), *Excavations 2001: Summary Accounts of Archaeological Excavations in Ireland*, 126–8. Dublin, Wordwell.

Cooney, G. and Grogan, E. (1999) *Irish Prehistory: A Social Perspective*. Dublin, Wordwell.

Cooney, G. and Mandal, S. (1998) *The Irish Stone Axe Project*. Monograph 1. Bray, Wordwell.

Cooper, J., Kelley, J., Belknap, D., Quinn, R., and McKenna, J. (2002) Inner shelf seismic stratigraphy off the north coast of Northern Ireland: new data on the depth of the Holocene lowstand. *Marine Geology* 186, 369–87.

Corlett, C. (1998) The Prehistoric Ritual Landscape of Croagh Patrick, Co. Mayo. *The Journal of Irish Archaeology* 9, 9–26.

Cotter, E. (2005) Bronze Age Ballybrowney, Co. Cork. In J. O'Sullivan and M. Stanley (eds), *Recent Archaeological Discoveries on National Road Schemes 2004*, 25–35. Archaeology and the National Roads Authority Monograph Series 2. Dublin, Wordwell.

Cunliffe, B. (1974) *Iron Age Communities in Britain: An Account of England, Scotland and Wales from the Seventh Century BC until the Roman Conquest*. London, Routledge.

Cunliffe, B. (2001) *Facing the Ocean: The Atlantic and its peoples, 8000 BC to AD 1500*. Oxford, Oxford University Press.

Cunliffe, B. (2003) *Danebury Hillfort*. Stroud, Tempus.

Curwen, E. C. (1938) The Hebrides: a cultural backwater. *Antiquity* 12 (47), 261–98.

Danaher, E. (2004) Ballinaspig More 5, Co. Cork. In I. Bennett (ed.) *Excavations 2002: Summary Accounts of Archaeological Excavations in Ireland*, 55–6. Dublin, Wordwell.

Davies, O. (1949) Excavations at the horned cairn at Ballymarlagh, Co. Antrim. *Ulster Journal of Archaeology* 12, 26–42.

Deevy, M. (2000) *Gorteen, Co. Limerick. Fulachta fiadh and stone-lined well*. In I. Bennett (ed.), *Excavations 1999: Summary Accounts of Archaeological Excavations in Ireland*, 166–7. Dublin, Wordwell.

Doody, M. (2000) Bronze Age houses in Ireland. In A. Desmond, G. Johnson, M. McCarthy, J. Sheehan, and E. Shee Twohig (eds) *New Agendas in Irish Prehistory*, 135–60. Bray, Wordwell.

Doody M. G. (1987) Ballyveelish, Co. Tipperary. In R. M. Cleary, M. F. Hurley and E. A. Twohig (eds) *Archaeological Excavations on the Cork-Dublin Gas Pipeline (1981–82)*, 9–22. Cork Archaeological Studies No. 1.

Doyle, L. and Moore, D. G. (1997) *Antrim coast and glens – a preliminary assessment of the archaeology*. Vol 1: Main Report. Queen's University Belfast/Environment and Heritage Service Belfast.

Edmonds, M. (1995) *Stone Tools and Society: Working Stone in the Neolithic and Bronze Age Britain*. London, Routledge.

Ellison, A. (1987) The Bronze Age settlement at Thorny Down. *Proceedings of the Prehistoric Society* 53, 385–92.

Eogan, G. (1964) The Later Bronze Age in Ireland in the light of recent research. *Proceedings of the Prehistoric Society* 14, 268–350.

Eogan, G. (1983) *Hoards of the Irish Later Bronze Age*. Dublin, University College Dublin.

Eogan, G. (1984) *Excavations at Knowth* 1. Dublin, Royal Irish Academy Monographs in Archaeology.

Eogan, G. (1993) Aspects of metal production and manufacturing systems during the Irish Bronze Age. *Acta praehistorica etarchaeologica* 25, 87–110.

Eogan G. (1998) Homes and Homesteads in Bronze Age Ireland. In H. Bernhard (ed.) *Mensch und Umwelt in der Bronzezeit Europas,* 307–26. Kiel, Oetker-Voges Verlag.

Eogan, G. and Roche, H. (1997) *Excavations at Knowth* 2. Dublin, Royal Irish Academy Monographs in Archaeology.

Francis, E. (1987) *The Palynology of the Glencoy Area.* Unpublished PhD thesis, Queen's University Belfast.

Gale, R. and Cutler, D. (2000) *Plants in archaeology. Identification of vegetative plant materials used in Europe and the southern Mediterranean to c. 1500.* West Yorkshire, Westbury Publishing.

Giles, M. and Parker Pearson M. (1999) Learning to live in the Iron Age: dwelling and praxis. In B. Bevan (ed.) *Northern exposure: Interpretative Devolution and the Iron Ages in Britain,* 217–31. Leicester, School of Archaeological Studies, University of Leicester.

Goddard, A. (1971) *Studies of the Vegetational Changes Associated with Initiation of Blanket Peat Accumulation in North East Ireland.* Unpublished PhD thesis, Queen's University Belfast.

Goddard, I. (1971) *The Palaeoecology of some sites in the North of Ireland.* Unpublished MSc thesis, Queen's University Belfast.

Gowen, M. (1988) *Three Irish Gas Pipelines: New Archaeological Evidence in Munster.* Wordwell, Dublin.

Gowen, M. and Tarbett, C. (1988) A Third Season at Tankardstown. *Archaeology Ireland* 8, 156.

Gowen, M., Ó Néill, J. and Phillips, M. (eds) (2005) *The Lisheen Mine Archaeological Project 1996–8.* Dublin, Wordwell.

Greig, J. R. A. (1991) The British Isles. In W. Van Zeist, K. Wasylikowa and K. E. Behre (eds) *Progress in Old World palaeoethnobotany,* 299–334. Rotterdam/Brookfield, Balkema.

Grogan, E. (2004a) The implications of Irish Neolithic houses. In I. Shepard and G. Barclay (eds) *Scotland in Ancient Europe,* 103–114. Edinburgh, Society of Antiquaries of Scotland.

Grogan, E. (2004b) Middle Bronze Age burial traditions in Ireland. In H. Roche, E. Grogan, J. Bradley, J. Coles and B. Raftery (eds) *From Megaliths to Metals. Essays in Honour of George Eogan,* 61–71. Oxford, Oxbow Books.

Grogan, E. (2005a) Appendix C. The pottery from Mooghaun South. In E. Grogan *The later prehistoric landscape of south-east Clare,* 317–28. Discovery Programme Monograph 6, Volume 1. Dublin, The Discovery Programme/Wordwell.

Grogan, E. (2005b) *The North Munster Project Vol. 1: the Later Prehistoric Landscape of Southeast Clare.* Discovery Programme Monograph 6. Dublin, Wordwell.

Grogan, E. (2005c) *The North Munster Project Vol. 2: The Prehistoric Landscape of North Munster.* Discovery Programme Monograph 6. Dublin, Wordwell.

Grogan, E. and Eogan, G. (1987) Lough Gur excavations by Seán P. Ó Ríordáin: further Neolithic and Beaker habitations on Knockadoon. *Proceedings of the Royal Irish Academy* 87C, 299–506.

Grogan, E. and Roche, H. (2004a) *The prehistoric pottery from Ballinaspig More 5, Ballincollig, Co. Cork.* Unpublished report prepared for Archaeological Consultancy Services Ltd.

Grogan, E. and Roche, H. (2006a) *The prehistoric pottery from Monanny, Co. Monaghan (03E0888).* Unpublished report prepared for Irish Archaeological Consultancy Ltd.

Grogan, E. and Roche, H. (2006b) *The prehistoric pottery from the M3 Testing. Preliminary Report.* Unpublished report prepared for Archaeological Consultancy Services Ltd.

Grogan, E. and Roche, H. (2007a) *The prehistoric pottery from Ballydrehid, Co. Tipperary (Site 185.5).* Unpublished report prepared for Margaret Gowen and Co. Ltd.

Grogan, E. and Roche, H. (2007b) *The prehistoric pottery assemblage from Darcytown 1, Balrothery, Co. Dublin (03E0067/03E0067 extension).* Unpublished report prepared for Judith Carroll and Company.

Grogan, E. Condit, T., O'Carroll, F., O'Sullivan, A. and Daly, A. (1996) *Tracing the later prehistoric landscape in north Munster.* Discovery Programme Reports 4, 26–46.

Guinan, B. (2003) *Carrowcor, Co. Mayo. Fulachta fiadh*. In I. Bennett (ed.) *Excavations 2001: Summary Accounts of Archaeological Excavations in Ireland*, 274. Dublin, Wordwell.

Halpin, E. (1995) Excavations at Newtown, Co. Meath. In E. Grogan and C. Mount (eds) *Annus Archaeologiae: Proceedings of the OIA Winter Conference 1993*, 45–54. Dublin, Office of Public Works and Organization of Irish Archaeologists.

Hanley, K. (2002) AR85/86, Knocksaggart. In I. Bennett (ed.) *Excavations 2000: Summary Accounts of Archaeological Excavations in Ireland*, 32–3. Dublin, Wordwell.

Hanna, S. A. (1993) *Blanket Mire Initiation in Ireland with special reference to upland sites in central Ireland and Donegal*. Unpublished PhD thesis, Queen's University Belfast.

Hawkes, J. (1941) Excavation of a Megalithic Tomb at Harristown, Co. Waterford. *Journal of the Royal Society of Antiquaries of Ireland* 71, 130–147.

Healy, F. (2000) Metal using societies of later prehistory. *Past: The Newsletter of the prehistoric society*, [online], No. 36 (December 2000). Lithics studies in the year 2000 Lithic Studies Society Conference 8–10 Sept 2000, Cardiff. Available from: http://www.ucl.ac.uk/prehistoric/past/past36.html#Lithics [Accessed 24/11/06].

Healy, F. (2004) After hunter-gatherers – lithics in a crowd scene. In E. A. Walker, F. W. S. Healy and F. Healy (eds) *Lithics in Action: Papers from the conference, lithic studies in the year 2000*, 183–4. Lithic studies society occasional paper No. 8. Oxford, Oxbow Books.

Herity, M. and Eogan, G. (1977) *Ireland in Prehistory*. London, Routledge and Keegan Paul.

Herring, I. (1937) The forecourt, Hanging Thorn Cairn, McIlwhan's Hill, Ballyutoag, Ligoneil. *Proceedings and Reports of the Belfast Natural History Philosophical Society* 1936–7, 43–9.

Hindle B. P. (1982) *Medieval Roads*. Aylesbury, Shire.

Hjelmqvist, H. (1980) An Irish cereal find from the transition between Bronze and Iron Age. In G. Burenhult (ed.) *The archaeological excavation at Carrowmore, Co. Sligo, Ireland. Excavation seasons 1977–79*, 130–2. (Theses and Papers in North-European Archaeology 9). Stockholm, Institute of Archaeology at the University of Stockholm.

Hull, G. (2007) Excavation of a Bronze Age round-house at Knockdomny, Co. Westmeath. *Journal of Irish Archaeology* XV, 1–14.

Hurl, D. (1994) Crossreagh West, Coleraine Road, Portstewart. www.excavations.ie.

Johnston, P. (2007) Analysis of carbonised plant remains. In E. Grogan, L. O'Donnell and P. Johnston *The Bronze Age Landscapes of the Pipeline to the West*, 70–9. Dublin, Wordwell.

Jordan, K. and O'Conor, T. (2003) Archaeological site of interest surrounding the Turoe Stone. *Journal of Galway Archaeological and Historical Society*, Vol 55, 110–116.

Kavanagh, R. (1976) Collared and Cordoned Urns in Ireland. *Proceedings of the Royal Irish Academy* 76C, 293–403.

Kelley, J., Andrew, J., Copper, G., Jackson, D., Belknap, D., and Quinn, R. (2006) Sea-level change and inner shelf stratigraphy off Northern Ireland. *Marine Geology* 232, 1–15.

Kelly, A. (2008) Interim Report on Grange 3. *Unpublished report prepared for Irish Archaeological Consultancy Ltd*.

Knarrström, B. (2001) *Flint: A Scanian Hardware*. Sweden, National Heritage Board, Archaeological Excavations Department.

Knight, J. (1993) *Technological Analysis of the Anvil (Bipolar) Technique, Lithic Studies: Looking Backwards – Looking Forwards*, 57–87. Oxford, Lithic Studies Society Anniversary Conference 2–4 April 1993. St. Hilda's College.

Knowles, W. J. (1886) Whitepark Bay, Co. Antrim. *Journal of the Royal Society of Antiquities of Ireland* 17, 104–25.

Kuijit, I. (2000) People and Space in Early Agricultural Villages: Exploring Daily Lives, Community Size and Architecture in the Late Pre-pottery Neolithic. *Journal of Anthropological Archaeology* 19, 75–102.

Ladle, L. and Woodward, A. (2003) Middle Bronze Age House and Burnt mound at Bestwall, Wareham, Dorset: An Interim Report. *Proceedings of the Prehistoric Society* 69, 265–77.

Lambeck, K. (1996) Glaciation and sea-level change for Ireland and the Irish Sea since Late Devensian/Midlandian time. *Journal of the Geological Society of London* 153, 853–72.

Lanting, J. and Brindley, A. (1996) Irish logboats and their European context. *Journal of Irish Archaeology* 7, 85–9.

Lawlor, D. P. (2000) *Inner Shelf Sedimentology off the North Coast of Northern Ireland*. Unpublished PhD thesis, University of Coleraine.

Linnane, S. J. (2002) *Tullyallen, Co. Louth*. Unpublished report prepared for Archaeological Consultancy Services Ltd.

Liversage, G. D. (1968) Excavations at Dalkey Island, Co. Dublin, 1956–1959. *Proceedings of the Royal Irish Academy* 66C, 53–233.

Logue, P. (2003) Excavations at Thornhill, Co. Londonderry. In I. Armit, E. Murphy, E. Nelis and D. Simpson (eds) *Neolithic Settlement in Ireland and Western Britain*, 149–55. Oxford, Oxbow Books.

Lynn, C. (2003) *Navan Fort: Archaeology and Myth*. Bray, Wordwell.

MacDonald, P. (2002) *Data Structure Report: Crossreagh West, Portstewart, County Londonderry:* http://64.233.183.104/search?q=cache:Jv5f_zn1RNMJ:www.qub.ac.uk/schools/ CentreforArchaeologicalFieldworkCAF/Reports/DataStructureReports/Filetoupload,64245,en. pdf+crossreagh+west&hl=en&ct=clnk&cd=8&gl=uk

Macdonald, P., Carver, N. and Yates, M. (2005) Excavations at McIlwhans Hill, Ballyutoag, County Antrim. *Ulster Journal of Archaeology* 64, 43–61.

Mallory, J. P. (1990) Trial excavations at Tievebulliagh, Co. Antrim. *Ulster Journal of Archaeology* 52, 15–28.

Mallory, J. P. and McNeill, T. E. (1991) *The Archaeology of Ulster: From Colonization to Plantation*. Belfast, Queen's University Belfast.

Mandal, S., Cooney, G., Meighan, I. and Jamison, D. (1997) Using Geochemistry to Interpret Porcellanite Stone Axe Production in Ireland. *Journal of Archaeological Science* 24, 757.

McCabe, S. (2005) *Report on the Archaeological Excavtion of a Bronze Age Settlement Site at Caltragh, Co. Sligo*. Unpublished report prepared for Archaeological Consultancy Services Ltd.

McConway, C. (2002) Troopersland, IDB Site. West Division, Co. Antrim. www.excavations.ie.

McLoughlin, C. (2002a) *Excavations at Kerlogue, Wexford*. Unpublished report prepared for Stafford McLoughlin Archaeology Ltd.

McManus, C. (2002) IDB (NI) Industrial Development Site, Ballyhenry. In I. Bennett (ed.) *Excavations 2000: Summary Accounts of Archaeological Excavations in Ireland*, 2–3. Dublin, Wordwell.

McQuade, M. (2005) *The N8 Cashel to Mitchelstown Road Improvement Scheme. Preliminary Report on Ballydrehid, Co. Tipperary (Site 185.5)*. Unpublished report prepared for Margaret Gowen and Co. Ltd.

McQuillan, L. (1999) Inch and Ballyrenan 1. www.excavations.ie.

McSparron, C. (2001) *Excavations at Crossreagh East, Portstewart, Co. Derry:* http://www.northarch. supanet.com/CRE%20Report.htm#Intro.

McSparron, C. (2003) The excavation of a Neolithic house in Enagh townland, County Derry. In I. Armit, E. Murphy, E. Nelis and D. Simpson (eds), *Neolithic Settlement in Ireland and Western Britain*, 172–5. Oxford, Oxbow Books.

Molloy, B. (2003) *Excavations at Charlesland Residential Development, Co. Wickow. Site D*. Unpublished report prepared for Margaret Gowen & Co. Ltd.

Moore, D. (2004) Hostilities in Early Neolithic Ireland: Trouble with the New Neighbours – The Evidence from Ballyharry, County Antrim. In A. Gibson and A. Sheridan (eds), *From Sickles to Circles: Britain and Ireland at the Time of Stonehenge*, 142–154. Oxford, Oxbow Books.

Moore, J. and Jennings, D. (eds) (1992) *Reading Business Park: a Bronze Age Landscape*. Oxford, Oxford University School of Archaeology.

Moore, J. (1992) Area 5. In J. Moore and D. Jennings (eds) *Reading Business Park: a Bronze Age Landscape*, 14–29. Oxford, Oxford University School of Archaeology.

Morahan, L. (2001) *Croagh Patrick, Co. Mayo: Archaeology, landscape and people*. Westport, The Croagh Patrick Archaeological Committee.

Mytum, H. (1987) *Excavations at the Iron Age fort of Castell Henllys in North Pembrokeshire: An interim report 1980–86*. York, Department of Archaeology, University of York.

Mytum, H. (1999) Castell Henllys. *Current Archaeology*, 161, 164–72.

Nolan, J. (2003) *Clare, Co. Mayo. Fulachta fiadh*. In I. Bennett (ed.), *Excavations 2001: Summary Accounts of Archaeological Excavations in Ireland*, 228. Dublin, Wordwell.

Nowakowski, J. (2001) Leaving home in the Cornish Bronze Age. In J. Brück (ed.) *Bronze Age Landscapes, Tradition and Transformation*, 139–48. Oxford, Oxbow Books.

Ó Drisceoil, C. (2003) Archaeological excavations of a Neolithic settlement at Coolfore, Co. Louth. In I. Armit, E. Murphy, E. Nelis and D. Simpson (eds) *Neolithic Settlement in Ireland and Western Britain*, 176–81. Oxford, Oxbow Books.

Ó Néill, J. (2001) A Glimpse of Wicklow's Past. *Archaeology Ireland* 58, 30–1.

Ó Néill, J. (2005) Killoran 8. In M. Gowen, J. Ó Néill and M. Phillips (eds) *The Lisheen Mine Archaeological Project 1996–8*, 288–90. Dublin, Wordwell.

Ó Néill, J. forthcoming *Inventory of Bronze Age Structures*. British Archaeology Reports. Oxford, Archaeopress.

Ó Nuallain, S. (1972) A Neolithic house at Ballyglass near Ballycastle, Co. Mayo. *Journal of the Royal Society of Antiquaries of Ireland* 102, 49–57.

Ó Ríordáin, A. B. (1967) Cordoned Urn burial at Laheen, Co. Donegal. *Journal of the Royal Society of Antiquaries of Ireland* 97, 39–44.

Ó Ríordáin, A. B. and Waddell, J. (1993) *The Funerary Bowls and Vases of the Irish Bronze Age*. Galway, Galway University Press.

Ó Ríordáin, S. P. (1954) Lough Gur Excavations: Neolithic and Bronze Age Houses on Knockadoon. *Proceedings of the Royal Irish Academy* 56C, 297–459.

Ó Ríordáin, S. P. (1953) *Antiquities of the Irish countryside*. London (3rd edn), Methuen and Co. Ltd.

O'Brien, W. (2000) Ballyrisode, Co. Cork. Early Bronze Age Copper Mine. I. Bennett (ed.) *Excavations 1999: Summary Accounts of Archaeological Excavations in Ireland*, 21–2. Dublin, Wordwell.

O'Donnell, L. (2007) Charcoal and Wood. In E. Grogan, L. O'Donnell and P. Johnston 2007 *The Bronze Age Landscapes of the Pipeline to the West*, 27–69. Dublin, Wordwell.

O'Hara, R. (2004) *Archaeological Excavations at Grange Rath, Colp West, Co. Meath*. Unpublished report prepared for Archaeological Consultancy Services Ltd.

O'Hare M. (2005) *The Bronze Age Lithics of Ireland*. Unpublished PhD thesis, Queen's University Belfast.

O'Hare, M. (forthcoming) *The Everyday Chipped Stone Technologies of the Irish Bronze Age: a Broader Regional Perspective* British Archaeological Reports, International Series. Oxford, Archaeopress.

O'Kelly M. J. (1989) *Early Ireland. An Introduction to Irish Prehistory*. Cambridge, Cambridge University Press.

O'Sullivan, A. (1998) *The Archaeology of Lake Settlement in Ireland*. Discovery Programme Monograph, No. 4. Dublin, Royal Irish Academy.

O'Sullivan, M. (2005) *Duma na nGiall. The Mound of the Hostages, Tara*. Dublin, School of Archaeology, University College Dublin/Wordwell.

Oppenheimer, S. (2006) *The origins of the British*. London, Constable.

Orme, B. J. and Coles J. M. (1985) Prehistoric Workworking from the Somerset Levels 2. Species selection and prehistoric woodlands. *Somerset Levels Papers* 11, 7–24.

Oswald, A. (1997) A doorway to the past: practical and mystic concerns in the orientation of roundhouse doorways. In A. Gwilt and C. Haselgrove (eds) *Reconstructing Iron Age Societies*, 87–95. Oxford, Oxbow Books.

Parker Pearson, M., Chamberlain, A., Craig, O., Marshall, P., Mulville, J., Smith, H., Chenery, C., Collins, M., Cooks, G., Craig, G., Evans, J., Hiller, J., Montgommery, J., Schwenninger, J-L., Taylor, G., and Wess, T. (2005) Evidence for mummification in Bronze Age Britain. *Antiquity* 79, 529–46.

Parker Pearson, M., Sharples, N. and Symonds, J. (2004) *South Uist: Archaeology and History of a Hebridean Island*. Stroud, Tempus.

Pendleton, C. (2001) Firstly, let's get rid of ritual. In J. Brück (ed.) *Bronze Age Landscapes: Tradition and Transformation*, 170–8. Oxford, Oxbow Books.

Plunkett, G. (1999) *Environmental Change in the Late Bronze Age in Ireland, 1200–600 cal BC*. Unpublished DPhil thesis, Queen's University Belfast.

Pollock, A. and Waterman, D. (1964) A Bronze Age habitation site at Downpatrick. *Ulster Journal of Archaeology* 27, 31–58.

Pope R. (2008) Roundhouses 3000 years of Prehistoric Design. *Current Archaeology*, Vol XIX (6), 222.

Pryor, F. (2001) *Seahenge: a Quest for Life and Death in Bronze Age Britain*. London, Harper Collins.

Purcell, A. (2002) Excavation of Three Neolithic Houses at Corbally, County Kildare. *Journal of Irish Archaeology* 11, 31–76.

Raftery, B. (1995) The Conundrum of Irish Iron Age Pottery. In B. Raftery, V. Megaw and V. Rigby (eds) *Sites and Sights of the Iron Age. Essays on Fieldwork and Museum Research presented to Ian Matheson Stead*, 149–156. Oxbow Monographs 56. Oxford, Oxbow Books.

Raftery, B. (1999) Paths, tracks and roads in Early Ireland. In A. F. Harding *Experiment and design: Archaeological studies in honour of John Coles*, 170–82. Oxford, Oxbow Books.

Raftery, B. (forthcoming) *Excavations at Rathgall, Co. Wicklow*. Dublin, School of Archaeology, University College Dublin/Wordwell.

Ramsay, G. (1995) Middle Bronze Age Metalwork: Are Artefact Studies Dead and Buried? In J. Waddell and E. Shee Twohig (eds) *Ireland in the Bronze Age*, 49–62. Dublin, Stationery Office.

Rathbone, S. (in prep) The Village People? A reconsideration of Neolithic and Bronze Age settlement patterns in Britain and Ireland.

Read, C. (2000) Neolithic/Bronze Age cemetery site at Ballyconneely, Co. Clare. *Archaeology Ireland* 54, 28–9.

Reilly, A. (2000) Magheramenagh, Co. Derry: souterrain, prehistoric house. In I. Bennett (ed.), *Excavations 1999: Summary Accounts of Archaeological Excavations in Ireland*, 38–40. Dublin, Wordwell.

Reynolds, P. J. (1979) *Iron Age Farm, The Butser Experiment*. London, British Museum Publications Limited.

Reynolds, P. J. (1982) Substructure to Superstructure. In P. J. Drury (ed.), *Structural Reconstruction: Approaches to the interpretation of the excavatin remains of buildings*, 173–199. British Archaeological Reports, British Series 110. Oxford, Archaeopress.

Roche, H. (2004) *The Prehistoric Pottery from Kerlogue, Co. Wexford*. Unpublished report prepared for Stafford McLoughlan Archaeology.

Roche, H. (forthcoming a) The prehistoric pottery assemblage from Ballyglass, Co. Mayo. Appendix. In S. Ó Nualláin *Excavations at Ballyglass, Co. Mayo*. Dublin, School of Archaeology, University College Dublin/Wordwell.

Roche, H. (forthcoming b) The prehistoric pottery assemblage from Rathgall, Co. Wicklow. Appendix. In B. Raftery *Excavations at Rathgall, Co. Wicklow*. Dublin, School of Archaeology, University College Dublin/Wordwell.

Roche, H. and Grogan, E. (2005a) *The N8 Rathcormac – Fermoy Bypass. The prehistoric pottery*. Unpublished report prepared for Archaeological Consultancy Services Ltd.

Roche, H. and Grogan, E. (2005b) *N2 Finglas – Ashbourne. Baltrasna, Co. Dublin (Site 17/18, 03E1354)*. Unpublished report prepared for CRDS Ltd.

Roche, H. and Grogan, E. (2005c) *N2 Finglas – Ashbourne. Kilshane, Co. Dublin (Site 5, O3E1359)*. Unpublished report prepared for CRDS Ltd.

Roe, F. (1966) The Battle-Axe Series in Britain. *Proceedings of the Prehistoric Society* 31, 199–245.

Roe, F. (1968) Stone maceheads and the Latest Neolithic Cultures of the British Isles. In J. Coles and D. D. A. Simpson (eds) *Studies in Ancient Europe*, 145–72. Leicester.

Roe, F. (1979) Typology of stone implements with shaftholes. In T. H. McK. Clough and W. A. Cumins (eds) *Stone Axe Studies: Archaeological, Petrological, Experimental and Ethnographic Vol 1*, 23–48. London, Council for British Archaeology.

Russell, I. and Ginn, V. (2006) *Interim Excavation Report on Adamstown 3, 03E1217, Co. Waterford*. Unpublished report prepared for Archaeological Consultancy Services Ltd.

Ryan, M. (1975) Urn Burial at Ballintubbrid, near Blackwater, County Wexford. *Journal of the Royal Society of Antiquaries of Ireland* 105, 132–38.

Sheridan, A. (1995) Irish Neolithic pottery: the story in 1995. In I. Kinnes and G. Varndell (eds) *Unbaked Urns of Rudely Shape*, 3–21. Oxbow Monograph 55. Oxford, Oxbow Books.

Sheridan, A., Cooney, G. and Grogan, E. (1992) Stone axes studies in Ireland. *Proceedings of the Prehistoric Society* 58, 389–416.

Sheridan, J. A. (1986) Porcellanite artifacts: a new survey. *Ulster Journal of Archaeology* 49, 19–32.

Shott, M. J. (1989) Bipolar Industries: Ethnographic Evidence and Archaeological Implications. *North American Archaeologist* 10 (1), 1–24.

Shott, M. J. and Sillitoe, P. (2005) Use life and curation in New Guinea experimental used flakes. *Journal of Archaeological Science* 32, 653–63.

Simpson, D. (1996) The Ballygalley houses, Co. Antrim, Ireland. In T. Darvill and J. Thomas (eds), *Neolithic Houses in Northwest Europe and Beyond*, 123–32. Oxford, Neolithic Studies Group Seminar Papers 1, Oxbow Monograph 57, Oxbow Books.

Simpson, D. D. A. (1988) The Stone Maceheads of Ireland. *Journal of the Royal Society of Antiquaries of Ireland* 118, 27–52.

Simpson, D. D. A. (1989) The Stone Maceheads of Ireland, Part II. *Journal of the Royal Society of Antiquaries of Ireland* 119, 113–26.

Simpson, D. D. A. (1990a) The Stone Battle Axes of Ireland. *Journal of the Royal Society of Antiquaries of Ireland* 120, 5–40.

Simpson, D. D. A. (1990b) Irish axe hammers. *Ulster Journal of Archaeology* 53, 50–6.

Smith, A. G. (1975) Neolithic and Bronze Age landscape changes in Northern Ireland. In J. G. Evans, S. Limbrey and H. Cleere (eds) *The effect of Man on the Landscape: the Highland Zone*, 64–73. London, Council for British Archaeology, Research Report No. 11.

Suddaby, I. (2003) The Excavation of Two Late Bronze Age Roundhouses at Ballyprior Beg, Co. Antrim. *Ulster Journal of Archaeology* 62, 45–92.

Taylor, C. (1979) *Roads and Trackways of Britain*. London, Orion.

Taylor, K. (2004) Knockuregare, Co. Limerick. Bronze Age ring-gullies and enclosures. In I. Bennett (ed.) *Excavations 2002: Summary Accounts of Archaeological Excavations in Ireland*, 331–33. Dublin, Wordwell.

Taylor, K. (2008) At Home and on the Road: Two Iron Age sites in Co Tipperary. *Seanda* Issue 3, 54–5.

Tinevez, J. Y. (2002) The Late Neolithic settlement of La Hersonnais, Plechatel in its regional context. In G. Varndell and P. Topping (eds) *Enclosures in Neolithic Europe*. Oxford, Oxbow Books.

Tobin, S., Swift, D. and Wiggins, K. (2004) *Greystones Southern Access Route (GSAR), Co. Wicklow. Sites 6/6a–g, Priestsnewtown. Excavation report. Licence no. 04E0401.* Unpublished report prepared for Judith Carroll and Company for Wicklow County Council.

Townsend, S. (2007) What have reconstructed roundhouses ever done for us? *Proceedings of the Prehistoric Socitey* 73, 97–111.

Waddell, J. (1983) Rathcroghan – a Royal Site in Connacht. *Journal of Irish Archaeology* Vol 1, 21–46.

Waddell J. (1991) The Irish Sea. *Prehistory Journal of Irish Archaeology* VI, 29–40.

Waddell, J. (1995) The Cordoned Urn tradition. In I. Kinnes and G. Varndell (eds) *Unbaked Urns of Rudely Shape*, 113–22. Oxford, Oxbow Monograph 55, Oxbow Books.

Waddell, J. (1998) *The Prehistoric Archaeology of Ireland*. Galway, Galway University Press.

Wainwright, G. and Smith, K. (1980) The Shaugh Moor Project: second report – the enclosure. *Proceedings of the Prehistoric Society* 46, 65–122.

Walsh, F. (2005) *N2 Carrickmacross–Aclint Road Re-Alignment. Site 110 Monanny (03E0888). Post-Excavation Assessment and updated Project Design.* Unpublished report prepared for Irish Archaeological Consultancy Ltd.

Weir, D. A. (1993) *An environmental history of the Navan Area, Co. Armagh.* Unpublished PhD thesis, Queen's University Belfast.

Weiss, B. (1982) The decline of Late Bronze Age civilization as a possible response to climatic change. *Climate Change* 4, 173–198.

Wilde, W. R. 1861 *A Descriptive Catalogue of the Anqituities of Stone, Earthen and Vegetable Materials in the Museum of the Royal Irish Academy.* Dublin, M. H. Gill.

Williams, B. (1986) Excavations at Altanagh, County Tyrone. *Ulster Journal of Archaeology* 49, 33–88.

Woodman, P. C. (1985) *Excavations at Mount Sandel 1973–77.* Belfast, The Stationery Office.

Appendix I

An analysis of the Radiocarbon Dates from Corrstown, Co. Londonderry by Cormac McSparron (Centre for Archaeological Fieldwork, School of Geography, Archaeology and Palaeoecology, Queen's University Belfast)

Introduction

In total 37 radiocarbon dates were obtained using samples from the excavations at Corrstown, Co. Londonderry (Table 4.3). A first batch of 29 dates was commissioned during initial post-excavation analysis by Archaeological Consultancy Services Ltd. The dates were funded by the Environment and Heritage Service of the Department of the Environment (now the Northern Ireland Environment Agency) and dated by the Chrono Centre, Queen's University Belfast (28 dates) and Beta Analytic Inc. (one date). A second batch of eight dates was selected from the remaining suitable charcoal samples by Victoria Ginn, and dated at and funded by the Chrono Centre for Climate, the Environment and Chronology, Queen's University Belfast. Overall, four of these dates were associated with the medieval features, one returned a Mesolithic date, and one returned an Iron Age date. This appendix examines the chronological implications of the 31 radiocarbon dates which fell within the Bronze Age period.

The results of the radiocarbon dating analysis suggests that there was an initial smaller scale 'Growth Phase' settlement at Corrstown which is likely to have commenced after 1550 BC, and probably after 1460 BC (Phase 1). This then became a fully-fledged 'Village Phase' sometime between 1360 and 1270 BC. This village settlement, Phase 2, is likely to have lasted between 10 and 200 years, although given the evidence for the repair and rebuilding of some structures several times (see particularly Chapter 2) it seems likely that the village was occupied for at least several generations. By the middle years of the twelfth century BC the site appears to have entered a period of decline – the 'Decline Phase' – where there may have been sporadic settlement for a considerable period after this. It is feasible that this final period of occupation could have lasted for centuries, although the small number of later dates makes a precise estimation impossible.

Methodology

Unfortunately, little information on the methodology of sample selection exists from the first batch of radiocarbon dates. Although there is a record of the structure and feature from which each dated sample was obtained, the lack of charcoal identification has obvious implications for defining the settlement's chronology. The second batch of dates tried to address some of these deficiencies by using identified wood charcoal samples; however, there was only a small amount of available material representing nine structures, eight of which were datable.

The dates from Corrstown were calibrated, sequenced and plotted using OxCal 3.10 (Bronk Ramsey 2005) using the IntCal 04 calibration curve (Reimer *et al*. 2004).

Sequencing is a technique which uses assumptions about the chronological sequence of a series of radiocarbon dates, and potentially other information, to statistically constrain the calibrated ranges of the dates and to make statistical estimates of the beginning, end, duration, etc. of the sequences. There are a number of approaches to sequencing. One approach frequently used in a site specific analysis is to take the stratigraphic information from a site to build a reliable sequence of events which can be compared with the radiocarbon evidence and used to statistically tighten the dating and phasing of a site. A second approach, the approach used in this analysis, can be used when there is no, or little, stratigraphic information but where we can make the assumption that all, or most, of the dates in the analysis belong to the same phase of activity or period under study. In this the dates are sequenced, in order of the earliest to latest radiocarbon date, having informed the computer program, using the Boundary command that the events belong to a period with a beginning and an end and not just randomly distributed through history. OxCal can then statistically test the proposition that the radiocarbon dates are likely to belong to a bounded period. It informs the user by way of Agreement Indices if the radiocarbon data fits the suggested model and can estimate the beginning, end and duration of the periods and phases of activity under study.

The analysis of the dating of a village, with little in the way of a stratigraphic sequence, is an ideal subject for this second type of analysis as we can assume that the village should have reasonably defined beginning and end points, with possible sub-phasing in between. The success of the analysis depends on using dates which date to the actual period of village use and correctly identifying and removing outliers, dates from residual samples, dates effected by contamination and identifying and dealing with dates subject to the 'old wood' effect (Warner 1990).

Although there is no substitute for using short-lived single entities, as defined by Ashmore (1999), in the Corrstown case it is possible that there were no short-lived single entities dated in the first batch of dates and there were no short-lived single entities available to date for the second batch of dates. Consequently, all the dates from Corrstown have the potential to be affected by 'old wood' latency and it is likely that most are affected to a greater or lesser degree. In an attempt to redress this, an 'old wood' correction, as suggested initially by Warner (1990) and updated for use in OxCal following suggestions by Richard Warner (Warner forthcoming), has been utilised. It is explained in more detail below.

Calibration and sequencing of Corrstown radiocarbon dates

At first the 31 Bronze Age dates from Corrstown were calibrated without further sequencing or data manipulation (Illustration AI.1). A sample from one of the Bronze Age roundhouses, S31, returned an early medieval date of AD 653–766 (UBA-16613;

Atmospheric data from Reimer et al (2004);OxCal v3.10 Bronk Ramsey (2005); cub r:5 sd:12 prob usp[chron]

S1 UB-6230 3556±34BP	
S19 UB-6247 3293±32BP	
S19 UB-6246 3256±32BP	
S21 UB-6379 3199±35BP	
S58 UB-6243 3178±32BP	
S47 UB-6382 3156±35BP	
S65 UB-6244 3153±32BP	
S43 UB-6239 3143±33BP	
S31 UB-6236 3141±33BP	
S76 UB-6251 3129±31BP	
S8 UB-6240 3120±33BP	
S33 UB-6235 3117±33BP	
S47 UBA-16608 Alder 3103±26BP	
S37 UB-6238 3101±32BP	
S4 UB-6231 3090±32BP	
S4 UBA-16615 Hazel 3089±24BP	
S17 UB-6381 3086±34BP	
S68 UB-6380 3076±34BP	
S30 UB-6234 3072±32BP	
S45 UB-6248 3068±31BP	
S17 UBA-16611 Hazel 3050±32BP	
S40 UB-6241 3048±32BP	
S15 UB-6378 3041±34BP	
S23 UB-6249 3041±32BP	
S37 UBA-16612 Alder 3024±22BP	
S40 UBA-16614 Alder 3003±24BP	
S23 UBA-16610 Hazel 2946±25BP	
S33 UBA-16609 Alder 2946±27BP	
S9 Beta-190132 2900±50BP	
S33 UB-6233 2932±33BP	
S13 UB-6245 2796±32BP	
S31 UBA-16613 Hazel 1326±22BP	

3000CalBC   2000CalBC   1000CalBC   CalBC/CalAD   1000CalAD

Calibrated date

Illustration AI.1: Corrstown radiocarbon dates sorted by date and calibrated

charcoal: hazel) which was most likely a result of intrusive material from the early medieval ringfort which truncated it. The earliest Bronze Age date UB-6230, obtained from S1, which has a calibrated range of 2016–1772 BC, seems significantly older than any of the other dates, from either the identified or unidentified charcoal samples. It seems too old to be a likely 'old wood' effect and seems likely to be the result of a fragment of old charcoal being residually deposited in a later feature, possibly at the time that the house and its surrounding ditch were constructed. These two dates have been excluded from further analysis of the data set.

An initial sequence, Sequence 1, of the 30 suitable dates, was carried out (Illustration AI.2). The OxCal 3.10 program (Bronk Ramsey 2005) tests the consistency of the proposed chronological sequence against the actual radiocarbon dates providing Agreement

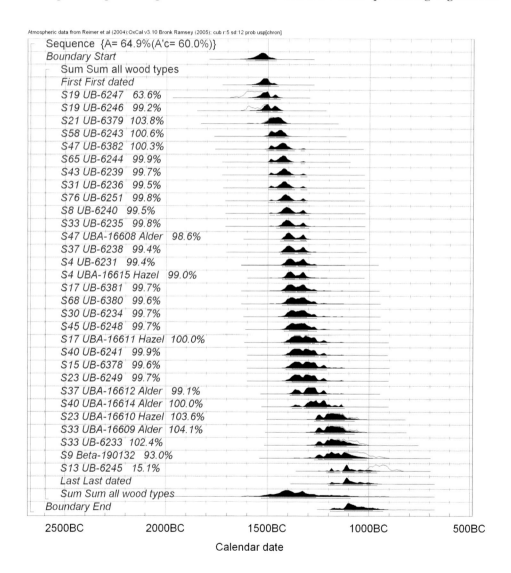

Illustration AI.2: Corrstown dates, outliers removed, calibrated and sequenced as a single phase of activity

Indices: figures which express, in the form of a percentage, the degree of overlap between what the model expects and what actually is the evidence of the radiocarbon dates. An Agreement Index of 60% or above is considered acceptable. Agreement Indices are produced for both the individual dates within the model and the overall model. If either the overall model or the individual dates within it have Agreement Indices which fall beneath the 60% level then the chronological model and the provenance of the material which provided the radiocarbon dates should be examined and if necessary revised. It is worth stating that an Agreement Index above 60% does not prove that a model is correct, it just shows that it *may* be correct, that the model and the radiocarbon dates are *compatible* with each other. The Agreement Index for the overall Sequence 1 at Corrstown was 65.1%, showing that OxCal finds that the suggestion that the dates are all part of a bounded episode of use compatible with the radiocarbon dating evidence. However, one date, the latest date in the sequence UB-6245 2796 ±32, which has a calibrated range of 1030 to 840 BC from S13 has an Agreement Index of only 15.1%, indicating that it is chronologically too far removed from the rest of the data set to be likely to be part of this bounded series of events. Given the unidentified, mixed, charcoal sample and the presence of early medieval structures within a few metres of this site this date seems a likely candidate for contamination and it has been excluded from further analysis.

With this date removed the samples from the excavation were again sequenced in OxCal, Sequence 2 (Illustration AI.3). As part of Sequence 2 OxCal was asked to quantify, using the Boundary command, the likely beginning and end dates for activity at the site, and the possible span of use of the site. OxCal estimated from this data set that activity at the site commenced between 1580 and 1450 BC and continued to between 1260 and 1110 BC. The estimated period of continuing activity at the village site was estimated, using the Span command, at between 210 and 400 years.

However, as mentioned above, three different types of samples were dated from Corrstown. Of the 30 samples dated and used in this analysis, 23 were from unidentified charcoal, four were from alder and three were from hazel. It is possible, in fact likely given their prevalence in Ireland, that many, if not most, of the unidentified samples come from long-lived wood species, probably oak. Consequently, it is best practice to assume that some of these samples have been affected by a considerable 'old wood effect' (Warner 1990). A brief examination of Sequence 2 indicates that none of the identified charcoal dates, both alder and also hazel, come from the earliest third of the date range, supporting this view. In fact it is even likely that the identified charcoal dates may be affected by some 'old wood effect' as alder can grow for up to 200 years and even hazel can potentially live for 50 years (Warner 1990).

To minimise the potential old wood effect it is possible to utilise only those dates which come from the shortest lived species, hazel with a life of only 50 years, is an obvious example. In the case of Corrstown; however, there are only three hazel dates available, the fourth being the probably contaminated early medieval date. This is clearly too few dates for a meaningful analysis of so complex a site.

A suggestion has been made by Richard Warner (1990) which can address this problem. Warner postulated that it might be possible to allow for potential 'old wood effect' in unidentified wood samples, or in samples which were potentially long lived. Warner used a computer simulation to combine the probability of an old wood effect,

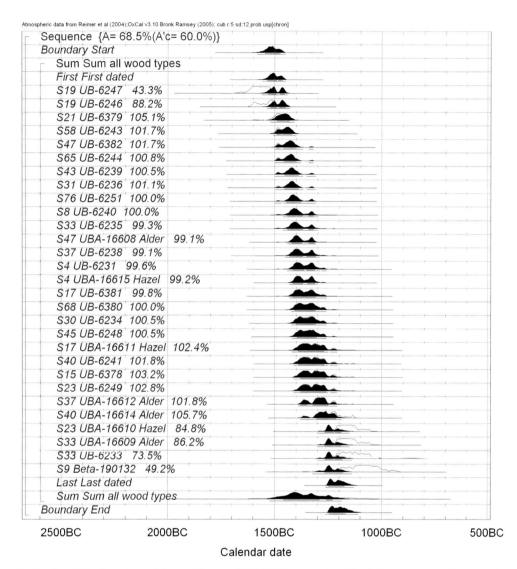

Atmospheric data from Reimer et al (2004);OxCal v3.10 Bronk Ramsey (2005); cub r:5 sd:12 prob usp[chron]

Sequence {A= 68.5%(A'c= 60.0%)}
Boundary Start
  Sum Sum all wood types
  First First dated
    S19 UB-6247 43.3%
    S19 UB-6246 88.2%
    S21 UB-6379 105.1%
    S58 UB-6243 101.7%
    S47 UB-6382 101.7%
    S65 UB-6244 100.8%
    S43 UB-6239 100.5%
    S31 UB-6236 101.1%
    S76 UB-6251 100.0%
    S8 UB-6240 100.0%
    S33 UB-6235 99.3%
    S47 UBA-16608 Alder 99.1%
    S37 UB-6238 99.1%
    S4 UB-6231 99.6%
    S4 UBA-16615 Hazel 99.2%
    S17 UB-6381 99.8%
    S68 UB-6380 100.0%
    S30 UB-6234 100.5%
    S45 UB-6248 100.5%
    S17 UBA-16611 Hazel 102.4%
    S40 UB-6241 101.8%
    S15 UB-6378 103.2%
    S23 UB-6249 102.8%
    S37 UBA-16612 Alder 101.8%
    S40 UBA-16614 Alder 105.7%
    S23 UBA-16610 Hazel 84.8%
    S33 UBA-16609 Alder 86.2%
    S33 UB-6233 73.5%
    S9 Beta-190132 49.2%
  Last Last dated
  Sum Sum all wood types
Boundary End

2500BC   2000BC   1500BC   1000BC   500BC

Calendar date

Illustration AI.3: Corrstown dates, outliers and UB-6245 removed, calibrated and sequenced as a single phase of activity

based on the probability of a piece of wood coming from a particular part of a tree, with the probability range of a given radiocarbon date. He presented the results of this simulation in a table (*ibid*.). Warner has subsequently suggested that using the Offset function in OxCal, an offset of 1/2 the potential age lapse with an error of 1/4 the potential age lapse for a type of wood would be a suitable correction for 'old wood effect' (Warner forthcoming). This would mean that for oak, which in an Irish context has a potential age lapse of 250 years, then an Offset of 125 years with an error of ± 63 years should be added to all oak charcoal dates. The potential age lapses and corrections applied to the calibrated date ranges as offsets for each wood type in this analysis are as follows:

Oak: potential 250 year age lapse, 125 year Offset, 63 year error
Alder: potential 200 year age lapse, 100 year Offset, 50 year error
Hazel: potential 50 year age lapse, 25 year Offset, 13 year error

Using this technique a new sequence, Sequence 3, was generated (Illustration AI.4). It is significantly different from either of the other two sequences. Interestingly, while it has an acceptable Agreement Index of 62.6% several of the dates at the extreme ends of the sequence, UB-6247 at the far end and UB-6233 and Beta-190132 at the near end, had unacceptable individual Agreement Indices. It is possible to remove these dates and recalculate the sequence; however, when this was attempted OxCal 3.10 found a further two dates not compatible with the sequence. There is a danger with this type of analysis that you keep removing dates which are incompatible with the model until you have a perfect sequence but where much of your data is rejected. In such a scenario it may be that the analyst is putting too much faith in the model; rather than rejecting data sometimes the model should be revised. In this case it appears as if the activity at Corrstown may not begin or end abruptly, as the model would like, but rather that the village may grow from an initial nucleus of structures, enter a main phase when most structures are constructed / in use and then decline with residual activity continuing for a number of decades leading to a 'tail' in the radiocarbon record. Consequently, the dates were not removed from the sequence but retained and the model revised.

   A potential difficulty of using the old wood correction technique was illuminated by this sequence. When you construct an OxCal sequence to model a coherent, bounded, period, where you have no other stratigraphic or chronological information, the dates, as mentioned above, should be ordered according to their uncalibrated age within the sequence. However, when using woods with different old wood offsets, which are applied after calibration in Oxcal, the estimated age range for woods most susceptible to old wood latency will be shifted more than the woods less susceptible or short-lived samples with no latency. While this does not affect the reliability of individual dates it does have an affect on the radiocarbon sequence. It is apparent from an examination of Sequence 3 that there are two hazel dates UBA-16608 and UBA-16615 which have each a lower, although still acceptable, Agreement Index. They also physically look out of place in the sequenced date plot. It was decided to move these dates within the sequence to a position which reflects their smaller 'old wood' correction offset. This is not a perfect solution as the correction for the offset is carried out pre-calibration where as the actual offsets are carried out post-calibration but the difference is relatively slight and it seems to be a lesser evil than leaving them in a position in the sequence which does not reflect the 'old wood' correction carried out upon them.

   Utilising these lessons a new multi-phase hypothesis model, Sequence 4 (Illustration AI.5), was developed with three distinct phases embedded within the wider sequence. This sequence used the same radiocarbon dates as Sequence 3. This sequence has an Agreement Index of 179.9% (the algorithm which calculates the level of agreement can,

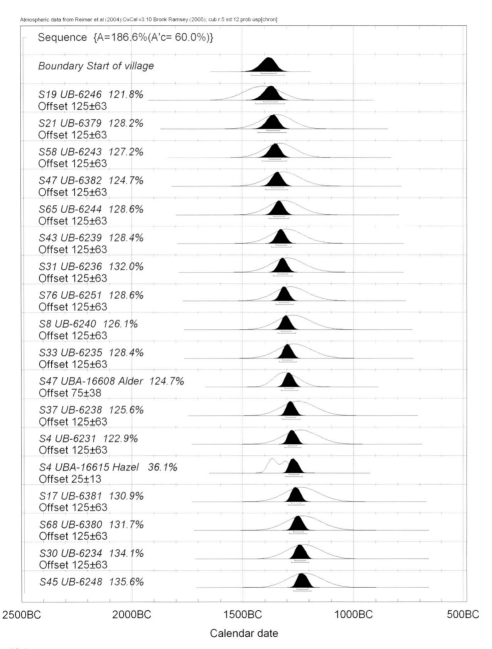

Atmospheric data from Reimer et al (2004);OxCal v3.10 Bronk Ramsey (2005); cub r:5 sd:12 prob usp[chron]

Sequence {A=186.6%(A'c= 60.0%)}

Boundary Start of village

S19 UB-6246 121.8%
Offset 125±63

S21 UB-6379 128.2%
Offset 125±63

S58 UB-6243 127.2%
Offset 125±63

S47 UB-6382 124.7%
Offset 125±63

S65 UB-6244 128.6%
Offset 125±63

S43 UB-6239 128.4%
Offset 125±63

S31 UB-6236 132.0%
Offset 125±63

S76 UB-6251 128.6%
Offset 125±63

S8 UB-6240 126.1%
Offset 125±63

S33 UB-6235 128.4%
Offset 125±63

S47 UBA-16608 Alder 124.7%
Offset 75±38

S37 UB-6238 125.6%
Offset 125±63

S4 UB-6231 122.9%
Offset 125±63

S4 UBA-16615 Hazel   36.1%
Offset 25±13

S17 UB-6381 130.9%
Offset 125±63

S68 UB-6380 131.7%
Offset 125±63

S30 UB-6234 134.1%
Offset 125±63

S45 UB-6248 135.6%

2500BC   2000BC   1500BC   1000BC   500BC

Calendar date

AI.4a

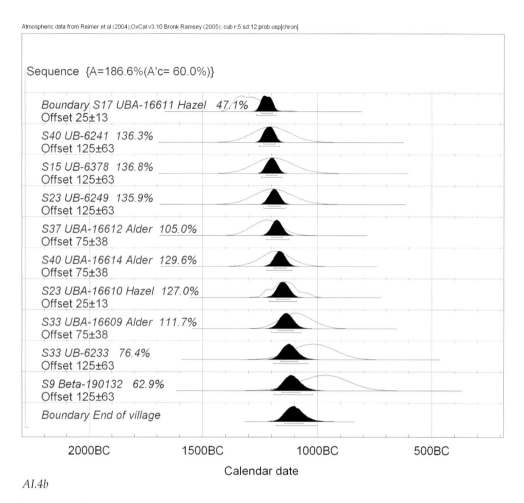

Atmospheric data from Reimer et al (2004);OxCal v3.10 Bronk Ramsey (2005); cub r:5 sd:12 prob usp[chron]

Sequence {A=186.6%(A'c= 60.0%)}

Boundary S17 UBA-16611 Hazel 47.1%
Offset 25±13

S40 UB-6241 136.3%
Offset 125±63

S15 UB-6378 136.8%
Offset 125±63

S23 UB-6249 135.9%
Offset 125±63

S37 UBA-16612 Alder 105.0%
Offset 75±38

S40 UBA-16614 Alder 129.6%
Offset 75±38

S23 UBA-16610 Hazel 127.0%
Offset 25±13

S33 UBA-16609 Alder 111.7%
Offset 75±38

S33 UB-6233 76.4%
Offset 125±63

S9 Beta-190132 62.9%
Offset 125±63

Boundary End of village

2000BC   1500BC   1000BC   500BC

Calendar date

AI.4b

Illustration AI.4a and b: Sequence 3, Corrstown radiocarbon dates, outliers and UB-6245 removed, calibrated, sequenced as a single phase of activity and corrected for 'old wood' latency

in the case of a good fit, produce Agreement Indices in excess of 100%), which suggests a high degree of compatibility between the model and the radiocarbon dates.

This model, Sequence 4, suggests that a 'Growth Phase' of activity at Corrstown is likely to have commenced between 1550 and 1300 BC (2 sigma) or 1460 to 1340 BC (1 sigma). The main phase of village life, the 'Village Phase' at Corrstown, to which most of the structures date, is likely to have begun 1360 to 1250 BC (2 sigma) or 1330 to 1270 BC (1 sigma). The final phase of decline, the 'Decline Phase', is likely to have commenced between 1270 and 1140 (2 sigma) or 1245 and 1175 (1 sigma) with the last occupation at prehistoric Corrstown sometime between 1170 and 760 BC (2 sigma) or 1120 and 920 BC (1 sigma). Using the Interval command, which estimates the period of time between boundaries in the model OxCal calculates that the Growth Phase lasted between 0 and

Atmospheric data from Reimer et al (2004);OxCal v3.10 Bronk Ramsey (2005); cub r:5 sd:12 prob usp[chron]

Sequence {A=179.9%(A'c= 60.0%)}

Boundary Begining Growth Phase

Phase Growth Phase

S19 UB-6247 81.2%
Offset 125±63

S19 UB-6246 106.8%
Offset 125±63

S21 UB-6379 124.6%
Offset 125±63

S4 UBA-16615 Hazel 107.1%
Offset 25±13

S58 UB-6243 122.7%
Offset 125±63

Boundary Begining Village Phase

Phase Village Phase

S47 UB-6382 105.6%
Offset 125±63

S17 UBA-16611 Hazel 97.8%
Offset 25±13

S65 UB-6244 107.3%
Offset 125±63

S43 UB-6239 115.6%
Offset 125±63

S31 UB-6236 117.2%
Offset 125±63

S76 UB-6251 124.4%
Offset 125±63

S8 UB-6240 128.6%
Offset 125±63

S33 UB-6235 129.3%
Offset 125±63

S47 UBA-16608 Alder 98.5%
Offset 75±38

S37 UB-6238 130.0%

2500BC   2000BC   1500BC   1000BC

Calendar date

Atmospheric data from Reimer et al (2004);OxCal v3.10 Bronk Ramsey (2005); cub r:5 sd:12 prob usp[chron]

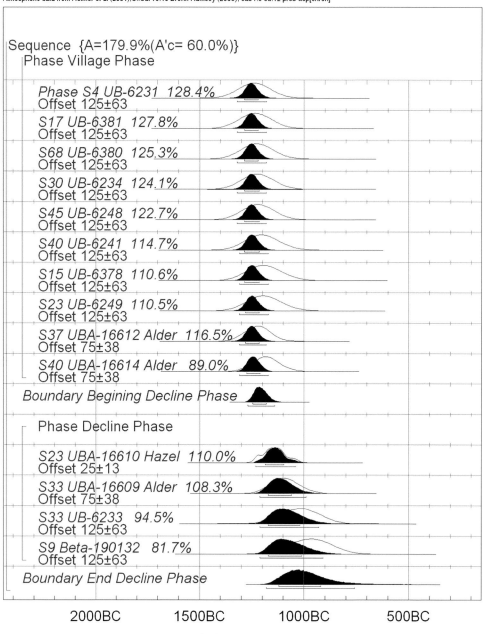

Sequence {A=179.9%(A'c= 60.0%)}
Phase Village Phase

Phase S4 UB-6231 128.4%
Offset 125±63

S17 UB-6381 127.8%
Offset 125±63

S68 UB-6380 125.3%
Offset 125±63

S30 UB-6234 124.1%
Offset 125±63

S45 UB-6248 122.7%
Offset 125±63

S40 UB-6241 114.7%
Offset 125±63

S15 UB-6378 110.6%
Offset 125±63

S23 UB-6249 110.5%
Offset 125±63

S37 UBA-16612 Alder 116.5%
Offset 75±38

S40 UBA-16614 Alder 89.0%
Offset 75±38

Boundary Begining Decline Phase

Phase Decline Phase

S23 UBA-16610 Hazel 110.0%
Offset 25±13

S33 UBA-16609 Alder 108.3%
Offset 75±38

S33 UB-6233 94.5%
Offset 125±63

S9 Beta-190132 81.7%
Offset 125±63

Boundary End Decline Phase

2000BC   1500BC   1000BC   500BC

Calendar date

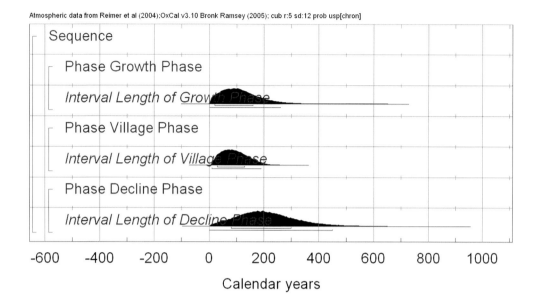

Atmospheric data from Reimer et al (2004);OxCal v3.10 Bronk Ramsey (2005); cub r:5 sd:12 prob usp[chron]

Illustration AI.5: Corrstown dates, outliers and UB-6245 removed, calibrated, corrected for 'old wood' latency and sequenced as a three-phase model of activity at the site

260 years (2 sigma), 20 and 160 years (1 sigma), that the Village Phase lasted between 10 and 190 years (2 sigma) and 35 and 155 years (1 sigma) and that the Decline Phase lasted between 0 and 450 years (2 sigma) or 80 and 300 years (1 sigma).

It is noticeable that the estimations of the length of the Growth Phase and Decline Phase are rather longer than the actual Village Phase at Corrstown. While this may possibly be the case it is also the true that OxCal will, because of the small number of dates available for analysis in these two phases, make the assumption that statistically it is less likely that the dates from these phases will actually be close to the real beginning and ends of activity at the site and will therefore mathematically extend its estimate of the length of these phases to compensate (if we have three dates from a phase it is less likely that we will have an even distribution of dates through the beginning, middle and end of the phase than if we have for example ten or twenty dates from that phase). Consequently, it is perhaps better to give more weight to the length of the Village Phase and note that the Growth and Decline Phases, may, as calculated by OxCal in this sequence, be somewhat longer than they actually are.

Conclusions

The mixture of sample types and the scale of the excavated remains make Corrstown a most challenging radiocarbon dating project. The problems of residuality, contamination and variant 'old wood'-type age lapses in the various samples dated called for a subtle

Illustration AI.6: Radiocarbon-dated structures from Corrstown. Green structures: Growth Phase; blue structures: Village Phase; red structures: Decline Phase

dating strategy. Initial radiocarbon calibration identified a number of outliers which were immediately removed from the data set. Using techniques developed by Richard Warner (Warner forthcoming) a series of corrections were made to each of the dated wood types to compensate for their potential 'old wood' effects. The dates were then sequenced. While a sequence modelling all the corrected dates as a single phase of activity at Corrstown provided an acceptable overall level of agreement with the radiocarbon data it had a low level of agreement with several dates at the beginning and end of the sequence. This suggested that there may be a separate initial phase of settlement at Corrstown followed by a main phase when Corrstown was a village and then a period of perhaps decline, or a lessening of construction / occupation at the site. When this model was sequenced with the radiocarbon data it provided a very acceptable fit indeed, both with the radiocarbon dates as a whole and also with the individual dates in the sequence.

The radiocarbon analysis of the dates from Corrstown seems to suggest that there was an initial nucleus, possibly a small settlement, around which the village at Corrstown grew. When structures from Corrstown are colour coded on plan (Illustration AI.6) according to phase it seems possible that the site has developed outwards from a fixed point, possibly the well-developed S19. Unfortunately, given the small number of dates available to date this Growth Phase the OxCal estimation of its duration is very long, up to 280 years. It is likely to be less.

The main phase of village life at Corrstown commenced between 1370 and 1250 BC, was up to 200 years long, and – given the evidence of repairs and rebuilds to several of the buildings – it seems that it is likely that the Village Phase lasted for no less than several generations.

The decline of activity at Corrstown had probably begun by the middle years of the 12th century BC although it is likely that there was continuing activity at the site for some time after. Given the small number of dates available this is difficult to estimate precisely although it is possible to accurately state that this phase of decline was less than 480 years long, in all probability much less.

Bibliography

Ashmore, P. J. (1999) Radiocarbon dating: avoiding errors by avoiding mixed samples. *Antiquity* 73, 124–30.

Bronk Ramsey, C. (2005). Oxcal v3.10.

Reimer, P. J., Baillie, M. G. L., Bard, E., Bayliss, A., Bayliss, A., Beck, J. W., Blackwell, P. G., Bronk Ramsey, C., Buck, C. E. Burr, G. S., Edwards, R. L., Friedrich, M., Grootes, P. M., Guilderson, T. P., Hajdas, I., Heaton, T. J., Hogg, A. G., Hughen, K. A., Kaiser, K. F., Kromer, B., McCormac, F. G., Manning, S. W., Reimer, R. W., Richards, D. A., Southon, J. R., Talamo, S., Turney, C. S. M., van der Plicht, J., Weyhenmeyer, C. E. (2009) IntCal09 and Marine09 Radiocaron Calibration Curves, 0–50,000 Years cal BP. *Radiocarbon* 51, 1111–50.

Warner, R. B. (1990) A proposed adjustment for the "Old-Wood Effect". In W. Mook and H. Waterbolk (eds) Proceedings of the 2nd Symposium of C14 and Archaeology, Gronigen, 159–72. *PACT Journal*, No. 29.

Warner, R. B., forthcoming An analysis of the radiocarbon dates from Dear Park Farms. In C. Lynn *Deer Park Farms: the Excavation of a Raised Rath in the Glenarm Valley, Co. Antrim.*

Appendix II: Medieval Corrstown
with contributions by Maria Lear

Three of the excavated structures and associated features belonged to the early medieval period. The eastern half of a ditched enclosure [1000] (maximum: 44m × 2.5m × 1.09m) with a possible entranceway in the northeast enclosed an area 25m northwest–southeast (Illustration AII.1). The western half was destroyed due to the presence of a modern culvert. Ploughing had removed any traces of a bank. These ploughed-out remains represent a ringfort or rath. In 1942 Ó Ríordáin described this monument type 'In its simplest form… as a space most frequently circular, surrounded by a bank and fosse or simply by a rampart of stone' (Ó Ríordáin 1991, 29). Stout maintains that this circularity, certainly a defining characteristic according to the seventh- and eighth-century law tracts, was achieved by using a line connected to a central stake (1997, 14–15), although such preciseness seems perhaps unlikely and more recent archaeological excavations have revealed a plethora of shapes. The majority of raths enclosed a space between 15m and 35m (Edwards 1990, 14; Barrett 1980, 42) and it would seem that the Corrstown example was no different. Artefacts, as at Corrstown, are generally few in number at rath sites and those that are recovered are of a primarily utilitarian nature. Although Limbert (1996) argues their origins began in the Iron Age, raths are more generally tightly dated to between the seventh and ninth centuries (Stout 1997). No direct date for the enclosure was obtained, although several dates for internal features were (see below).

Raths functioned as early medieval homesteads and many examples contained houses in the enclosed area. The remains of a possible rectangular house foundation, represented by a linear gully and a line of four postholes, were recovered from near the centre of the rath at Corrstown. Ploughing had removed much of the immediate sub-surface remains; however, traces of the continuation of the rectangular ground plan were visible on an oblique photograph. The ground plan, seen from above, was not complete and the dimensions of this structure remain uncertain. It was apparent, due to the similarity in the fills, that this possible structure was associated with a souterrain.

Inside the enclosed space of a rath at Lisnagun, Co. Cork, three souterrains were discovered (O'Sullivan *et al.* 1998). At Corrstown, a single example was observed (Illustration AII.2). The Corrstown souterrain was a simple construction, L-shaped (north–south passage: 3.68m × 1.76m; east–west passage: 4.4m × 1.9m), predominantly of dry-stone construction (surviving to between two and three courses) although the west return of the passage was set on natural rock, and had a ramped entranceway (Clinton 2001, 99). The majority of souterrains (95%) were predominantly dry-stone built (*ibid.* 36) and, as was possibly the case at Corrstown, in the known examples where the souterrain opens directly from an associated structure, that structure will be rectangular (Edwards 1990, 31). Unfortunately, the inability to determine the dimensions of the Corrstown structure precludes the possibility of making any viable comparisons. Souterrains are not commonly found in isolation and the Corrstown example was no exception. Northern Archaeological Consultancy Ltd found an additional two and re-located a third example (SMR LDY 003:023) in the neighbouring townland of Magheramenagh

Illustration AII.1: Ringfort with northeast entranceway, internal kiln [1109] and souterrain

(Reilly 2000), close to the excavation site. Unlike the Corrstown example, these nearby souterrains were not enclosed. A fourth souterrain exists in Clogghorr (SMR LDY 006:014). Counties Londonderry and Antrim had a particularly dense distribution of souterrains and for some writers (e.g. Buckley 1986, 108) the souterrains in this area could be related and equated to the territory of Dal Riata. For others (e.g. Warner 1986) such a concentration transcended political borders. Despite this widespread and concentrated distribution not only on the north coast but also in the rest of Ireland, the function of souterrains remains enigmatic: certain archaeologists maintain they primarily fulfilled a storage function (Evans 1966; Thomas 1972) although some suggest this is only true of the more simple types (Macalister 1949; de Paor and de Paor 1958) while others suggest they were used uniquely for refuge (Warner 1979). Ultimately though, souterrains could have been used for either function, or both (deValera 1979; Lucas 1971–3; Ó Ríordáin 1953).

Material from the souterrain walls at Corrstown was radiocarbon dated to AD 552–654 (UB-6237) (Table AII.1). Radiocarbon dates from the excavations at Magheramenagh were provided by Stephen Gilmore in advance of publication and demonstrate that the adjacent souterrains were later than that at Corrstown. Two were dated to AD 790–1000 (Beta-186549, 1160±40 BP) and AD 670–800 (Beta-186551, 1280±40 BP). The early medieval structure of Corrstown (see below) may have been contemporary with the later of two Magheramenagh souterrains.

The rath also enclosed a kiln [1109] which had two parallel linear features extending from it, one or both representing its flue, or successive flues (Illustration AII.1). Kilns in the interior space of raths are not unknown and a possible cereal-drying kiln was excavated in the central space at Letterkeen, Co. Mayo (Edwards 1990, 32). A radiocarbon date was returned for this Corrstown kiln and it was identical to that of the souterrain, AD 552–654 (UB-6232) (Table AII.1).

Two sections of ditch that were only 0.30m in depth formed the third medieval structure (Illustration AII.3). There may have been fences or wind-breaks which followed the line of these shallow ditches but there was no extant evidence for them. The ditches appear too inadequate to have definitely supported walls and the absence of any associated postholes suggests that the 'structure' was not roofed either. There was no evidence for a formal entrance. Two alternative possibilities for the early medieval structure can be presented: it was a possible corrale / animal pen, or its remains form a system of drains that defined an area which could have been used as an open-air threshing floor. If the latter was true then the pair of large pits that cut through the outer ditch of the S39 could have been contemporary with this square enclosure; indeed, they certainly do not seem contemporary with S39 which has a suspected Bronze Age date. One of these pits [8044] contained approximately 2,000 cereal grains, most being oat (*Avena*), but a small proportion was hulled barley (*Hordeum distichon/vulgare*). There were also several fruit segments (mericarps) of wild radish (*Raphanus raphanistrum* L.), fruits of knotgrass (*Polygonum*) and caryopses of wild grasses (Poaceae). The fill was radiocarbon dated to AD 772–941 (UB-6377) (Table AII.1).

The discovery of early medieval structures and features on this predominantly Bronze Age site is not surprising and certainly the early medieval north coast of Co. Antrim and Co. Londonderry was no less active than its Bronze Age counterpart.

Indeed, a previous landscape study completed in 1984 noted an enclosure on the site of the Corrstown excavations, SMR LDY 003:026, supposedly situated within the upper northwestern area of the site. Subsequent visits to the site in the years preceding the ACS excavations found that the area was heavily ploughed and that there were no

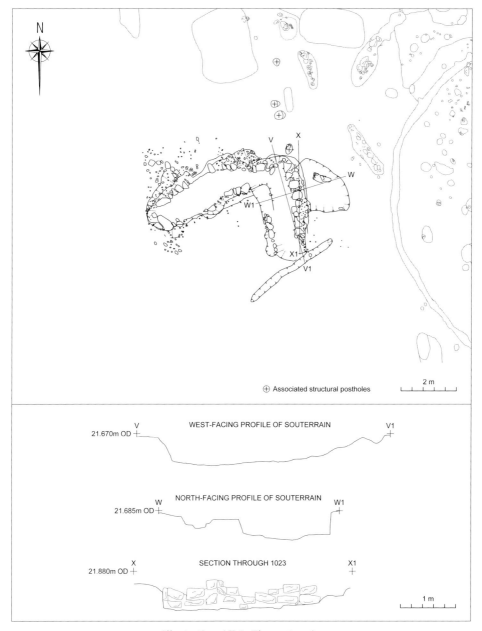

Illustration AII.2: The souterrain

Context	Material	Lab	Lab Code	Date Type	Calibrated Date	Conventional Date (BP)	13C/12C
Souterrain walls	Charcoal	UB	6237	AMS	AD 552–654	1447±30	N/A
Kiln	Charcoal	UB	6232	AMS	AD552–654	1447±30	N/A
Fill of pit [8044]	Charcoal	UB	6377	AMS	AD 772–941	1185±31	-24.6
Pit (S31)	*Hazel*	*UBA*	*16613*	*AMS*	*AD 653–766*	*1326±22*	*-26.2*

IntCal 09
Reimer, P. J., Baillie, M. G. L., Bard, E., Bayliss, A., Bayliss, A., Beck, J. W., Blackwell, P. G., Bronk Ramsey, C., Buck, C. E. Burr, G. S., Edwards, R. L., Friedrich, M., Grootes, P. M., Guilderson, T. P., Hajdas, I., Heaton, T. J., Hogg, A. G., Hughen, K. A., Kaiser, K. F., Kromer, B., McCormac, F. G., Manning, S. W., Reimer, R. W., Richards, D. A., Southon, J. R., Talamo, S., Turney, C. S. M., van der Plicht, J., Weyhenmeyer, C. E. (2009) IntCal09 and Marine09 Radiocaron Calibration Curves, 0–50,000 Years cal BP. *Radiocarbon* 51, 1111–50.
Dates in italics were funded by Chrono as part of Ginn's PhD research.

Table AII.1: Radiocarbon dates

obvious traces of the monument remaining visible on the ground. Nevertheless, it may be suggested that the Corrstown enclosure was in fact the monument which had been recorded in 1984. In addition to the above-mentioned neighbouring souterrains, other nearby early medieval sites include an enclosure (SMR ANT 003:019) located to the southeast of the site at Corrstown and aerial photographs taken in the Crossreagh townland depict the presence of a possible enclosure (SMR ANT 006:020) located *c.* 1km to the east of Corrstown. Additional aerial photographs of Corbally demonstrate the existence of a possible barrow or small enclosure (SMR ANT 006:019) as well as a site noted in Clogghorr townland, listed as SMR ANT 006:014 and given the description of a souterrain and possible enclosure. While it is not certain, it is a distinct possibility that some of these sites would have been occupied or in use contemporaneously with the early medieval features at Corrstown.

Bibliography

Barrett, G. F. (1980) A field survey and morphological study of ringforts in southern Co. Donegal. *Ulster Journal of Archaeology* 43, 39–51.
Buckley, V. M. (1986) Ulster and Oriel souterrains – an indicator of tribal areas? *Ulster Journal of Archaeology* 49, 108–10.

Clinton, M. (2001) *The Souterrains of Ireland*. Bray, Wordwell.

de Paor, M. and de Paor, L. (1958) *Early Christian Ireland*. London, Thames and Hudson.

deValera, R. (ed.) (1979) Antiquities of the Irish countryside, by SP Ó Ríordáin (5th edn). London, Routledge.

Edwards, N. (1990) *The Archaeology of Early Medieval Ireland*. London, Routledge.

Evans, E. E. (1966) *Prehistoric and Early Christian Ireland: a Guide*. London, BT Batsford.

Limbert, D. (1996) Irish ringforts: a review of their origins. *The Archaeological Journal*, Vol. 153, 243–90.

Lucas, A. T. (1971–73) Souterrains: the literary evidence. *Béaloideas*, 39–41, 165–91.

Macalister, R. A. S. (1949) *The archaeology of Ireland* (2nd revised edn). London, Methuen.

Ó Ríordáin, S. P. (1953) *Antiquities of the Irish countryside*. London (3rd edn), Methuen and Co. Ltd.

Ó Riordáin, S. P. (1991) *Antiquities of the Irish Countryside*. London (1942 edn), Routledge.

O'Sullivan, J., Hannon, M. and Tierney, J. (1998) Excavation of Lisnagun ringfort, Darrava, Co. Cork, 1987–89. *Journal of Cork Historical and Archaeological Society* Vol. 103, 31–66.

Reilly, A. (2000) Magheramenagh, Co. Derry: souterrain, prehistoric house. In I. Bennett (ed.), *Excavations 1999: Summary Accounts of Archaeological Excavations in Ireland*, 38–40. Dublin, Wordwell.

Stout, M. (1997) *The Irish Ringfort*. Dublin, Four Courts Press.

Thomas, C. (ed.) (1972) *The Iron Age in the Irish Sea Province*. Research Report No. 9. London, Council for British Archaeology.

Warner, R. B. (1979) The Irish souterrains and their background. In H. Crawford (ed.) *Subterranean Britain: Aspects of Underground Archaeology*, 100–44. London, Baker.

Warner, R. B. (1986) Comments on 'Ulster and Oriel souterrains'. *Ulster Journal of Archaeology*, 49, 111–12.

Appendix III: Cappagh Beg

Steve Linanne with contributions by Victoria Ginn

Excavations at Cappagh Beg (NGR: 8240 3656; Portstewart, Co. Londonderry) in 2003 for Kennedy Holidays (Coleraine) Ltd revealed the remains of two or three houses, two boundary ditches and a single cremation pit with a possibly associated hearth (Illustration AIII.1). The site was situated about 1.6km from the coast and from the north of the River Bann and the features were located in a low-lying area (31m OD) consisting of soft, orange sand which overlay the limestone bedrock. It is possible that both the sand deposit and the settlement area had been more extensive in prehistory. Various sites and monuments are recorded in the vicinity of the site, including two unlocated standing stones and one prone stone (1.1m in length) located to the southeast (SMR LDY 003:020; LDY 003:021; LDY 003:074). Two further standing stones are situated to the west (SMR LDY 003:004; LDY 003:005). There was also a prehistoric settlement site on the coast, although its location is unknown (SMR LDY 003:043).

Structure A

A series of pits, postholes and ditch sections formed an oval structure *c.* 9m north–south by *c.* 7m west–east (Illustration AIII.2). Structure A had a similar footprint to many of the Corrstown Type 1 structures and the segmented ditch segments and pits formed an external perimeter. These features were filled with silty sands and varying amounts of charcoal flecks and inclusions; burnt limestone was also noted in some of the fills. Charred cereal grains, including barley and wheat, along with charcoal identified as hazel (*corylus*), and alder/hazel (*alnus/corylus*), were recovered from the fill of one of the ditch segments (identified by Palaeoecology Services). Within the fill and lying against the outer face of another ditch segment was a portion of carbonised wood which appeared to be wattle (Illustration AIII.3). This would suggest that the walls of the structure were constructed of wattle and daub and that the building had been destroyed by fire. The charred twig wood was identified as alder/hazel and willow/poplar/aspen (*salix/populus*) as well as hazel twig (Palaeoecology Services). An 11g sample of this material (*alnus/corylus*) returned a radiocarbon date of 1491–1058 BC (Beta-188622) (Table AIII.1).

A series of features indicated that there was at least one further and later phase of construction. One of the ditch segments was cut by further ditch segments and pits. A spread of mixed material which was similar to the ditch segment fills was also associated with this phase.

A series of five postholes ran around the western internal perimeter and may have supported the roof structure. They appeared to be associated with the first phase of construction but this is by no means certain. Three stakeholes and three pits were also apparent in the interior.

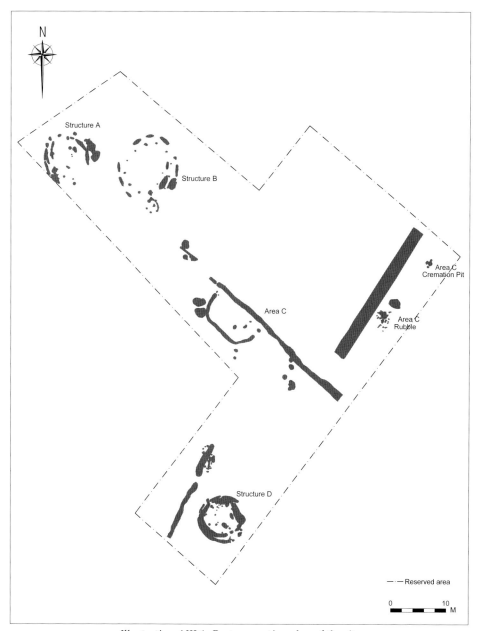

Illustration AIII.1: Post-excavation plan of the site

Structure B

A sequence of eight ditch segments formed a structure *c.* 11m in diameter (Illustration AIII.4). The fills of all the ditch sections were similar and consisted of near-black silty sand with occasional lenses of red silty sand. Large twig/small roundwood material

Illustration AIII.2: Post-excavation plan of Structure A

of hazel and willow/poplar/aspen (*salix/populus*) and some detached fragments of bark were noted in the fill of one of the ditch segments (identified by Palaeoecology Services). A sample of this material was sent for radiocarbon analysis and returned a date of 1433–1122 BC (Beta-188623) (Table AIII.1).

An internal postring comprised 11 postholes which formed a circle with a diameter of *c*. 8.5m. The postholes were spaced at *c*. 2.2m intervals except in the southwestern section where there should have been a twelfth posthole but where instead there was a gap. It is believed that the gap would have been left as an entrance into the circle's interior even though such a large gap would have compromised the stability of a roof structure (if there was one). Three charred cereal grains (two barley and one wheat) were identified within a sample from one of the postholes along with alder/hazel charcoal (identified by Palaeoecology Services).

There was only one internal feature and this consisted of a ditch section, *c*. 1.4m in length. The ditch was identical to those on the exterior but served no obvious function.

Structure C

Situated *c*. 32m to the south of Structure A and *c*. 30m to the northeast of Structure D was a D-shaped ditch (0.6m wide × 0.05–0.2m deep) forming an enclosure which represented Structure C. It may have been used for the containment of livestock. Structure C was built against a boundary formed by three north–south ditches.

Nearby features

Situated in the southeastern part of the site was a circular pit which contained significant quantities of burnt bone, occasional small stone fragments and charcoal flecking which represented a cremation pit.

Illustration AIII.3: Carbonised wattle fill

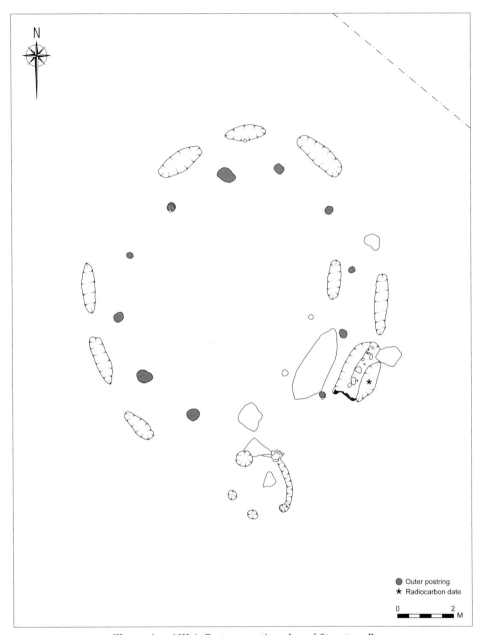

Illustration AIII.4: Post-excavation plan of Structure B

The well-preserved and well-burnt cremation (614.5g; some 60% of the cremated skeleton) was analysed by Malin Holst, Allan Hall and John Carrott (Palaeoecology Research Services). A total of 64% of the bone fragments were identifiable and 40% of these were cranial fragments and 34% were long bone shaft fragments. A few of the facial bones and some of the teeth were not recovered but otherwise the skull was almost complete. Rib fragments, spine vertebral bodies and arches and parts of the pelvis represented the remains of the torso. Tarsals were identified, although only one of the toe bones was present. No grave goods were identified; however, the present of charcoal flecks in the backfill of the pit suggests that some of the pyre debris had been included in the burial. Malin Holst, Allan Hall and John Carrott (Palaeoecology Research Services) also suggested that the individual was a juvenile, aged between six and 12 years and that the association of the child cremation and Structure D could suggest that the child was of importance to the community. They concluded their analysis with the indication that the Cappagh Beg burial may represent an unusual, possibly ritual, function or be of high status.

Situated to the north, west and east of the cremation pit were three depressions. These bowl-shaped pits were circular with an average diameter of *c.* 0.3m and a maximum depth of *c.* 0.08m. The pits were filled with very soft medium-brown silty sand with no inclusions of bone, stone or charcoal. It is possible that the pits were caused by tree root activity (the northern pit has been disturbed by such activity) but their proximity to the cremation pit might suggest otherwise.

Situated *c.* 7m to the north of the cremation pit was a circular area of red (oxidized) subsoil (1m diameter). It is a possibility that the hearth area is connected with the cremation as the site was not characterised by tree or bush burning.

A possible pond was situated to the south of the site and contained layers of sand as well as a layer of limestone rubble; the pond may have existed during the same period as the other features on the site.

Structure D

Structure D was situated on ground rising towards the west where the subsoil (a very soft orange/brown sand) petered out onto the underlying limestone bedrock (Illustration AIII.5). The structure is another circular house with two phases of construction, both of which consist of a series of irregular ditch sections, pits and occasional stake- and postholes forming circular enclosures of *c.* 6.5m internal diameter. Phase 2 is positioned slightly to the west and south of Phase 1 and there is considerable cross-cutting between the ditches of the two phases. The Phase 1 structure comprised five ditch segments (into which stakeholes were cut), two pits and a depression. This was replaced by the Phase 2 structure, which comprised one pit, eight ditch segments (some of which contained stones), two postholes, and a depression. The internal features included a hearth with a thin band of blackened subsoil around its perimeter, as well as further postholes and pits.

Within the interior were a number of pits, postholes, stakeholes and a hearth. In all cases, it was impossible to allocate these internal features to a specific construction phase. Unless otherwise stated, all fills were identical and consisted of soft medium-red/brown silty sand with only occasional small stone inclusions and with charcoal practically absent. The position of doorways in both phases was not made obvious by any structural features but the absence of any major features to the south of the structure would suggest that the doorways lay in that area.

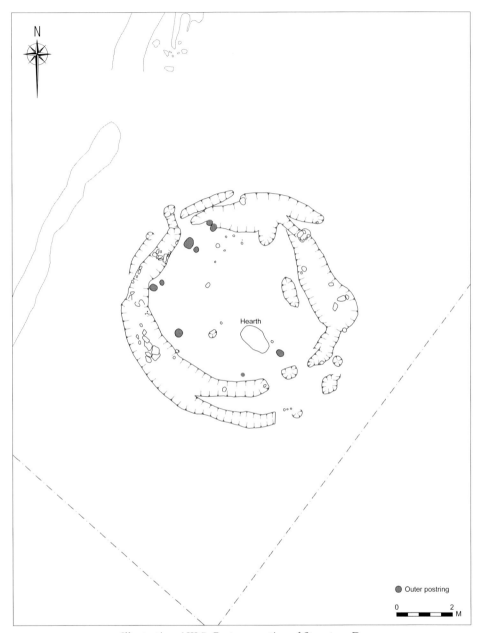

Hearth

Outer postring

0   2
          M

Illustration AIII.5: Post-excavation of Structure D

Large quantities of flint and approximately 100 pottery sherds were recovered during the excavation, including 36 from topsoil. No post-excavation analysis was carried out and it is unknown if the lithics and the sherds are prehistoric.

Discussion

Structures A and C appear to be houses of a type common in the Bronze Age with a single outer footing trench and internal posts to support the roof structure.

The absence of internal features within Structure B appears to indicate that this may never have been roofed (the diameter, at *c.* 8.5m, seems too great to span without internal supports). If Structure B is to be considered of ritual significance, then the proximity of the cremation pit and associated hearth may be significant.

Segmented boundary ditches are common features within the Bronze Age landscape and the two excavated on this site would again appear to be part of the same landscape as the structures. The wet area to the south of the site with possible hard standing could again be part of the same landscape and may indicate why the area was considered a viable settlement site.

Context	Material	Species id/Weight	Lab	Lab Code	Date Type	Calibrated Date	Conventional Date (BP)	13C/12C
117: fill of ditch, SA	Charred material	11g alder/ hazel	Beta	188622	AMS(Std)	1491–1058 BC two sigma	3050±70	-26.8
231: fill of ditch, SB	Charred material	40g twig/ roundwood fragments: hazel and willow/ poplar/ aspen	Beta	188623	AMS(Std)	1433–1122 BC two sigma	3040±60	-26.2

tCal 09

imer, P. J., Baillie, M. G. L., Bard, E., Bayliss, A., Bayliss, A., Beck, J. W., Blackwell, P. G., Bronk Ramsey, Buck, C. E. Burr, G. S., Edwards, R. L., Friedrich, M., Grootes, P. M., Guilderson, T. P., Hajdas, I., Heaton, J., Hogg, A. G., Hughen, K. A., Kaiser, K. F., Kromer, B., McCormac, F. G., Manning, S. W., Reimer, R., chards, D. A., Southon, J. R., Talamo, S., Turney, C. S. M., van der Plicht, J., Weyhenmeyer, C. E. (2009) tCal09 and Marine09 Radiocaron Calibration Curves, 0–50,000 Years cal BP. Radiocarbon 51, 1111–50.

Table AIII.1: Radiocarbon dates